DATE			

Conrad's Heroism
A Paradise Lost

Studies in Modern Literature, No. 43

A. Walton Litz, General Series Editor

Professor of English
Princeton University

Thomas C. Moser

Consulting Editor for Titles on Joseph Conrad
Professor of English
Stanford University

Daniel Mark Fogel

Consulting Editor for Titles on Henry James
Professor of English
Louisiana State University
Editor, The Henry James Review

Other Titles in This Series

Conrad's Heroism
A Paradise Lost

by
Michael P. Jones

UMI RESEARCH PRESS
Ann Arbor, Michigan

Produced and distributed by
UMI Research Press
an imprint of
University Microfilms International
A Xerox Information Resources Company
Ann Arbor, Michigan 48106

Library of Congress Cataloging in Publication Data

Jones, Michael P. (Michael Pusey), 1948-
Conrad's heroism.

(Studies in modern literature ; no. 43)
Revision of thesis—Boston College, 1974.
Bibliography: p.
Includes index.
1. Conrad, Joseph, 1857-1924—Criticism and interpre-
tation. I. Title. II. Series.

PR6005.04Z7493   1984   823'.912   84-8764
ISBN 0-8357-1596-5 (alk. paper)

To my mother and my father

Contents

Foreword

In this book, I address the present-day audience for Joseph Conrad—students, teachers, professors, and readers who enjoy good stories that present an intellectual challenge—and convey to them both the excitement of better understanding Conrad and the delight that can be taken in reading some of the greatest adventure stories in the English language. *Conrad's Heroism* is, of course, a scholarly book in that it grew out of a doctoral dissertation and was originally intended exclusively for an academic audience. My methods rely on my critical readings of the stories I discuss and my arguments remain close to the texts. I believe that this is a book accessible to those who not only enjoy reading Conrad but who are interested in looking for critical commentary that may help to heighten their appreciation of one of the foremost novelists in English literature.

The four main chapters of this book follow the development of Conrad's heroic imagination from 1897 to 1909 by examining the dialectics of the heroic journey in four of his adventure tales. Framing these chapters are more general discussions of Conrad and other heroic writers of the nineteenth and early twentieth centuries. For those readers who are less interested in literary history, it is possible to read only the chapters on Conrad's stories and emerge with a way to read Conrad that will, I hope, make him more fun and more comprehensible. The first and last chapters reveal some of my historical concerns and attempt to show how my reading of Conrad may contribute to our understanding of heroic literature and help us better to define Conrad's "place" in literary modernism.

Foremost among the people who deserve my special thanks for their help during the writing of this book is James Guetti, whose criticism, advice, and encouragement have meant more to me over the years than I can express; and this book truly would not have been possible without the support of Thomas Moser, who was generous and largeminded in both his praise and his criticisms of my manuscript. To Helmut Gerber, David Leon Higdon, C. B. Cox, Emerson R. Marks, and Thomas R. Edwards I am grateful for encouragement and suggestions on matters relating to his book.

My wife Eleanor deserves my gratitude not only for her editorial help, but also for her critical reading of the manuscript in the early stages of my writing. Finally, I am indebted to my former professors at Rutgers and Boston College, whose influence upon me cannot always be represented in footnotes. I hope my own book does some small measure of justice to such tutelage.

Introduction

According to H. G. Wells, an exasperated Joseph Conrad once demanded, "What is all this about Jane Austen? What is there *in* her? What is it all *about*?"[1] Whether or not this short anecdote is true, it serves the purpose of Wells's joke. Conrad may as well have asked, "What is all this about the English novel? What is it all about?" Fortunately those questions do not have to be answered thoroughly before we may see some important differences between Conrad and his predecessors in English fiction, especially if we take Jane Austen as an example of the classic English novelist. Assume for a moment, with F. R. Leavis, that Conrad does belong to a great tradition in English fiction. Immediately we have to dismiss much of Conrad's adventure fiction as "minor work" uncharacteristic of the great tradition. Moreover, we have to reject a way of talking about human experience that to Leavis represents "an adjectival and worse than supererogatory insistence" on "the presence of what he can't produce." We would praise *Nostromo* for its "firm and vivid concreteness," but we would puzzle ourselves that "for all the rich variety and the tightness of the pattern, the reverberation of *Nostromo* has something hollow about it; with the colour and life there is a suggestion of a certain emptiness." We are reminded, metaphorically, of our uneasiness over "Heart of Darkness," and we are left to invoke critical standards implied by the great tradition. "There is no intimate sense of the day-by-day continuities of social living," Leavis says of *Nostromo*—and we are back, with H. G. Wells, to Jane Austen as an exemplar of the classic English novel.[2]

It is commonly accepted that since it began taking on the characteristics of a genre—in the early eighteenth century—the English novel has been predominantly a "social" form of literature in its language, its audience, and its subject matter. While the history of great poetry is a cumulative body of highly technical language, replete with indigenous images and metaphors, special modes of expression, and stylized patterns of speech, and has been read, even in its more public forms, by a relatively small, educated, and esoteric audience, the novel in its eighteenth-century forms shared the language used by people in ordinary social discourse. Poetry, in other words, developed a language traditional and special unto itself, and if that language was modified during the course of years, for example, if it became politicized after the English revolution, "romanticized" after the French, it still changed for the most part within its own conventions and accumulated meanings, and it echoed past voices within the range of its own vocabularies. Poetry has had a history of its own, an existence in many ways independent of society and its institutions.

As the novel developed, on the other hand, journals and diaries, travelogues, letters, and written confessions became the property of authors like Defoe, Richardson, and Sterne, who made use of them in the writing of fiction. Doubtless, it would be naive to ascribe to the novel a greater literary freedom than to poetry, whatever that would mean. And surely the novel developed its own conventions and formal prescriptions, its own stylistic procedures and determined modes of thought. It even assimilated, parodied, and commented upon some of the conventions of the theater, of heroic poetry, of religious allegory, and of popular romance. But the novel has been directly responsive to extra-literary pressures, too, which is to say that the novelist's business was "public" language, language subject less to the conventions of a literary genre than to social realities and the history of public events. It follows that one effect of this language and its conventions was social realism, and that another was the novel's emphasis upon human relationships as they occurred in everyday life.

In the eighteenth century, this appropriation of nonfictional forms of literature into the form of the novel served yet another important purpose in legitimizing the novelist's "insight" into the private thoughts of his characters. The novelist employing such forms did not have to make any unusual claims to narrative authority. Richardson appears to be present in *Pamela* and *Clarissa* only as an editor; Defoe apparently allows Robinson Crusoe to "speak for himself." If the imaginative relationships between these authors and their characters are more complex than such formalistic distinctions allow for, these forms nonetheless were studiously maintained in order to determine the claims an author may have made about his knowledge of his fictional world. In this regard, even Fielding stops short of asserting any omniscient knowledge of Tom Jones's thoughts. Fielding's narrator is a public figure, intelligent and urbane, an astute observer of the human condition, an informed and self-conscious man of letters, a storyteller capable of reporting, inferring, and commenting upon the history of a young man's life. But no more.

With Jane Austen, the role of the novelist significantly changed. For the first time in English fiction the novelist's authority rested upon a claim to semi-omniscience — to a special narrative insight into the minds of her characters. With the development of this convention it was no longer necessary for the novelist to rely upon the appropriation of popular literary conventions to represent a character's most private life. Through the eyes of the semi-omniscient, and later the omniscient, narrator, the novelist acquired a seemingly unlimited freedom to explore both the private and the public lives of his characters. Nevertheless the novel remained and flourished as a "social" literature. While there were various forms of prose fiction in the eighteenth and nineteenth centuries — romances, satires, Gothic tales — all of which may loosely be called novels, the most remarkable and prolific achievements in English fiction came in the fulfillment of the novel's potential as social fiction: in the presentation of ordinary characters dramatically interacting among one another, sometimes seen in conflict between the private and public lives, usually shown in situations that readers could identify with the public and domestic realities of their own lives. In a literature of such particularity, the hollowness and emptiness that F. R. Leavis talks about really has no place.

Leavis has been attacked for his parochialism much too often and in ways that do not always attest to his critical insight. Despite his notorious selectivity, I think he is largely correct in identifying the "great tradition" in English fiction. Certainly among the many critics of Joseph Conrad, he remains one of the most astute. But aside from attributing to Conrad "a marked moral intensity," Leavis is mistaken in some crucial ways in placing Conrad next to Austen, Eliot, and James — the giants of the English social novel. After all, Conrad does not promise to examine the personal and social lives of his characters by rendering them in the context of public and historical institutions. Rather he promises to "render the highest kind of justice to the visible universe, by bringing to light the truth, manifold and one, underlying its every aspect." This statement, sometimes read as part of a realist's manifesto, is not written in the language of a social novelist. Nor does it sound quite like the language of a symbolist or an impressionist.[3] Rather, Conrad's promise reverberates in a vocabulary of an earlier era: *bringing to light the truth*, the truth *underlying* the visible universe, and the truth *manifold and one*. These are decidedly romantic locutions, closer to the language of the early nineteenth-century English poets than to anything written by Austen or Eliot or even James. In Conrad's fiction, the language of public discourse — the medium of the Great Tradition — is often subsumed within the effort to "penetrate" and enhance the visible universe and is manifested in narrators like Marlow, who serve to mediate between Conrad's readers and "the chaos of dark thoughts," the moral "abyss," "the night of first ages," and the "heart of darkness." These latter terms are the ones with which Conrad addresses an area of experience posited to exist beyond society, history, and human consciousness. If we are to find precedents for this language — if literary history will help us understand the vocabulary of Conrad's fiction — we must look to a literature other than social fiction.

This book has been written on the assumption that Conrad does partake in a special historical imagination, and that without some study of this imagination, we may risk some of Leavis's confusing talk about the paradoxical richness and hollowness of Conrad's work. I have given prominence to the heroic tales in my study, both because these stories have not received detailed critical attention as a sequential group and because the shape of Conrad's romanticism is best seen in the developments that occur within this sequence of heroic adventures. In providing a context for our understanding of Conrad's fiction, particularly his heroic tales, I have turned primarily to two traditions of heroic literature that speak to matters central to Conrad's imagination. One tradition, partly identified by Conrad himself, I have represented in a discussion of Richard Henry Dana, James Fenimore Cooper, Rudyard Kipling, and Stephen Crane. This strain of fiction involves a physical and metaphorical journey from a known world to an unknown or from civilization to the frontier. The second tradition links Milton and Wordsworth in a visionary journey, either into divine matters or into the mind of man.[4] Broadly common to both traditions is the assumption of a state of order, simplicity, or perfection destroyed, often of a heroic society dissolved by time, self-consciousness, or human corruption. Appearing also in modern literature in various forms, especially in Lawrence, Yeats, and Eliot, this is the myth of a paradise lost, the evocation of a nonhistorical community—sometimes rendered as a kind of pastoral world—that may be said to exist, if at all, only in the imagination of man.[5] For those adventure writers, such a paradise is expressed usually as a social ideal, an image of a unified and harmonious community uncorrupted by historical change, one in which the individual is in perfect accord with his fellow man. For Wordsworth, this ideal, much less social, is associated with the innocence of pastoral folk, all of whom are in close touch with nature and who comprise the human symbols of an almost mystical perfection in which the world is at one with itself. The journey undertaken under the fallen conditions of man is restorative in purpose. For the writers of adventure fiction, the object is to discover and perfect the virtues fundamental to a social ideal. For Wordsworth, it is to uncover in the darkness of human consciousness the sublime and visionary self. In Conrad, both of these traditions may be seen to intersect, both their journeys synthesize, and both of them fail. It is the sources, the processes, the character, and the implications of this failure with which I am concerned.

In establishing a link between Conrad and these two traditions, I have employed two kinds of documentation which are not always simultaneously possible, and two different notions of what a literary "influence" means. In the first instance, documentation is mostly external. There is no doubt that Conrad was well acquainted with the fiction of heroic adventure: he himself expressed his familiarity in stating his admiration for *The Red Badge of Courage*, *Captains Courageous*, and Cooper's *The Sea Lions*, three novels I will discuss in relation to Conrad's tales. While I can find no direct proof that Conrad was familiar with Dana's *Two Years Before the Mast*, he is known to have been an avid reader of travel journals and the autobiographies of adventurers. This fact should justify the inclusion of Dana within this tradition and as a part of the imagination I will suggest that they represent. By including Dana, however, I am beginning to suggest that literary influence is also a phenomenon of cultural imagination, not subject to a kind of documentation or proof that conventional scholarship sometimes demands: namely, an author's explicit reference to other literary figures in his essays, journals, notebooks, or letters; the titles and contents of an author's private library; or the personal connections between an author and his immediate circle of literary friends. Influence may also be traced through internal and textual evidence—through structural, metaphorical, etymological, and tonal connections—a method which may apply to both traditions I have mentioned.

Without challenging the validity of conventional wisdom, such a method suggests a different notion of what tradition and influence may mean for historical literary studies. The following and relatively simple example, relevant to the substance of my argument, illustrates my case. Near the end of *Paradise Lost*, Milton's narrator promises Adam and Eve that "The World was all before them, where to choose/Their place of rest." It is now commonly accepted that in the beginning of *The Prelude*, Wordsworth echoes those words and claims to inherit the burden of such a quest:

> What dwelling shall receive me? in what vale
> Shall be my harbour? underneath what grove
> Shall I take up my home? and what clear stream
> Shall with its murmur lull me into rest?
> The earth lay all before me.

The English novel, as I have remarked, did not share Wordsworth's romanticism, but it did quite often and for its own purposes adopt the idiom of the romantic quest. In *Great Expectations*, Pip on the way to London at the end of the first stage of his adventures, declares that "the mists had all solemnly risen now, and the world lay spread before me." In *The Portrait of a Lady*, Isabel Archer, who harbors her own expectations, bids farewell to her family at Euston Square thinking that "The world lay before her—she could do whatever she chose." Shortly thereafter, Gilbert Osmond rephrases Isabel's dreams in his characteristically languid and elegant way: "My dear girl, I can't tell you how life seems to stretch there before us – what a long summer afternoon awaits us." And in the last chapter of that novel, Casper Good-wood offers his own version of the romantic ideal, "The world's all before us – and the world's very big. I know something about that." This preoccu-pation with a lost paradise and with the discovery of a "paradise beyond" is part of a pervasive if often subliminal strain of romanticism in nineteenth-century English literature and may be identified quite apart from the kinds of external evidence I mentioned earlier. The examples of James and Dick-ens that I have mentioned are curious instances of novelists whose language is derived from Milton probably without their being consciously aware of that influence. Although it will jar some readers of Conrad to see him identified as part of a high romantic literary tradition, his place in that tradition depends no more upon his direct knowledge of Milton or Wordsworth than does the place of Dickens or James, however familiar any of them were with English romantic poetry. Language accumulates its meanings and assumes its forms as a result of historical pressures, and in that sense the relationship between history and language is deterministic. By inheriting a language, writers assume the past without being aware of all the ways in which language can define, limit, or generate thought. No writer can escape the fluid and mysterious configurations of prior literature in some combination or other, but among those who exert a counter-pressure against their historical predicament are those who become known as origi-nal. Some novelists seem almost instinctively aware of an historical situa-tion that makes prior modes of expression both inescapable and anachronis-tic. D. H. Lawrence in *The Rainbow* tells us that for Lydia and Tom Brangwen, "Everything was lost, and everything was found. The new world was discovered, it remained only to be explored." Here Lawrence, in 1915, is locating a moment in literary history, significantly in the middle of the nineteenth century and midway through his novel, when the promise of Wordsworth seemed about to be fulfilled.

But as Lawrence knew, it was not fulfilled, or at least not in a way that the modern novel could build upon. Like the story of the Brangwen family in *The Rainbow*, the record of nineteenth-century romanticism is insinuated most strikingly in its failures, or at best in its ambiguous success. Although Isabel Archer's disappointment ends in another kind of triumph of knowl-edge and feeling distantly associated with her youthful dreams, the expecta-tions of all the characters I have mentioned dissolve in some way; from Pip's mortification in the knowledge that his benefactor is a criminal to the loss of Tom and Lydia's covenant in the second generation following them. By the early twentieth century, the hope of a romantic paradise as the earlier century had imagined it had to be radically redefined, as in Lawrence, or expressed only as a parody, as in Joyce. Stephen Dedalus, contemplating his breakfast of sausages, eggs, and pudding in *A Portrait of the Artist as a Young Man*, exults, "How simple and beautiful was life after all! And life lay all before him."[6] Eventually the trauma of the lost paradise was itself to become lost, and with Joyce the British novel would take a different direction from the one anticipated early in *The Rainbow* and consummated in more modern terms in *Women in Love*. To understand Conrad within the context of English and American literature that I have defined is to identify a moment in literary history when the cumulative pressure of nineteenth-century romanticism emerges only to undergo romanticism's most spectacular collapse.

Romanticism, of course, is a word that may serve many critical purposes, and discussions of Conrad's heroic imagination tend to draw into competition notions of romanticism derived from very different sources. Sometimes he is seen in the context of a Polish nationalism that looks back nostalgically upon an aristocratic and chivalric world that has disappeared into the past.[7] Other times he is compared to Wordsworth in the way that each ostensibly celebrates an ideal of human solidarity and a harmony with nature.[8] He may also be discussed in relation to the romanticism of nineteenth-century France.[9] It is not my purpose to discount or to disagree with these other historical theories, but I have tried to be at once more selective and more complete than some of them in sketching Conrad's literary background. One of the reasons I refrain from talking about Flaubert, Du Maupassant, Schopenhauer, Pater, and Hardy, for example, is that an effort to discuss the comprehensive literary and intellectual backgrounds of Conrad's work is apt to blur rather than to clarify what I consider to be his most important historical precedents. Partly, too, Conrad's inheritances, like those of any major writer, are so extensive that it is likely to seem pretentious and at the same time mechanical to begin cataloguing all of them. But there is still a more important reason for my selectivity, and this stems from my desire not merely to "place" Conrad in literary history but also to account for the radical nature of his skepticism and the decisiveness of his failures to imagine a spiritual fulfillment in his version of the romantic quest. No doubt Conrad had strong affiliations with French aestheticians from Rousseau to Baudelaire, and that he partook in the imaginative climate that gave rise to modernism in France. Certainly Conrad's significance in English literature, like that of Henry James, Ford Madox Ford, and James Joyce, has much to do with his enrichment of it through the introduction of modern European ideas. But the transcendental romanticism of English and American literature, the personal and historical myth of a paradise lost, and the responsibility to the idea of a reality posited to exist beyond the imagination together hold Conrad in an even closer contact with the English. Similarly, the idea of the heroic journey in Conrad seems to respond most to English and American romanticism. For that reason, I place my greatest emphasis upon the imaginative processes in Conrad's work: upon the fate his fiction suffers in the rhetorical development of his stories, upon the ramifications of the heroic journey in his fiction, and upon the nature of Conrad's modern imagination, which I think is not so much opposed to Wordsworthian romanticism as it is an extension and a fulfillment of the most disquieting implications of the romantic quest.

If nothing else could make replication in literature impossible, cultural and literary history would. To say that Conrad is like Wordsworth in the way I am proposing is not to write an equation between them. It is not even to say that Conrad may be associated with Wordsworth in the same way that Wordsworth is associated with Milton, as a writer consciously trying to lay claim to the frontiers of his predecessor's territory. I am, rather, trying to isolate the historical development of a mode of imagination. The poet I call "Wordsworth" is to some extent an abstraction from the Wordsworth I would characterize in a work dealing exclusively with his career. I am interested primarily in those elements of Wordsworth that represent the apocalyptic and visionary strain of English romanticism and in the historical displacement, the logical extension, and the despiritualization of this romanticism in Conrad's heroic fiction. To read Conrad as a romantic is to see rhetorical and stylistic connections between him and earlier romantic writers, and to use stylistic analysis as a vehicle to understand the forces that organize an historical imagination. I assume what literary historians increasingly are insisting upon: literary history cannot invariably be made to observe even the most intelligent critical schemes. Distinctions among genres, literary periods, literary movements, and national literatures must necessarily be matters of some convenience, generalizations that run the risks of all generalizations in becoming too simple or too broad. The danger for scholarship is in any tendency to reify historical categories—to act as if a generalization is a tangible reality and functions as a rigid fact. What I find especially remarkable about Conrad is the extent to which he serves as a watershed for so many of romanticism's subconscious traumas, and the way he becomes a conduit for so much of nineteenth-century thought. In part, Conrad's imaginative make up may be explained by his international background, in part by biographical circumstances that lend themselves to expression in various romantic modes. I have speculated upon some of the reasons for Conrad's romanticism, but I have also held that the study of Conrad's literary performance is more practical and fecund than an explanation for its cause. It is in the spirit of this attitude that I make my historical connections.

My generalizations about Wordsworth are based upon selective examples from his writing, the scholarship of other critics, and my sense of what he means for Conrad, without much regard for the differences between the poet's earlier and later work. My specific quotations come primarily from the Preface to the *Lyrical Ballads* (which I compare to Conrad's Preface to *The Nigger of the "Narcissus"*); from some of the early short poems; from Books I and VI and Books XII-XIV of *The Prelude*; and from Book I of *The Recluse*, where I think the currents between Wordsworth and Conrad run deepest. My choice of nineteenth-century adventure stories has been partly determined by Conrad himself.

Thus, in my first chapter I will define a literary context and complete my introduction to Conrad. In the succeeding four chapters I will discuss the progress of Conrad's heroic imagination from 1897 to 1909, along a route which itself becomes a journey into the modern world. My last chapter, finally, has three purposes. The first is to offer some conclusions about the adventure tales as a group. The second is to carry my arguments to Conrad's political novels and in a relatively brief discussion to demonstrate how such a seemingly different kind of fiction from that of the adventure tales actually shares common assumptions about language, heroism, and human experience. My analysis of these later novels is necessarily shorter than my readings of the adventure tales, not because the political novels are less important, but because a detailed study of them would either be repetitious of my earlier arguments or would lead to other matters beyond the scope of this book. I have tried, rather, to discuss the points of comparison between the earlier tales and the later novels in order to extend the ideas I develop in the preceding chapters. Finally, I conclude this book by briefly examining in terms of my study the relationship between Conrad and other modern novelists, particularly Lawrence and Joyce. Like my first chapter, my concluding pages are not intended to define comprehensively the literary matrices of an historical period. I try to show, instead, that Conrad's romanticism both allies him with and distinguishes him from other modern novelists. And I suggest that we may look at Conrad's career in the same way that Marlow imagines his adventures in the Congo: as a heroic journey unsuccessfully completed, but one, we should add, that only he had the courage to make.

1

Culture and the Heroic Self

> There is something in the first gray streaks stretching along the eastern horizon and throwing an indistinct light upon the face of the deep, which combines with the boundlessness and unknown depth of the sea around, and gives one a feeling of loneliness, of dread, and of melancholy foreboding, which nothing else in nature can. This gradually passes away as the light grows brighter, and when the sun comes up, the ordinary monotonous sea day begins.

The voice that meditates in the first sentence of the previous passage over the boundlessness of the ocean at dawn could be the voice of Melville's Ishmael. The imagery, shadowy, illusive, and immense, could be that of Conrad's first narrator in "Heart of Darkness." But the last sentence of the passage is strangely settled and unruffled over the whole episode and reports the passing of this almost cosmic loneliness as if it were a slight case of nausea or a transient morning shower. It is a sentence spoken by one who believes that the world is a soluble mystery, one who is not easily shaken from his conception of himself or his confidence that time and patience will return him to the familiar and the conventional. This writer has survived the terrors of the sea without suffering so much as a ripple in his imagination.

Two Years Before the Mast, the book from which this passage is taken, has become a classic among both autobiographies and sea adventures, largely because its story of a young man's initiation into manhood is a trial, not only of the man's physical endurance and adaptability, but of the resilience of his culture as well. Going to sea to improve his health, Dana at the same time reminds us that his voyage requires numerous, and at first liberating, changes in the cultural identity he brought with him aboard the brig *Pilgrim*. He describes to us how he replaces his frock coat and kid gloves with a checked shirt and duck trousers, how he must eat salt beef instead of sweetmeats and in effect learn a new language to become one of the crew, and how his work aloft is rewarded with a "Well done" from the mate instead of a "*Bene*" at the foot of a Latin exercise at Harvard. Dana humorously describes his seasickness ("there could be none worse than mine"[1]) as an initiation into the hardy life of the sea. And after the first few days of the voyage, he proclaims, "I was a new being . . . I felt somewhat like a man" (p. 10). Yet, once arrived in California, Dana begins to worry that more than two years (seemingly an arbitrary figure that he nonetheless insists upon) away from Harvard might irreparably change his character and his mind, that psychologically and imaginatively, if not in physical fact, he may never be able to return. Happily for him, then, he manages to secure an early passage on another vessel and, once again, saves himself from the inner terrors of a life at sea.

The purpose of this paraphrase is to begin defining what in the nineteenth century had become a cultural myth that informed the fiction of heroic journeys. That Dana is writing nonfiction in his autobiography is not at all beside the point for it will help establish that in these adventure stories, life and art share a common form and a common destiny. Dana becomes typical of what I characterize as the hero of nineteenth-century adventure journeys when he proclaims, "I was separating myself from all the social and intellectual enjoyments of life. Yet, strange as it may seem, I did then and afterward take pleasure in these reflections, hoping by them to prevent my becoming insensible to the value of what I was losing" (p 6). Although he changes his clothes, delights in a new language, and adapts to a physically demanding style of life, in the most important ways Dana never really leaves Boston behind him. Throughout the course of both his voyages, he comes alive for us as an impressively intelligent young gentleman educating himself, not in a Harvard classroom to be sure, but in much the same style upon the sea. We are always aware of his decent, idealistic mind, his well-trained eye for sociological observations, his future lawyer's zeal for possible defenses of and reforms for seamen's legal rights. During the tedious days of the return voyage, he comforts and entertains himself with private recitations straight from years spent in New England Yankee schools and hours compiling notebooks and journals during the voyage: "the multiplication table and the tables of weights and measures; the Kanaka numerals; then the states of the Union, with their capitals; the counties of England, with their shire towns; and the thirty-ninth chapter of Job. . . . Cowper's 'Castaway'" (p. 341). Dana possesses a vault of cultural wealth which he may draw upon with a resourcefulness that is awesome in itself. He is never at a loss for the appropriate quotation, the suitable literary allusion, or timely social and political analogies that serve as his map and compass to keep him well-located. He is what D. H. Lawrence contemptuously and admiringly describes in his fine essay on Dana as a "knower" who "must conquer the sea in his consciousness."[2] He makes his voyage another of his intellectual acquisitions, even when his experience of the sea seems to resist the kind of mental exercises he is intent upon performing. It is no wonder to us that, returning to Boston, his health apparently restored, he reenters Harvard, graduates, takes his law degree, and becomes a prominent public figure in mid-nineteenth century America. The sea adventure has become part of his cultural life, memorialized in this book and rendered further into terms he can understand, when he writes *The Seaman's Friend*—a description of seamen's duties and a summary of shipboard law. Dana becomes an example of the nineteenth-century man who turns his adventures and their moral implications (his "health" is not simply a physical condition) into an education and initiation—not into a life beyond the codes and conventions of his cultural background but ultimately into the life we might expect him to have lived had he not gone to sea.

Half a century later, at the height of the Victorian empire and in the same year that Conrad completed *The Nigger of the "Narcissus,"* Rudyard Kipling wrote his memorable adventure story, *Captains Courageous.* Although often considered a children's book, in its own way it is as serious as *Gulliver's Travels* or *Huckleberry Finn.* The story is familiar to most of us. The wealthy, soft, arrogant son of an American railroad tycoon falls overboard from an ocean liner and is picked up by a Gloucester fishing schooner, the *We're Here,* where he becomes subject to the rigors and disciplines of a life in the fishing fleet, emerging at the end of the voyage what Kipling would call a "man." Like Dana, Harvey Cheyne learns to imitate the habits, manners, and speech of the fishermen, and also like Dana he feels all this to be a liberating experience. His identity more than Dana's is dressed out in externals: he learns to steer the vessel, he has to clean fish, he participates in the schooner races, he confronts a dead seaman snagged on his line—all of which require performances different from the ones he is accustomed to. But Harvey never really becomes one of the fishermen. His summer aboard the *We're Here* is an almost pastoral experience among tough, hard-working, even-tempered men who collectively serve him as part of his education into a more sophisticated society. When Harvey returns, he is ready to become the kind of man whom, oddly enough, his father can finally admire.

Toward the end of the novel, father and son hold a long conversation on the subject of manhood. "'Men can 'most always tell when a man has handled things for himself,'" says Cheyne Sr., "'and then they treat him as one of themselves.'"[3] Self-reliance, physical and moral toughness, a view of life as hard work, all seem to characterize this fraternity that Cheyne Sr. talks about. But what has Harvey Jr. really learned? That his father after all holds the same values of rugged individualism that Harvey himself has acquired on the Grand Banks. Kipling obviously admires the elder Cheyne, because his rags-to-riches success is the story of how a basically good man excelled by his own hard work. If his wealth became tainted in his son's hands, the reason is that Harvey had yet to go through the same learning process as his father and had yet to learn what a morally debilitating environment could not teach. For its services to Harvey Cheyne and the social ideal, the pastoral world of Captain Disko Troop is rewarded by the elder Cheyne's patronage. Dan, the captain's son, becomes through the elder Cheyne's influence a second mate in a west coast shipping line. Thus the two boys, Harvey and Dan, grow closer to one another. And, as Harvey goes to college to complete the other part of his education, the world of the fishermen seems to fade into the past, leaving the best of its values behind.

As the pairing of Dana and Kipling suggests, the type of hero I am concerned with for now is not the Byronic or the Promethean hero of Romantic poetry. And although I am talking about heroic journeys, the heroes I discuss have little in common with Odysseus, Aeneas, Galahad, or the knights of *The Faerie Queene*. The nineteenth-century hero of adventure journeys travels not in the company of great warriors but in the shadows of Bunyan's Christian and Scott's "mediocre prosaic hero."[4] Certainly, too, he is related to Robinson Crusoe. He is a man who ventures outside of his conventional social and cultural environment to experience some ordeal that challenges his culturally-derived moral beliefs and sense of himself. And he is a man who, if successful, returns to reject whatever was extraneous or imperfect in his own social identity and to reassert the ideal values and mores fundamental to his society. It is appropriate that the impulse behind this kind of story is frequently a sense of cultural nostalgia, a feeling that society has betrayed what is indispensable to its moral order, and that a model citizen is necessary to reassert whatever has been lost. Scott, the nineteenth-century father of the citizen-hero, associates heroic conduct almost exclusively with events of the past, while deliberately populating his history with men who are timelessly bourgeois in their conduct and values.[5] Scott writes with a mission to redeem order from possible chaos, to resolve social and political conflicts, to make peace with historical change. Unsurprisingly, the adventure story that takes its cue from Scott is not as likely to renounce a degenerate society as it is to find ways to reform it.

Conveniently, like the environment of Christian in *The Pilgrim's Progress*, that of the hero in this tradition facilitates his reassertion of cultural values. Though in some ways hostile, the geography of the journey is ideal to provide the hero with the right kind of trial: to lead him through a struggle whose moral logic is already laid down, to offer him choices whose right and wrong are made obvious by whatever survival (both physical and moral) under such conditions requires. To succeed, the hero must fall back upon the ideals of his culture; often he must, in effect, bring that culture with him. And what he doesn't already know about the ideals of his society, he must learn by his intuitive adaptations to the rigors of the adventure. The heroic journey, then, becomes not so much a departure from his culture as it is a rediscovery of it in its ideal form.

One implication of this kind of heroism is ultimately to deny heroic individuality to the hero in most conventional senses of the term. Rather than becoming a paragon who stands above his peers or a Prometheus who stands beyond them, this hero adopts a more commonplace identity sanctioned by various social, professional, religious, governmental, and literary institutions of the society from which he comes. What in the imagination of Tennyson might have been a world of a heroic aristocracy becomes in nineteenth-century fiction a social and public world in a more realistic sense; and what had been heroic virtues in the greater adventure stories of earlier centuries become the public, middle class virtues of a nineteenth-century society.

One of the best examples of this middle class myth of heroism is to be found in a novel by James Fenimore Cooper called *The Sea Lions*. In an article included in his *Notes on Life and Letters* called "Tales of the Sea," Conrad spends lavish praise upon Cooper and Frederick Marryat. Of Cooper he says:

> It is hard to believe that Manual and Borroughcliffe, Mr. Marble of Marble-Head, Captain Tuck of the packetship Montauk, or Daggett, the tenacious commander of the Sea Lion of Martha's Vineyard, must pass away some day and be utterly forgotten.6

The similarities between Conrad and Cooper are more numerous than may be at first apparent. Both had a professional and first hand knowledge of seamanship and delighted in maritime literature. Both were preoccupied with the idea of a journey beyond the civilized world. Both (though Conrad in a more complicated way), were essentially conservative in their values and shared an aristocratic nostalgia for a simple and timeless past. In the passage I have quoted, moreover, it is evident that Conrad admired one of Cooper's more obscure works, *The Sea Lions* (1849), which bears some resemblance to Conrad's heroic fiction in both its intention and in the problems it encounters.

The official hero of *The Sea Lions* is one Roswell Gardiner, a young sea captain from the village of Oyster Pond, New York, who sets out on a seal hunting expedition to the Antarctic regions. Gardiner's schooner, the *Sea Lion*, is financed by Deacon Pratt, a caricature of sham Puritanism, whose niggardly interests are excited by reports of an uncharted sealing island in the South Atlantic and a buried treasure on an island in the West Indies, both of which he has learned about from a dying seaman. Gardiner, like Natty Bumppo, is courageous, honest, naive, charitable, a little headstrong, but above all uncorrupted by any mean or selfish ambitions. He consents to carry out Pratt's treasure hunt, not from a desire for the pirated wealth, but primarily out of loyalty to his patron. Gardiner's character does, however, have one flaw, and that is in his freethinking, rationalistic rejection of Trinitarian Christianity. To Cooper, his freethinking is seen as egocentric pride and heresy, and in this novel it prevents Mary Pratt, the deacon's niece and ward and a picture of orthodox Christian piety, from consenting to marry Gardiner, whom she otherwise loves.

Gardiner's counterpart and competitor in his adventure is Jason Daggett of Martha's Vinyard (the character Conrad mentions), a nephew of the dead seaman and a man who seeks the same islands as Gardiner. Daggett commands a second schooner, also, by virtue of its same commercial use, and Cooper's intended symbolism, called the *Sea Lion* of Martha's Vineyard. The two schooners proceed to the southern Atlantic, Daggett most of the time following Gardiner, who knows the exact location of the islands. The result of this pairing is a relationship sometimes antagonistic, sometimes symbiotic, sometimes, during Daggett's manipulations of Gardiner's goodwill, parasitic, and one upon which the allegory of the novel largely depends.

Briefly, Gardiner's prudent management of his affairs results in a full load of seal skins and oil, while Daggett's vessel takes weeks longer to obtain a reasonable catch. Because Gardiner stays longer in the southern seas to help Daggett, whose schooner is damaged by ice, the two crews have to spend the winter near the Antarctic Circle. During an ordeal of incredible hardship, Gardiner lives and Daggett dies, confessing his sins on his death bed. The experience of ordeal and adventure makes Gardiner reassess his religious beliefs, and he comes to accept the Trinity on faith, after which he returns to marry Pratt's niece and make a small fortune from his cargo of furs. The treasure, which turns out to be a rather modest amount of gold, Gardiner finds and delivers to Pratt, but the deacon, who has been long ill, dies before his reaction can be fully observed. Gardiner then gives up the life of the sea and leaves Oyster Pond, settles down, becomes a miller in western New York state, and with Mary lives happily ever after.

The novel is governed by a scheme which encompasses the conventions of an adventure story, a Christian allegory, and a fairy tale, and at the same time works itself into political and social resolutions. Good and bad are duly rewarded. Commercial enterprise comes to express a larger physical and moral ordeal of men against the elements, which in turn leads to the religious conversion of Gardiner. And finally, Gardiner's courage is demonstrated to be at the service of essentially institutional values, though not necessarily values to be found practiced elsewhere in his society. He becomes a good Christian, attains some wealth, becomes a steady family man, and learns a trade which is much less mobile and adventuresome than that of a seaman. Gardiner's courage, in short, helps him to find his place in a stable and ideal corner of society. And, similar to Dana's story, the sea adventure in *The Sea Lions* is ultimately valued not as an initiation into exotic or esoteric experiences, nor even as individual self-discovery, but rather as an investiture of a young man into the ideal structure of his society.

So far, we can see the similarity in pattern between this novel and the works of Dana and Kipling that I have mentioned. We can also anticipate some of the differences between this kind of work and Conrad's adventure stories, particularly *Lord Jim* and "Heart of Darkness." But *The Sea Lions* yields even richer material than *Two Years* or *Captains Courageous* for an understanding of Conrad, particularly on the level of cultural myth. Throughout *The Sea Lions*, Roswell Gardiner represents the American capable of redemption. Coming from a fundamentally simple, pastoral New York maritime community, he is in touch with America's grass roots culture and serves as a link between the contemporary America Cooper imagines as disordered and corrupt and the old America of Cooper's political mythology, a kind of Jeffersonian paradise. Conrad's Jim is of a similar ilk; Gardiner is "one of us" as we would like to be.

Cooper is also much like Kipling in the latter's cultural conservatism and in his myth of initiation into a social ideal. But Cooper's imagination is less ordered than Kipling's, and his sense of the heroic ordeal is, like Conrad's, less easily contained by literary structures. According to the novel's moral scheme, Daggett represents all that has gone wrong with America in his unthinking, reckless, self-centered ambitions. Throughout the book, "Vineyarder" becomes a metaphor for unscrupulous democratic commercialism. Yet there is something which for Cooper is dangerously exciting about Daggett—something like the qualities Marlow sees in Kurtz—which makes him, dramatically at least, a more appealing character than the almost saintly Gardiner. It suggests a heroism of sorts is to be found beyond the moral framework of the "mediocre prosaic hero." When in one instance the two men compete for a whale that is finally killed by Gardiner, an argument over right to the whale ensues. Daggett's guileful claims are answered by Gardiner's lecture on American shipping law, during which the narrator interrupts to remark about Daggett, "it seemed to him un-American, un-Vineyard, if the reader please, to 'give up'; and he clung to his error with as much pertinacity as if he had been right."[7] Following a description of both men standing by the carcass of the whale with their lances imbedded in the animal's blubber to steady themselves, Daggett's "clinging" to his error is virtually literalized by his hold on the lance. There is an intensity about Daggett, and a kind of dramatic as well as commercial opportunism expressed even in this relatively minor scene, which brings him out in striking relief, while the morally upright Gardiner, though described in exactly the same pose, stands overshadowed, as if off in the distance.

While the moral conflict of the novel is abstractly and allegorically represented by the opposing ethical principles of Daggett and Gardiner, it is the Vineyarder who provides the impetus for the dramatic conflict. He stalks Gardiner through the southern Atlantic, persuades, manipulates, and cajoles him into helping him hunt seals, and constantly plays upon his sense of duty as a brother seaman to distract him from returning home with a cargo of seal skin and oil. In the most intensely dramatic moments of the novel, Daggett usually dominates the action with his reckless but practiced daring and his superior seamanship. And almost by this energy alone, Daggett resists Cooper's categorical judgments: even Cooper confesses to Daggett's complexity. In fact, when the novel's mythical dimensions are most fully realized, the standards of conduct implicit in Cooper's allegorical scheme become practically irrelevant to the demands of the environment. The following passage, which extends an analogy between the icebergs and a painting of a ruined town of alabaster suggests an experience disassociated from the common, homespun, theological directives that shape the course of Cooper's adventure story:

> As the vessels came driving into the midst of the bergs, everything contributed to render the movements imposing in all senses, appalling in one. There lay the vast maze of floating mountains, generally of a spectral white at that hour, though many of the masses emitted hues more pleasing, while some were black as night. The passages between the bergs, or what might be termed the streets and lanes of this mysterious-looking, fantastical, yet sublime city of the ocean, were numerous, a league in length; others winding and narrow; while a good many were little more than fissures, that might be fancied lanes. (pp. 281–82)[8]

While reading this passage we tend to forget the modest and sober analogy to the painting that Cooper makes in prefacing this description, even when he reminds us that he is still making it. The effect, instead, is a vision of a spectral city, a beautiful, frightening, and awesome spectacle which seems to depict both nature and the civilized world in a lonely twilight, on the extreme edge of the human predicament. On this frontier of the known world near the Antarctic Circle, the two vessels and their crews seem to enact a treacherous and symbolic voyage through both earthly and spiritual experience. The dramatic and the symbolic qualities of this passage are indistinguishable. The ordeal of the schooners is both one of seamanship and physical endurance and one of moral fortitude in meeting the challenge of a vast, empty, and impersonal universe which does not seem to lend itself to ideological oratory. On these waters Daggett is a worthy competitor of Gardiner's, in fact, he appears to be Gardiner's superior. Seemingly by his very energy and resourcefulness Daggett threatens not only to usurp the seat of dramatic interest from Gardiner, but also to subvert his moral position as well, for the outcome of this ordeal will certainly carry a moral significance. Therefore, in order to deal out the proper rewards and punishments and to make the novel illustrate his theological doctrines, Cooper has to destroy Daggett and vindicate Gardiner. Both are accomplished by the winter episode and the subsequent religious conversions.

Thomas Philbrick, who has written the most extensive critical account of *The Sea Lions*, notes that the theological voice of the sea adventure is dramatically represented by an old seaman named Stimson, who may perhaps be seen as a forerunner of Conrad's Singleton. In a series of fatuous sermons, Stimson, as Melville says in a review appearing in *Literary World* (April 28, 1849), "discourses unctuously upon various dogmas."[9] While Stimson is for Cooper the archetype of the good Christian, for us he represents the major flaw in the novel. Just as Daggett is unintentionally made appealing, Stimson is unintentionally made a bore. "Stimson," Philbrick remarks, "is unalloyed by human failings; he never blunders, never swears, never drinks, never even chews tobacco."[10] Aside from reminding Gardiner to observe the Sabbath, Stimson is constantly making what for us appear ludicrous suggestions, such as recommending that the men bathe themselves in snow and wear fewer clothes to harden themselves to the Antarctic winter. Like a medieval monastic, Stimson directs the pattern of the redemptive ordeal.

During the winter sequences the novel thus begins to take a different shape, announcing more insistently the differences between the protagonist and the antagonist. Gardiner and Daggett gravitate in different directions, with Gardiner retreating into his makeshift shelter to read the Bible Mary gave to him and to listen to Stimson preach, and Daggett withdrawing to his schooner, wrecked upon the ice. Refusing to leave his hopeless wreck and his dreams of success, refusing even to use his vessel for firewood, Daggett, who now sounds even more like Kurtz, becomes isolated from the rest of humanity and increasingly distinguishable from Gardiner, who believes that his own survival signifies the mercy of God. Two kinds of isolation are thus examined: the isolation of the vain, worldly man, and that of the contemplative, religious man. Literally Daggett dies because he lets his fire go out, and Gardiner lives because he is prudent enough to keep his going. Symbolically, Daggett dies because of his unyielding egocentricity, while Gardiner survives because he learns to adjust to the spiritual order of the universe. To assert this allegorical strategy in the novel, however, Cooper has to separate the two men from direct competition, strip them of their material possessions, divest the novel of its dramatic conflicts, and destroy Daggett in both his death and in his pathetic, demeaning, and uncharacteristic confession of his sins. And while Cooper thereby remains true to the theological implications of each man's conduct, the logic of these implications is founded upon his abstract doctrines in which good and evil are justly rewarded. The field of moral conflict is no longer to be found among spectral images of a frozen sea, but in Stimson's oratory and in Cooper's revived allegorical plan.

The ways in which Marlow's survival and Kurtz's death in "Heart of Darkness" are prefigured in the fates of Gardiner and Daggett will become clearer in chapter 3, as will Conrad's departure from Cooper's conservative myth of heroic adventure. For now, it is important to understand what course this conservative myth has taken in *The Sea Lions*. At a moment of extreme hardship, Gardiner is described as reacting in this way: "But pride of profession, ambition, love of Mary, dread of the deacon, native resolution, and the hardihood produced by experience in dangers often encountered and escaped, nerved him to the undertaking" (p. 203). Gardiner's courage plays into Cooper's scheme; it consists of an appeal to prior experiences, an abstract and generalized motivation, and an established social background and code of ethics, all of which suggest common social values that exist apart from any individual man. There is nothing reckless or even particularly daring about Gardiner's courage, as there is about Daggett's. And while Daggett may be a representative Vineyarder, a type of American who dies because he refuses to relinquish his obsessions, his character eventually isolates him from Martha's Vineyard, from his culture, and even from his generalized and abstract moral traits. Gardiner, on the other hand, subscribes to a moral code that may be conveniently reasserted in times of danger. He hardly seems like an individual at all, but rather an institutional self, an embodiment of moral abstractions who is given very little dramatic strength or public expression. What Gardiner does learn from his experience in the South Atlantic is that he ought to become more orthodox and conformist than he already is. The frigid winter threatens his life, and he responds by reasserting that institutional identity, which is the only way in which "life" for him has any meaning. He is thus a hero, not so much because he dares to perform, but rather because he conforms and endures.

In the end, *The Sea Lions* serves to create a sense of cultural permanence out of rural, pastoral America engaged in Christian trials, exotic adventures, and conventional economic enterprise. Roswell Gardiner and Mary disappear into the history of the "new" America Cooper imagines. Oyster Pond becomes a railroad depot, the citizens change its name: the old pastoral America is dead. But the Gardiner family reestablishes a new kind of permanence in western New York, in a life that combines the virtues of honest labor, the moral purity and simplicity of rustic America, and a traditional faith in God. Cooper's heroic doctrine returns the hero from the frontier to the fireside, and in doing so, he has sacrificed the best of his creative imagination to his lukewarm sense of the social ideal.

Like the other books I have discussed, *The Sea Lions* makes its appeal to us in part as a form of cultural reinforcement. In some important ways, however, Cooper responds to more complex pressures than Dana or Kipling, because he is much less sure of the culture he is trying to defend, and because he is much more sensitive to the risks to which he exposes his imagination of order. In the end he cannot cope with the full burden of his spiritual ordeal. His idea of order falsifies what we feel after the Antarctic voyage: the pastoral simplicity of the old Oyster Pond and the pastoral life of Gardiner's post-heroic vocation in New York state impose comfortable boundaries upon the most intense experiences in the novel. Both exist almost outside the novel as models of an image reminiscent of an eighteenth-century version of the ideal country life. Thus, at both ends of the story Cooper is anchored to literary versions of social harmony, while the novel makes us aware of a contrived plot and prescribed ideology to settle its hero's confrontation with a nature we have come to see as threatening to all forms of self-identification.

For Kipling, this threat is never posed. Like several English adventure writers of the late eighteenth and early nineteenth centuries (Frederick Marryat, for instance, in *Mr. Midshipman Easy*), Kipling portrays an individual acting against a historical background to which he must finally conform. In such a novel the destiny of the hero seems to recapitulate the historical progress of the ideal society: Harvey Cheyne's education begins with a discovery of pastoral prototypes whose work ethic he carries over to a more complex and historically advanced society. Although *Captains Courageous* is a story about Americans, its idea of the self (and its generally comic atmosphere) is typically English in the ways Harvey makes amends for his early blunders by becoming a member of a traditional fraternity of men. Dana, at the other extreme, triumphs in characteristically American terms. Dana is an embodiment of a culture that, through his consciousness, is capable of assimilating and controlling that which is alien or threatening. The American mind in this instance becomes strengthened in its own values by passing the test of its durability and plasticity, proving its ability to expand without altering its composition. Cooper in this spectrum falls somewhere in between. In Cooper, nature and its spiritual significance are beyond the egocentric controls of man, and so man must find ways to submit to and retreat from it. Gardiner's shelter is in prearranged images of social order, in rigidified theological doctrine, in comfortable but barren evocations of the individual in harmony with society. One might say, therefore, that the risks Gardiner takes are essentially American, while the adjustments he makes for survival are typically English.

In all cases, though, what the Americans have in common with the English is the need to remain in touch with institutionalized forms of behavior. Dana's greatest fears, like those of Gardiner, are of losing his social and ideological bearings. How incidental the fear of physical danger is to that of moral and imaginative collapse in such cases is illustrated by Dana's fear of drowning. For Dana, death by drowning is particularly horrifying, because instead of a corpse, a wake, and a formal burial, only the empty sea remains: "A man dies on shore; his body remains with his friends and 'the mourners go about the streets'. . . . A man is shot down by your side in battle and the mangled body remains an object, and a real evidence; but at sea, the man is near you — at your side — you hear his voice, and in an instant he is gone, and nothing but a vacancy shows his loss" (p. 37). The environment — the nonhuman, noncultural, natural environment — invades man's imagination of himself and triumphs. The powers of consciousness, in Lawrence's terms, fail to conquer the sea. Although similar fears in English fiction are generally not expressed in the same ways — in fact, are usually not even considered — it is worthwhile to note that Robinson Crusoe's greatest terrors are of drowning, cave-ins, and cannibalism: death by physical self-dissolution. The territory of Crusoe's self-aggrandizing projects is much more limited than that of Dana — in fact, he marks it off and throws walls up around it to protect himself and his microcosm of the English economic system. And unlike Dana, Crusoe maintains a sense of himself that is almost always a tangible, material, measurable manifestation of his cultural ideology. But the object of each character's efforts is essentially the same: to make an alien environment part of the cultural self and to resist any encroachment upon that self-identity that cannot be consciously absorbed.

Although *The Sea Lions* is a minor novel by most standards and is much less impressive than *Robinson Crusoe* or *Two Years Before the Mast*, it is symptomatic of a crucial change in the tradition of heroic journeys, one that develops more in America than in England. Because the heroic journey in Cooper nearly ends — both literally and symbolically — in the depths of the Antarctic sea, Cooper must invent a way to rescue his hero and his allegory, which, as I have shown, after much contrivance he does. But it is precisely because the journey becomes a device intended to rescue the hero rather than to challenge him, and because this device requires the further help of an imposed ideology to make it work, the whole idea of the journey as a heroic ordeal may be called into question. In other words, the idea of such heroism presents itself as something artificial—a plot in a book, a myth of social order, a falsification of heroic ordeal, perhaps even as a lie. When conventional heroism becomes suspect in this way, we are moving closer to the heroic imagination of Joseph Conrad.

More than any book I have discussed, there is one that celebrates the ordeal of the nineteenth-century hero at the same time that it explodes the myth that sustained him. Stephen Crane's *The Red Badge of Courage* luxuriates in all the apparatus of heroic initiation and cultural reinforcement: like *The Sea Lions*, it takes the common man as its hero, it follows the pattern of trial and redemption, it asserts the concept of the individual as a cultural creation, and it is extravagantly self-oriented in a way that makes it typically American. But at the same time the novel is suffused with the light of irony. It is comic in a way that keeps it vaguely in touch with Kipling, but ultimately its comedy embraces not only Henry Fleming but the entire mode of experience represented by Fleming's (and, analogously, Cheyne's) adventure. In Crane, as in Cooper and Kipling, a young man becomes a hero in order to become a part of a society. His journey through the heroic ordeal also reinforces the codes and conventions of the popular imagination, and his heroism is not simply in his display of courage but in his implicit defense of the common man. Crane, after all, is willing to leave his readers feeling happy about Henry Fleming's initiation into "life." Most of his readers do. But if you care to inquire about heroism, Crane implies, this initiation has little to do with individual human will and nothing to do with private self-discovery. If you're happy with Henry Fleming at the end of the novel, then you are looking at him merely through the rose-colored glasses of a Kipling-esque social myth.

Crane's authorial voice in *The Red Badge of Courage* seems unobtrusive and objective. There is very little about it that calls attention to itself as a presence in the novel, and there is virtually no explicit authorial commentary. Apparently what we hear is a recounting of the youth's contemplation of his experience from what usually appears to be a neutral point of view:

> From his home his youthful eyes had looked upon the war in his own country with distrust. It must be some sort of a play affair. He had long despaired of witnessing a Greeklike struggle. Such would be no more, he had said. Men were better or more timid. Secular and religious education has effaced the throat-grappling instinct, or else firm finance held in check the passions.[11]

There is some slight irony here: the reminder of Fleming's "youthful eyes" and of his perspective, "from his home," is mildly indulgent. His pronouncements on history may seem amusingly pompous in their distinctions between the bygone days when men were men (or perhaps when men were barbarians — the youth is philosophically noncommittal) and the debased, or more civilized, present. But the narrator doesn't make much of the irony and soon goes on to talk about the mother's reactions to her son's enlistment. Then, a couple of pages later, we hear something oddly familiar:

> He was brought then gradually back to his old ideas. Greeklike struggles would be no more. Men were better, or more timid. Secular and religious education had effaced the throat-grappling instinct, or else firm finance held in check the passions. (p. 29)

The last two sentences of this short paragraph are, of course, exact repetitions of those sentences three pages earlier — and how strange is the effect. Earlier, in the first appearance of this passage, the youth seems to be making an effort to rise above the limited perspectives of his social and cultural predicament by commenting upon these limitations. His attempt there is only slightly comic. But by virtue of the second occurrence of the passage, the observation that earlier seemed an effort of his reflection now seems merely a conditioned response, a mechanical formula that he repeats to himself under certain conditions of introspection. The narrator's role also appears changed. While he is still reporting the youth's reflections upon war with only a touch of irony, whatever sense of authorial neutrality we felt earlier now has to be reevaluated. When Kipling simply "reports" Harvey Cheyne's experiences, we are never in doubt that he fully supports Cheyne in the boy's initiation into life, even when he jokes about his naivete. Every step of the way Kipling is sympathetic towards Cheyne. Similarly, Cooper helps his hero Gardiner by giving us a sense that everything which happens to him will finally be all for the best. Crane's "reporting," however, leaves us feeling that young Fleming is, with respect to the narrator, on his own, subject to ironies not entirely of the narrator's making. The mere reporting of such ironies becomes a way in which the narrator implicitly withdraws the authorial sympathy that is given by his counterparts to Gardiner and Cheyne. When we look for this sympathy, the best we sense is a faint, indulgent smile. And as the preceding passage shows, the second time around, we don't even imagine the smile; we listen, rather, to a mechanical and impersonal voice. Crane creates a narrative language that sounds very knowing and worldly-wise, yet is above human affairs in a way that relegates feelings and emotions to a lower order of experience. At the same time, this language refrains from commenting upon the workings of the human mind, perhaps from disdain for commentary, perhaps from an implicit reverence for the impersonality to which these workings seem subject.

The effect of Crane's writing throughout the novel is similarly impersonal. It is a commonplace that nature in Crane is indifferent to the trials of the youth and the horrors of the battle: "As he gazed around him the youth felt a flash of astonishment at the blue, pure sky and the sun gleaming on the trees and fields. It was surprising that Nature had gone tranquilly on with her golden process in the midst of so much devilment" (p. 70). At times, however, nature holds faint echoes of a magical, pastoral nature that cooperates with man in his endeavors, or of a heroic nature that heralds his achievements. But even then, Crane teases us by evoking natural images that do not conjure up feelings associated with conventional man-nature formulas:

> The cold passed reluctantly from the earth, and the retiring fogs revealed an army stretched out on the hills, resting. As the landscape changed from brown to green, the army awakened, and began to tremble with eagerness at the noise of rumors. It cast its eyes upon the roads, which were growing from long troughs of liquid mud to proper thoroughfares. A river, amber-tinted in the shadow of its banks, purled at the army's feet; and at night, when the stream had become a sorrowful blackness, one could see across it the red, eyelike gleam of hostile camp fires in the low brows of the distant hills. (p. 21)

In the personifications of nature and the army, one might expect that nature has something to do with the affairs of men, as one might read about a mythical nature which is responsive to the actions of heroes. The metaphors of the passage create subtle and intricate relationships between nature and man: the fog "retires," as if it might be the army, while the army is "stretched out" on the hills, in terms that could equally apply to a fog. The suggestion of a subdued metaphorical equation between the landscape and the army continues as the stream momentarily becomes human with its "sorrowful blackness," while the campfires gleam "eyelike" in the "low brows" of the hills.

Yet Crane somehow does not establish these metaphorical equations securely. Certainly the heroic proportions are there, but the suggested logic of the analogies between man and nature is never more than a suggestion: "The cold passed . . . *and* the retiring fogs revealed an army," and "*As* the landscape changed . . . the army awakened," with nothing in the conjunctions "and" and "as" more than the hint of a sympathetic cooperation between nature and the affairs of men. Though epic in their proportions, the terms of this passage don't seem to unite into an epic order. As the passage continues, nature undergoes strange and disquieting metamorphoses whose significance is unclear, from muddy roads to "proper thoroughfares," from amber-colored waters to those of a "sorrowful blackness." These transformations are remarkably rich in the variety of sensations and kinds of experiences they suggest (the oppressive filth of "liquid mud" against the urban picture of "proper thoroughfares" that may also contain a hint of an ironical cultural progress). But this suggestiveness is matched by Crane's restraint. He makes no case, no argument, no comprehensible pattern out of his language that would give meaning to these scenes. Ultimately, the imagery of the passage carries evocations of unrest and even hostility, making many of these personifications seem threatening. Yet the threat is not so much in nature's possible foreboding of the battle or of its direct antagonism to man, but rather in its lack of definition, its vague, mutable, and oppressive suggestions of a force uncontrolled by and indifferent to man. The narrator does not seem to acknowledge nature as either reassuring or threatening, but only as something mysteriously present as part of the drama of warfare.

This impersonality carries still further in the fictional world of the novel, affecting the way we look at the novel's hero. Fleming is often described as belonging to a "vast blue demonstration," and his individuality seems threatened by forces that he cannot understand:

> He was bewildered. As he ran with his comrades he strenuously tried to think, but all he knew was that if he fell down those coming behind would tread upon him. All his faculties seemed to be needed to guide him over and past obstructions. He felt carried along by a mob. . . . But he instantly saw that it would be impossible for him to escape from the regiment. It enclosed him. And there were iron laws of tradition and law on four sides. He was in a moving box. (p. 48)

Throughout the novel, the individual self becomes absorbed into the mob. Fleming's behavior is determined by irrational mass movements, his information on the course of the battle is supplied by rumors, and he becomes the puppet of generals who are never seen and whose judgments, if any are discernible, seem senseless and chaotic. All of these characteristics of Fleming's experience belie the occasional hints of some logic or reason in the personifications of the army that impute to it some immanent and overseeing mind that determines how the troops act. Even the repeated metaphor of the army as a "machine" fails to organize the overwhelming bulk of detail that appears mindlessly to sweep the youth up in the frenzy of combat. Most disturbing of all, Crane once again does not seem to legislate between these conflicting suggestions of order and disorder.

Despite our intimate knowledge of his thoughts, Fleming presents us with general, rather than individual characteristics. He is introduced to us with an almost fairy-tale indefiniteness ("There was a youthful private who listened with eager ears to the words of the tall soldier"), and throughout the story he is only two or three times called by his name, and then only by his companions. His mother is the universal mother, tender, protective, and a little sad. His friends, who are assigned common names, are more often known by their titles which Crane dispassionately deals out to them: the "tall soldier," the "loud soldier," the "tattered soldier," that once again generalize the scenario of the battle which itself is given no specific time or location. Finally, even in the introspection of Henry Fleming, the celebrated naturalism of the novel is in apparent competition with the profusion of literary images and allusions that shape the imagination of the youth and the course of his adventures. Throughout the story, that is, the youth's ideas about heroism, when he does think about it, are grounded in stories and history books, in legends, songs, myths, and tales of heroic conduct told to wide-eyed listeners back at home. A large part of Crane's impressionism thus draws upon prior cultural and particularly literary experience.

Because the pattern of the novel implies an initiation into the stark realities of war and the demands of heroism, we expect that the youth will learn something about himself through a series of realizations. And indeed, these realizations seem to begin early in the novel. He discovers that he cannot prove to himself "mathematically" that he will not run from a battle, and he admits that "he knew nothing of himself." He discovers that the personal identity he had conceived throughout his younger days is not relevant to the challenges of this battle:

> He felt that in this crisis his laws of life were useless. Whatever he had learned of himself was here of no avail. He was an unknown quantity. He saw that he would again be obliged to experiment as he had in early youth. He must accumulate information of himself, and meanwhile he resolved to remain close upon his guard lest those qualities of which he knew nothing should everlastingly disgrace him. "Good Lord!" he repeated in dismay. (p. 31)

Crane seems to bestow upon his hero a self-consciousness which the heroes of Cooper and Kipling lack. Fleming here seems to sense the radical implications of heroic endeavor: the confrontation with previously unknown qualities of the self, the need to reinvent oneself when one's past experience fails to provide the moral foundation for heroism. Unlike Roswell Gardiner, in moments of extreme crisis, the youth feels that he cannot call upon those institutional qualities of self acquired through conventional experience. The youth's textbook empirical approach to the problem ("He must accumulate information") appears to parody the immense difficulties we expect he will have. And when he does become more ambitious in his introspective language (talking about "everlasting disgrace"), we must feel that he has amusingly overshot his mark. The tone of his "Good Lord!" fittingly characterizes a boy-soldier who is simply bewildered by matters too large for him to handle. Thus, what finally seems to be emphasized about the youth's experience is, once again, the mindlessness of the whole thing.

When he runs, his flight is the result of impulse. People start running, and suddenly he is running, too. Crane does not dwell upon the moment of the flight. It passes incidentally, and to all in the novel except the youth, insignificantly. The pacing of the narrative (often associated with its "impressionism") gives no single moment or any one feeling the time to take hold of the reader. Crane ignores the rhythms of dramatic narrative, which try to emphasize and heighten certain moments over others. We are aware, rather, of a narrator to whom heroism and cowardice seem to mean very little. There are no heroes except in the eyes of the mere mortals whose trials and miseries the narrator regards with a cool eye.

Fleming's red badge of courage is an ironical one. He receives it before he acts in the least bit courageously, and he returns to his fellow men, led by a soldier whose face he never sees, with a lie on his lips that he received the wound from a bullet. When he finally fights courageously in battle, it is with a swell of overpowering emotions and often "blind" and uncomprehending rage, as he is compared to a hunting dog, a war devil, and a beast. When he has time to contemplate himself again, even he is incredulous over his new role of hero:

> It was revealed to him that he had been a barbarian, a beast. He had fought like a pagan who defends his religion. Regarding it, he saw that it was fine, wild, and in some ways, easy. He had been a tremendous figure, no doubt. By this struggle he had overcome obstacles which he had admitted to be mountains. They had fallen like paper peaks, and he was now what he called a hero. And he had not been aware of the process. He had slept and, awakening, found himself a knight. (p. 150)

The promise of a great moral struggle has evaporated, and there has been no self-conscious act of will. Fleming's reversion to the primitive, both physically and morally, is "in some ways, easy." The youth's heroism, finally, in his leading the charge with flag in hand and in his contemplating himself as if he were a performer, even seems rather theatrical. Indeed, the suggestions of theatricality are repeated in no uncertain terms:

> Regarding his procession of memory he felt gleeful and unregretting, for in it his public deeds were paraded in great and shining prominence. Those performances which had been witnessed by his fellows marched now in wide purple and gold, having various deflections. They went gaily with music. It was pleasure to watch these things. He spent delightful minutes viewing the gilded images of memory.
>
> He saw that he was good. He recalled with a thrill of joy the respectful comments of his fellows upon his conduct. (p. 197)

The youth's mind, like his flight from and return to the front lines, has virtually made a full circle. From the fantasies (awakening as a "knight") the youth's self-discovery becomes a parade, a procession accompanied by public accolade, while the narrator remains aloof and ironical, speaking only a little more pointedly when he parodies the youth's god-like pretensions in a paraphrase of Genesis, "He saw that he was good." We know from the next paragraphs that the youth has to suppress "the ghost of his flight" and the "specter of reproach" that privately haunt him and make his public images into a sham. But Fleming drops these troubling thoughts. His fantasies of heroism are now much less self-questioning than at any time in the novel, and the most probing questions about what it means to be heroic are forgotten.

All these final acts of courage and heroism may, of course, be taken as real heroism. Indeed, there is no reason to suppose that the youth is not a hero, even to the impersonal narrator. When the narrator drily remarks, in a tone that barely suggests parody, "He was a man," we cannot deny that he is, in the only terms that the novel offers for a definition of manhood. But unlike Kipling, Crane seems to view this manhood as a cultural fantasy devoid of the moral accomplishment we usually credit to supreme personal endeavor. Henry Fleming has achieved manhood, but we have to feel disappointed that he did not achieve something more.

Crane's purpose in *The Red Badge of Courage* seems guided, at least in part, by a calculated attack upon the reader's sensibilities. And in the atmosphere thus created, the ending of the novel, which superficially sounds reassuring, is really only an extension of the sham sentiments that Crane subtly discredits throughout:

> So it came to pass that as he trudged from the place of blood and wrath his soul changed. He came from hot plowshares to prospects of clover tranquilly, and it was as if hot plowshares were not. Scars faded as flowers.

> It rained. The procession of weary soldiers became a bedraggled train, despondent and muttering, marching with a churning effort in a trough of liquid brown mud under a low, wretched sky. Yet the youth smiled, for he saw that the world was a world for him, though many discovered it to be made of oaths and walking sticks. He had rid himself of the red sickness of battle. The sultry nightmare was in the heat and pain of war. He turned now with a lover's thirst, to images of tranquil skies, fresh meadows, cool brooks — an existence of soft and eternal peace.

> Over the river a golden ray of sun came through the hosts of leaden rain clouds. (pp. 199–200)

If we had just read these paragraphs alone, without reading the rest of the novel, we might not take these sentences ironically. But nowhere in the course of the narrative do we hear without some twist exerted by the context such biblical tones as in "So it came to pass" and "hot plowshares to prospects of clover,"[12] and as I have argued, there is in that course no credible pastoral language the likes of "tranquil skies, fresh meadows, cool brooks." Here it seems the youth has adopted still another mode of literary self-identification, imagining himself a lover in a lyric poem. We have been educated, of course, into reading such sentiments ironically, and certainly the simile "scars faded as flowers" (which reminds me of Andrew Marvell's ironic turns upon pastoral lyrics) adds a subversive touch of humor to the narrative perspective here. In the very act of reassuring us of an eternal spring, the analogy reminds us of frailty and death. Why, if we are to be reassured, should scars and flowers be compared in the first place? Then, Crane reminds us of the "liquid brown mud" of the beginning of the novel, once again cranking up his mechanical rhetoric. The metamorphosis here, however, is to even more artificial formulas, to "*images* of tranquil skies, fresh meadows, cool brooks" when the youth, in his naive egocentricity, "saw that the world was a world for him." In short, the narrator, as he has throughout the novel, reminds us that the youth and his fellow soldiers are only actors on their own imagined stages.

Historically, Crane's first contribution to this tradition of adventure fiction is to turn the question of heroism inward. What Cooper, Kipling, and even Dana denied their heroes was an inner life, something underneath the tarpaulin hats and duck trousers, the codes of rugged individualism and Christian pietism, the cultural accoutrements and moral weaponry their protagonists brought with them into combat with the unknown. In their performances under physical and emotional stress, they were able to call unquestioningly upon styles of the self sanctioned and institutionalized by the societies from which they emerged and back into which they eventually disappeared. They are heroes finally because they had rescued their cultural identities from threatened annihilation. Crane, on the other hand, propels his hero into momentary chaos and allows him to dwell there long enough to discover what it is like. The youth may run because he falls victim to a mass hysteria, but after that, he finds himself alone with the consciousness of his isolation. When he realizes what has happened, he feels angry, then defensive, then guilty, then jealous of the dead. It is Crane's achievement in the fiction of heroism to express cowardice as a psychological rather than a moral condition. In one unthinking moment the youth cuts himself off from morality, tradition, and the fellowship of his peers. It is his moment in the abyss.

But when the screw turns once again and matters of ethics and morality return as issues in the novel, the dictates of Fleming's conscience are to be found in his need to become once again a member of the community he had impulsively rejected. For the youth it all too easily follows that the style of heroism he finally adopts conforms to prevailing social conventions, which Crane takes pains to show may be formed by cultural fictions. Crane's look inside of the heroic mind thus reveals the machinery of social psychology and communal fantasies. The result of this inquiry is that Crane's hero, like the heroes of the other stories I have discussed, finally has no inner life. When he is conscious of his heroism, he imagines himself simply playing a role, one that he has adopted and, in effect, internalized, after his comrades call him "hero." The important difference between Crane and his predecessors is that in Crane we are made aware of the youth's private failings that the novel's social mechanisms have covered up.

To see both culture and history as essentially literary forms in the way that Crane does is not, to the twentieth-century mind, to do anything unfamiliar. It is not difficult for us to live with the idea that a hero is an invented presence in a world of inventions. The problems in more recent fiction, however, are importantly different from those of the writers I have described in at least one respect. The burden of the conflicts in Nabokov, Mailer, and Pynchon, for instance, rests upon individuals trying to find expression for their inner selves in a world populated by things, forms, and styles. Unlike Fleming or Gardiner or Dana, the characters of more recent fiction are not propelled beyond their cultural limits and exposed to formlessness. The idea of the isolated hero in twentieth-century literature is modified in that the voids of man's consciousness are invariably filled with images from a world abundant with objects, forms, and inventions. Man's inner energies, if they aspire to heroic expression, must create and invent, must take some form by externalizing themselves among the accumulations of his culture.[13]

The heroic mind of the nineteenth century, as I have discussed it, is presented with a different problem. For this mind, chaos is not a matter of disorder or a threat of a kind of suffocation among cultural artifacts. It is, rather, the threat of nothingness once culture disappears. Crane, like our contemporary novelists, sees the self as a repository of cultural fictions, but unlike the culture of contemporary fiction, Crane's images of culture only tenuously sustain the individual against the terror of what exists "beyond." What is most strongly felt in the undertones of Crane's novel is what has been peripheral and implicit in the other American writers I have discussed. There is an area of individual experience apart from that which is controlled by man-made myths and ideologies, where heroism as the nineteenth century knew it is meaningless and in contrast to which the world of society shrinks in size and importance. Dana, the most self-assertive of these writers, retreats from the very idea of drowning, because drowning means the disappearance of the self into nothingness. Drowning disarms him of his moral weaponry and suggests that the self has no recognizable existence apart from its public images and modes. It is not a mere physical death that Dana fears, but a dissolution into chaos. Somewhat similarly, Cooper's fear of "America" as a formless entity without any cultural stability may be seen in part as a fear of anticultural forces that eradicate forms and structures of a traditional society. His pastoral evocations of order at the beginning and the end of his novel seem to be the only ways he can exempt culture from his imagination of historical change. What remains unimaginable for Cooper and Dana is the loss of any cultural identity in an unconstructed world. The image of man momentarily isolated in a stark, immense, lifeless nature becomes an expression for the nonhistorical, noncultural condition of the self — which is virtually to say that the self, under such conditions, no longer exists. It is no wonder that Dana, Cooper, and (though engaged in subtle parody) Crane either fail or refuse to follow the logical developments their journeys seem to demand.

Thus, throughout the course of the nineteenth century, the literature of heroic adventure had taken man beyond the limits of his civilization and had returned him without making the confrontation between man and "nothingness" complete. The struggle of the hero had always been seen as a fundamentally conservative and defensive maneuver to preserve and reinvigorate a constituted society, not really as an ordeal of the isolated self. The full risks to the hero, as they are implied in this fiction, had not been taken, had barely been conceived of. The possibilities for a modern heroism had not been explored.

Joseph Conrad comes at the end of this tradition of heroic adventure journeys, and no less than his predecessors he undertook that journey to restore social harmony. But by the late nineteenth century, the redemptive myth behind the journey verged upon failure. If Conrad were not consciously aware of this failure, he nonetheless could understand the necessity to examine the hero where his predecessors left off — isolated, and beyond the limits of civilization. While the impulse behind this examination overlaps Cooper's desire to recover a lost cultural order, because of the hero's forced isolation, the nature of his ordeal is significantly changed. Indeed, the areas of heroic adventure are now turned inward, and the idea of a journey becomes a metaphor not simply for the rediscovery of a cultural order, but also, in its most radical extensions, for the metaphysical exploration of the mind. This is a crucial development not only in the fiction of heroic adventure, but also in the English novel, because it thrusts the novel into experiences alien to its nineteenth-century social and literary conventions. From a strictly literary perspective, Conrad's problem is to find a language to talk about such experience; from a moral or metaphysical perspective it is to decide whether such a journey is possible in the first place. I think Conrad's solutions to both problems are highly problematic, clouded with ambiguities, marked by false starts and occasional retreats, and often evasive enough to prompt critics such as F. R. Leavis to deny that such problems exist at all. But they do exist, and if I am right about Conrad's historical importance, I suspect that what makes his idiom indecipherable within one heroic tradition permits it to be conversant, if not comfortably at home, within another.

With that premise in mind, I will turn to the high romanticism of English poetry. As I stated earlier, the connections between Conrad and the English romantics are more obscure than his ties to English and American adventure fiction only because they are more oblique — because they are in large part a matter of a literary heritage that Conrad chose even as he adopted the English language. If such a claim appears to be deterministic, I do not mean it to be exclusive. That the English language and its literature both shaped and responded in complex ways to Conrad's education and temperament does not imply that Conrad had somehow cast off his affinities with Polish, French, and Russian literature. It means, rather, that only within certain English traditions did Conrad most fully express an imagination that becomes, in his most extreme works, so inhospitable to any literary expression, so subversive of all nineteenth-century literary traditions, so transcendently international in its scope.

The great consolation for Adam and Eve at the end of *Paradise Lost* is in the archangel Michael's promise that the fallen couple, expelled from Eden, will nonetheless come to "possess/A Paradise within thee, happier far" (XII, 586–87). Milton does not elaborate much upon the nature of this paradise, but its discovery involves a journey both out into the world ("The World was all before them, where to choose/Their place of rest," XII, 646–47) and into themselves. Either way, the course is indirect, dialectical, and perhaps paradoxical, for paradise must be found in a fallen world, and human community must be restored by looking first within the isolated self. For Milton, humanity is presented with new and seemingly limitless possibilities to transcend the confines of the fallen world. The dissolution of the archetypal and prefallen human society makes possible an epic search for its restoration. For Adam and Eve, the heroic journey has begun.

Perhaps the English poet in closest touch with the imagination of Milton is Wordsworth, who, in the beginning of *The Prelude*, implicitly declares his intention to continue the journey adumbrated at the end of *Paradise Lost*:[14]

> What dwelling shall receive me? in what vale
> Shall be my harbour? underneath what grove
> Shall I take up my home? and what clear stream
> Shall with its murmur lull me into rest?
> The earth is all before me. (I, 10–14)

Indeed, Wordsworth's major poetic project may be described as a search for paradise in the fallen world:

> I looked for universal things; perused
> The common countenance of earth and sky:
> Earth, nowhere unembellished by some trace
> Of that first Paradise whence man was driven;
> And sky, whose beauty and bounty are expressed
> By the name she bears — the name of Heaven.
> I called on both to teach me what they might;
> Or, turning the mind in upon herself,
> Pored, watched, expected, listened, spread my thoughts . . .
> (III, 109–17)

But as Wordsworth describes the project of "turning the mind in upon herself" in *The Recluse*, he redefines the terms of Milton's epic and he elaborates upon his allusion in *The Prelude* to "*that* beauty, which, as Milton sings,/Hath terror in it":

> Not Chaos, not
> The darkest pit of lowest Erebus,
> Nor aught of blinder vacancy, scooped out
> By help of dreams — can breed such fear and awe
> As fall upon us often when we look
> Into our Minds, into the Mind of man —
> The haunt, and the main region of my song.
> (The *Recluse*, I, ii, 788–94)[15]

The claims that Wordsworth makes do not simply echo Milton's declaration that he will explore the darkness and pursue "Things unattempted yet in Prose or Rime" (I, 16), but also, in his series of negatives ("Not Chaos . . . ") promises that he will extend the journey of his poetic father in making his own descent into the unknown.[16]

The imaginations which make possible the poetic visions in Milton and Wordsworth share certain broad assumptions about language and poetry, which, at the risk of simplification, may be stated briefly as aesthetic attitudes. First of all, for both poets language, though endowed with special powers, is seen also as a product of a fallen world, an instrument of man's imperfect vision. Images, metaphors, poetic form — the components of literature — are unable in themselves to embody or to reveal paradise, which exists "beyond" or "beneath" this language and may only be implied or evoked indirectly (when the poet is "by rules of mimic art transferred/To things above all art" in *The Prelude*, XI, 111–12). It follows that one of the dominant metaphors each poet uses to characterize his own enterprise is (analogous to the journey metaphor in nineteenth-century adventure fiction) that of some movement beyond, either in flight or in descent or in some other kind of solitary journey (as in *The Prelude*, when the poet follows a road that "Beyond the limits that my feet had trod,/Was like an invitation into space/Boundless, or guide into eternity," XIII, 149–51). Secondly, because this journey must evoke that which it cannot contain — because the end of the journey may be said to exist only as an evocation — the language of each poet appears to exhaust itself before the "vision" of paradise is fully attained. Thus in their journeys both Milton and Wordsworth rely upon an almost mystical vision that Cooper and Dana did not possess. Such a vision is something other than the visualization of images and is something that resides beyond the constructs of literary form. Such a vision is necessary to realize that divine state that exists beyond culture and that transcends human understanding. The claim each makes, in other words, is to a special "insight" into matters incomprehensible to normal human beings.

Clearly Wordsworth supposes his own imaginative journey to be immensely difficult, awesome, frightening, and demanding of heroic resolve. But the rewards of this experience, he would have us believe, are not finally terrifying, as he proclaims in the lines from *The Recluse* following those quoted above:

> —Beauty—a living Presence of the earth,
> Surpassing the most fair ideal Forms
> Which craft of delicate Spirits hath composed
> From earth's materials—waits upon my steps.
> (I, 795–98)

If the risks of this journey are great, for Wordsworth the rewards are greater; for his probing into the depths of the mind is enhanced by the awe and fear it provokes and is ennobled by its heroic demands. Wordsworth has internalized Milton's vision of paradise, so that the poet of the subconscious becomes the hero of modern epic. Exploring the mind, the poet hopes to discover "a living Presence" which surpasses art and "waits" upon his steps as both the attendant and the object of his imaginative odyssey. There appears to be a sublime pleasure in both the process and the substance of self-discovery, for in venturing beneath his mortal consciousness, Wordsworth implies he will fulfill the archangel's promise, regain paradise for English literature, and find for himself that which is permanent and divine.

Scholars of romanticism, however, are divided in their opinions on the exact character of Wordsworth's enterprise. David Ferry argues that Wordsworth's great undertaking is both sacramental and mystical in nature: sacramental because nature and the external world offer him signs and symbols of eternity; mystical because he desires to transcend these symbols and discover a union between the deepest powers of the mind and the essence of the universe. It follows from this duality that the processes of exploring the mind and the natural world are problematical: each may be seen as both a medium to the eternal and as an obstacle in the poet's path. Thus, self-consciousness may be painful for the poet when knowledge of self leads to an awareness of one's limitations and of the separation of man from eternity. Yet the profoundest knowledge of the self in Wordsworth carries with it "intimations of immortality," giving credence and conviction to his assumption that a union between the individual self and the infinite universe is possible. This is what Ferry calls Wordsworth's "mystical yearning."[17]

Geoffrey Hartman, on the other hand, believes that in Wordsworth's poetry there are "moments of semi-mystical fulfillment,"[18] but he insists that Wordsworth feared the power of his imagination to abstract itself from nature. What Hartman calls the apocalyptic powers of the imagination desire unmediated contact with the essence of things, in much the same manner that Ferry describes. And like Ferry, Hartman observes that nature is sacramental for the apocalyptic visionary. But Wordsworth is wary of this state of pure consciousness, according to Hartman, and he realizes that a fulfillment of his visionary longings would mean a severance between the poet's imagination and the natural world, a condition Hartman describes as solipsism. Reflecting on the writing of *Wordsworth's Poetry, 1787–1814* in the 1971 edition of that book, Hartman remarks:

> Wordsworth insisted on the creativeness of the mind and foretold its wedding to nature, yet what I saw mainly was the solipsism inherent in a great imagination, the despair tracking apocalyptic hope, the disabling shadow of ecstatic memories, and passion betrayed into empathy. All that could be said with certainty was that the antithetical resided inside life, that strength somehow obstructed itself, and that to heighten consciousness was to intensify rather than assuage the sense of isolation.

It is not necessary for my purposes to resolve these differences of opinion, and indeed such differences themselves suggest an ambiguity and instability in Wordsworth's vision that is important to my argument. Both Ferry and Hartman seem to agree that this tension between the mind and the external world is a central characteristic of Wordsworth's poetry. "The metaphysical experience," Ferry says, "is that moment in which the eternal world and this deepest and holiest region of man's mind merge, fuse, and as it were become identified. But this is rarely possible — Wordsworth is always a little obscure about whether it is in fact possible at all."[19] Hartman prefers to call Wordsworth's ideal relationship with nature a "blending" rather than a "fusion." To blend the mind with nature is to maintain a dialectical relationship between the two. Hartman's Wordsworth tries to mediate between the natural and the supernatural worlds, and his poetry is that mediation. Ferry's Wordsworth harbors a submerged antipathy to nature and to art, because as mediators they are also barriers to the eternal. According to Ferry, the natural world is more like a trap for Wordsworth; according to Hartman it becomes something of a refuge.

The sources of this disagreement are easy enough to understand if we look at a couple of crucial passages from *The Prelude* (a diabolical version of which will appear in "Heart of Darkness"). The first is from Book VI, where Wordsworth describes the Imagination as he feels its powers in the Alps:

> Imagination — here the Power so called
> Through sad incompetence of human speech,
> That awful Power rose from the mind's abyss
> Like an unfathered vapour that enwraps,
> At once, some lonely traveller. I was lost;
> Halted without an effort to break through;
> But to my conscious soul I now can say —
> "I recognize thy glory:" in such strength
> Of usurpation, when the light of sense
> Goes out, but with a flash that has revealed
> The invisible world, doth greatness make abode,
> There harbours; whether we be young or old,
> Our destiny, our being's heart and home,
> Is with infinitude, and only there;
> With hope it is, hope that can never die,
> Effort, and expectation, and desire,
> And something evermore about to be.
> Under such banners militant, the soul
> Seeks for no trophies, struggles for no spoils
> That may attest her prowess, blest in thoughts
> That are their own perfection and reward,
> Strong in herself and in beatitude
> That hides her, like the mighty flood of Nile
> Poured from his fount of Abyssinian clouds
> To fertilise the whole Egyptian plain.
> (VI, 592–616)

The second passage describes Wordsworth's vision of nature from Mount
Snowdon, when

> the full-orbed Moon,
> Who, from her sovereign elevation, gazed
> Upon the billowy ocean, as it lay
> All meek and silent, save that through a rift —
> Not distant from the shore whereon we stood,
> A fixed abysmal, gloomy, breathing-place —
> Mounted the roar of waters, torrents, streams
> Innumerable, roaring with one voice!
> Heard over earth and sea, and, in that hour,
> For so it seemed, felt by the starry heavens.
>
> When into air had partially dissolved
> That vision, given to spirits of the night
> And three chance human wanderers, in calm thought
> Reflected, it appeared to me the type
> Of a majestic intellect, its acts
> And its possessions, what it has and craves,
> What in itself it is, and would become.
> There I beheld the emblem of a mind
> That feeds upon infinity, that broods
> Over the dark abyss, intent to hear
> Its voices issuing forth to silent light
> In one continuous stream; a mind sustained
> By recognitions of transcendent power,
> In sense conducting to ideal form,
> In soul of more than mortal privilege.
> One function, above all, of such a mind
> Had Nature shadowed there, by putting forth,
> 'Mid circumstances awful and sublime,
> That mutual domination which she loves
> To exert upon the face of outward things,
> So moulded, joined, abstracted, so endowed
> With interchangeable supremacy,
> That men, least sensitive, see, hear, perceive,
> And cannot choose but feel. The power, which all
> Acknowledge when thus moved, which Nature thus
> To bodily sense exhibits, is the express
> Resemblance of that glorious faculty
> That higher minds bear with them as their own.
> (XIV, 63–90)

Both these passages express something very close to mystical experience,
and if Hartman is right, Wordsworth approaches the terror of apocalypse in
the arresting moment on the Alps, when he says, "I was lost." Yet in both
passages, it is difficult to decide whether Wordsworth desires mystical tran-

scendence or not: both slide into retrospective commentaries that impose an organization and control upon these experiences not suggested by the images of nature immediately preceding them. Ferry suggests that in Book XIV Wordsworth "has returned to nature, but he cannot tell whether it is the eternal nature as exhibited through the articulate processes of the natural scene or the pure mystery of things which is not to be distinguished from self-obliteration. . . . " Wordsworth can "only yearn for [immortality] from the top of Mount Snowdon, remembering that he had once been one with the things of nature and had required no symbols. Not clarity but mists attend his vision."[20] Hartman, on the other hand, argues that Wordsworth saves himself from "self-obliteration" by finding in nature a power answerable to his own imagination: "the poet comes face to face with his Imagination yet calls it Nature. It is the *Prelude's* supreme instance of the avoidance of apocalypse."[21] This complex dialectic, this precarious blending of the imagination and nature, becomes, according to Hartman, Wordsworth's ideal.

One is tempted to ask whether such a delicate state of consciousness, whether such ambiguities, are not essential to Wordsworth's sense of the sublime. Hartman defines the apocalypse as self-consciousness intensified beyond control. What would it be like if the poet *were* to become "lost"? Then the conditions that make "hope" necessary in Book VI would be eliminated. Then Wordsworth could no longer speak of "a mind sustained/ By recognitions of transcendent power." Then there remains only "that awful Power [that] rose from the mind's abyss," in which case the character of Wordsworth's romanticism would be radically altered. It may be possible to distinguish between the promises and the implications of Wordsworth's vision — the promises of immortality and the implications of an apocalyptic self-destruction, the first sustained by faith and the second realized through the logic of the heroic journey. In order for the heroic quest to remain viable, and in order for paradise to remain an imaginative possibility, the journey into darkness must continue unfulfilled, for the end of the journey implies the horrors of annihilation. One of the most telling remarks Hartman makes is to propose that Wordsworth "was at a turning point in history which would see either a real marriage of the mind of man with nature or their apocalyptic severance." In this respect, we may begin to link the romanticism of Wordsworth with that of Conrad.

Near the end of the century which in poetry was immeasurably influenced by Wordsworth, Conrad, then a virtually unknown and anomalous figure in English fiction, wrote that "the artist descends within himself, and in that lonely region of stress and strife, if he be deserving and fortunate, he finds the terms of his appeal" (XXIII, xi-xii). Conrad knew enough about his "place" in literary history to imagine the ghost of Flaubert on the deck of the *Adowa* (Conrad's last ship) in his recollections of the winter of 1894: "for was not the kind Norman giant with enormous moustaches and a thundering voice the last of the Romantics? Was he not, in his unworldly, almost ascetic devotion to his art a sort of literary, saint-like hermit?" (VI, 3). But if by implication Conrad sees himself as the literary hermit of the postromantic world, it seems to me his lonely romanticism is based not so much upon his ties with Flaubert as upon his peculiar relationship to Wordsworthian romanticism that make him, in the late 1890s, unique in English fiction.[22] Although separated in time and genre, Conrad and Wordsworth seem notably similar in the ways they talk about "the region of my song" and "that lonely region of stress and strife," which is the mind of man. Yet, finally, it is difficult to think of two writers whose initial similarities end in more pronounced differences.

Perhaps the best places to begin comparing Conrad and Wordsworth are their most famous critical statements: The 1897 Preface to *The Nigger of the "Narcissus"* and the Preface to the *Lyrical Ballads*.[23] In his Preface, Conrad begins by defining two kinds of fidelity: one to thought and science, and the other to feeling and art. Such a bifurcation seems to be a characteristically Victorian variation upon Wordsworthian aesthetics ("pleasure" and "fact" in Ruskin, "idea" and "fact" in Arnold). In Conrad, the scientist, the logician, the philosopher endeavor to explore the facts of human existence and "those heartless secrets which are called the 'Laws of Nature.'" The artist, on the other hand, "appeals to that part of our being which is not dependent on wisdom" to discover "what is enduring and essential." But with an almost visionary quality, more probingly inward than the language of Arnold or Hardy and with certainly less emphasis upon society and culture, Conrad's language throughout the Preface reiterates his proximity to the Wordsworthian imagination. His metaphor for the imagination, "the secret spring of responsive emotions" recalls Wordsworth's "spontaneous overflow of powerful feelings." And his claim that the artist "shall awaken in the hearts of the beholders that feeling of unavoidable solidarity," echoes Wordsworth's declaration that "the poet binds together by passion and knowledge the vast empire of human society, as it is spread over the whole earth, and over all time." There is, of course, much about Wordsworth's Preface peculiar to his occasional needs, particularly his discussions of poetic diction and meter. But when he and Conrad make their most general claims for art, the postures, sentiments, vocabulary, and even the weighty and eloquent rhythms of the prose in the two prefaces are very much alike. In the likenesses, Conrad departs from Victorian aestheticians and, more especially, from nineteenth-century English novelists as well.

Now, the similarities between Wordsworth and Conrad in their respective apologies for their art suggest what might be called Conrad's orthodox romanticism—his allegiance to what he described as "the 'ideal' value of things, events, and people."[24] Conrad as a romantic is devoted to the idea that man may look within his own mind and, beyond the consciousness of his isolation, discover something eternal and some spiritual bond uniting him with the rest of humanity. The inner journey, in other words, reveals a truth that becomes the basis both for a spiritual and aesthetic ideal and for the followship of mankind. If Conrad's expression of this idea is not precisely Wordsworthian, the two writers appear often enough almost indistinguishable in their ideals and objectives.

But in other statements Conrad makes, there seems to be no similarity at all. There appears on many occasions almost to be another Conrad talking—the one known for the "heart of darkness" that Arthur Symons attributed to him and for his character of Kurtz memorialized in the epigraph to Eliot's "The Hollow Men." This Conrad is a prophet of despair, one evident in both his fiction and in his personal correspondence with close friends, particularly between 1895 and 1900—during the same period that Conrad was announcing his romantic doctrines in the Preface.[25] Some of the most pressing problems in reading Conrad are a result of this self-contradiction, this apparent clash between a romantic and a "modern" voice, each of which seemingly affirms what the other denies. But in quoting from several of his letters, where he is most unequivocal in his despair, and in placing them next to Wordsworth, I think Conrad's departures from the nineteenth century may be seen to rely less upon a failure than upon a terrifying fulfillment of Wordsworthian romanticism. I have numbered these excerpts for convenient reference:

1. What makes mankind tragic is not that they are victims of nature, it is that they are conscious of it. . . . We can't return to nature, since we can't change our place in it. Our refuge is in stupidity, in drunkenness of all kinds, in lies, in beliefs, in murder, thieving, reforming, in negation, in contempt—each man according to the promptings of his particular devil. There is no morality, no knowledge and no hope: there is only the consciousness of ourselves which drives us about a world that, whether seen in a convex or a concave mirror, is always a vain and floating appearance.[26]

2. Even writing to a friend—to a person one has heard, touched, drank with—does not give me a sense of reality. All is illusion—the words written, the mind at which they are aimed, the truth they are intended to express, the hand that will hold the paper, the eyes that will glance at the lines. Every image floats vaguely in a sea of doubt—and the doubt itself is lost in an unexplored universe of incertitudes.[27]

3. Of course reason is hateful—but why? Because it demonstrates (to those who have the courage) that we, living, are out of life,—utterly out of it.[28]

4. When once the truth is grasped that one's own personality is only a ridiculous and aimless masquerade of something hopelessly unknown the attainment of serenity is not very far off. Then there remains nothing but the surrender to one's impulses, the fidelity to passing emotions which is perhaps a nearer approach to truth than any other philosophy of life.[29]

There is a considerable variety of metaphors in these letters and, if they may be looked at scientifically, a range of ideological statements sufficient to justify separate commentaries on each. But despite their variety, all these passages fall within the spectrum of ontological stances made possible by English romanticism, and in that way they include Conrad with Wordsworth in the same imaginative milieu.

What is most obviously present in these letters is a Wordsworthian detestation of the finite and temporal self; but what is most conspicuously missing is his celebration of the possibilities of transcending the self. In the Preface to the *Lyrical Ballads*, Wordsworth says that "man and nature are essentially adapted to each other, and the mind of man is naturally the mirror of the fairest and most interesting properties of nature." If Wordsworth's poetry expresses the relationship between man and nature in more complicated terms, it never despairs that the world "whether seen in a convex or a concave mirror, is always but a vain and floating appearance" (No. 1).

Wordsworth's "mirror" metaphor is a way of talking about the mind's power to select the most spiritual qualities of the natural world and a way of expressing a faith that man's discovery of eternity will also be a discovery of his deepest and most abiding self. Nature for Wordsworth may contain a fund of symbols and metaphors that point the way towards the imagination of the sublime. For Conrad, though, the mind seems to become almost literally a perspective glass — a reflector of images that are distorted by the shape of the glass's surface. There is "only the consciousness of ourselves": consciousness is the only reality.

Consider, too, the ways "life" and "truth" are talked about. There are the life and truth of a seemingly ideal world and the life and truth of a "fallen" world. In this distinction Conrad is very much like the Wordsworth of *The Prelude*. The difference in part is that the life Conrad evokes most passionately is that which apparently includes the range of all man's physical and intellectual activities in the fallen world, from "beliefs" to murder (1), and which consists of a kind of bizarre circus where the self is merely a "masquerade" (4) of some ideal reality. When Conrad asserts that we are living "out of life" (3), as if we are alienated from an ideal world, such a world cannot be even vaguely imagined or defined, cannot in fact, be posited with anything like a Wordsworthian conviction.[30] Having thus failed to conceive of the unities of self, nature, and mankind, Conrad is driven to present man seeking "drunkenness of all kinds" (1), reminding us of *The Prelude's* scenes of violent confusion in London and Paris. All that exists for heroic man is the consciousness and the confession of his own isolation and mortality. Finally, the masquerade of our present life and the ideal unity of a higher reality are *both* illusions, the first a pretentious vulgarity, the second a noble dream.

In Wordsworth, the imagination is both terrifying and beautiful, for it makes all else seem unreal. When the self is lost, divinity and self-destruction are implicated with each other. In Conrad, however, the imagination becomes terrifying without redemption, because it is raised to such self-consciousness that terror is the only possible response. There is no sense of dialectic in these letters, no feeling of the imagination's great potential. Conrad is devoid of the enormous spiritual resources that seem to reside in the ambiguities of Wordsworth's poetry. Nature itself seems deadened, neither symbolic nor sacramental, unresponsive to man. Hence, the great energies of Conrad's imagination are turned in against themselves masochistically, such that their resolution points to death without divinity. But what is especially important to realize is that the distinctions between the "two Conrads" are not between a "false" Conrad and a "true" Conrad, or between a romantic and a modern: these contradictions are contained within the same man whose imagination of chaos is so bizarre precisely because his romantic impulses end in literalizing the terrors described metaphorically in *The Recluse*. Conrad, in short, has raised introspection and imaginative self-consciousness to such intensity that the imagination becomes the only reality. Hence, the "self," in this most extreme form of romanticism, is, as Hartman anticipated, destroyed.

Returning to Conrad's Preface now, we may see why the romantic idiom I noted earlier sounds deflated, almost despondent at times. The logical implications of the romantic imagination make it impossible for Conrad to invest his vision with Wordsworth's aspirations, and so a new set of conditions for romantic heroism is created in a world despiritualized and devoid of divine powers, a world in which divinity is replaced by the "darkness," against which, recoiling and struggling for survival, remains the heroic self. That the Preface does not express Conrad at his most heroic — that it presents a Conrad elegiac and nearly resigned — offers evidence even at this early stage in Conrad's career that his heroes will from the beginning of their journeys be reeling in the aftershocks of romanticism's greatest dreams.

These new resonances are perhaps most clearly inferred from the differences between Wordsworth's idea of "vision" and Conrad's famous promise that art will "make you *see*." Wordsworth's Preface is less useful to me in this comparison than a passage from *The Recluse*, where the poet calls upon his Muse:

> upon me bestow
> A gift of *genuine insight*; that my Song
> With star-like virtue in its place may *shine*,
> *Shedding benignant influence*, and secure,
> Itself, from all malevolent effect
> Of those mutations that extend their sway
> Throughout the nether sphere! — And if with this
> I mix more lowly matter; with the thing
> Contemplated, describe the Mind and Man
> Contemplating, and who, and what he was —
> The transitory Being that beheld
> The *Vision*; when and where, and how he lived; —
> Be not this labour useless. If such theme
> May sort with highest objects, then — dread Power!
> Whose gracious favour is the primal source
> Of all *illumination*, — may my Life
> Express the *image* of a better time.
> (I,i, 840–56, italics mine)[31]

Here Wordsworth invokes a dual sense of vision as both visualization and visionary apprehension. Wordsworth's double nature of "The Vision" — both the act of seeing and that which is seen — suggests the ideal Oneness of man and nature: "the thing Contemplated" and "the Mind and Man/Contemplating." The poet suggests that even if he remains a mortal, that of "lowly matter" and "transitory Being" — his imaginative experience through his art nonetheless approaches the perception of this ideal union. Although he is conscious of his mortality and of the cognitive gap between a perception of the finite and a visionary perception of the divine, and although his poetry, like his "life," is merely an *image* of a better time, Wordsworth can still gain an imperfect glimpse of this paradise within. His imaginative "insight" is thus very close to a mystical vision of a union just beyond the limits of his mortality. And yet it appears that for this vision to remain compelling, it must be left mediated by language, dialectical, unfulfilled.

In Book V of *The Prelude*, an even closer relationship between words and visionary power is suggested:

> Visionary power
> Attends the motions of the viewless winds,
> Embodied in the mystery of words:
> There, darkness makes abode, and all the host
> Of shadowy things work endless changes, — there

As in a mansion like their proper home,
Even forms and substances are circumfused
By that transparent veil with light divine,
And, through the turnings intricate of verse,
Present themselves as objects recognised,
In flashes, and with glory not their own.
(V, 595–605)

Here the poet is able to draw his visionary power from nature, or from nature acting in concert with his imagination. Nature is infused with divine powers, and words are able to "embody" divine light.

Conrad, in the beginning of the preface, speaks of "vision" in a way that requires some rather subtle distinctions to reveal how different it has become from that implied in Wordsworth:

> And art itself may be defined as a single-minded attempt to render the highest kind of justice to the *visible universe*, by bringing to light the truth, manifold and one, underlying its every aspect. It is an attempt to find in its form, in its colours, in its light, in its shadows, in the aspects of matter and in the facts of life what of each is fundamental, what is enduring and essential—their one *illuminating* and convincing quality—the very truth of their existence. (XXIII, xi; italics mine)

Clearly Conrad intends to "bring to light the truth" in more than an impressionist's sense of "vision," and apparently he seeks a truth which is an ideal essence of reality, uniting the "manifold and one." But if the stance Conrad takes is Wordsworthian, if his conception of the artist's vision reminds us of the passage from *The Recluse*, Conrad never endows it with Wordsworth's visionary conviction. What is involved here, however, is not simply a loss of faith but also a shift in weight within Conrad's romantic imagination that distinguishes it from, at the same time it allies it with, that of Wordsworth. When the Preface elaborates upon its opening definition of art, we are told that the artist's "appeal is made to our less obvious capacities . . . for delight and wonder, to our sense of pity, and beauty and pain . . . to the subtle but invincible conviction of solidarity . . . in dreams, in joy, in sorrow." Everywhere in his Preface Conrad suggests that the artist's appeal is an emotional one, but nowhere does it become a visionary one. Emotional solidarity is poignant, suggestive. It even resembles some spiritual bond among human beings. But this "solidarity that knits together the loneliness of innumerable hearts" nevertheless reminds us of our loneliness and never denies it. At best the truth of art may be in an intimation of a tenuous human brotherhood (only a "conviction" of solidarity"), but never of immortality, or eternity, or the visionary ideal. In a way Conrad accords to art a burden equal to that of Wordsworth, but he endows it with a lesser ability to perform its moral task. Man is tragic—and this is the crucial part of it—because human fellowship relies solely upon art, not upon a divine spirit present in art.

In light of these implications, it is easier to understand why Conrad's attack upon scientific judgment, temporality, and short-sightedness, couched as it is in romantic rhetoric, is also framed in elegy and informed by a sense of loss. The great accomplishment of art is "a moment of vision, a sigh, a smile—and the return to eternal rest." The human community is bound together by a vision that defies the laws of nature, but one that is no more than a futile hope, because both the vision and the community are subject to those laws. Nature, fact, and reason become unequivocal antagonists to a diminished version of the visionary imagination. In contrast, we may recall that in Wordsworth's Preface, the poet "binds together by passion *and* knowledge" the community of man, because all human truths, whether scientific or artistic, are imperfect models of a perfect universe. Thus Wordsworth, unlike Conrad, tells us that the passions are "*connected . . .* with the operations of the elements," implying a continuity or a reciprocity between the motions of the mind and those of nature. Conrad, once again, tells us that the artist speaks to our "solidarity in dreams . . . in illusions," basing this solidarity not upon man's relationship to the universe, but upon his relationship to other human minds. Hence science and art are explicitly set against each other by Conrad in a way that Wordsworth did not imagine was necessary.

In this context of a failing romanticism, we should rightly wonder how "the truth underlying [the visible universe's] every aspect" could have any meaning at all in the Preface, or at least the meaning that Conrad suggests that it has. The romantic tenor of this language becomes lost in the vagueness of an aesthetic cut loose from its origins in Wordsworth, one seemingly based upon an emotional and sentimental "truth" which is finally imposed upon the impersonal operations of nature, giving life to an otherwise dead world. Conrad's assertion of brotherhood is at best a concession to a decent hope and an artistic illusion, and as such it represents the failure, not the revival, of English romanticism.[32] It is the juncture at which the temptation to escapism in art is counterbalanced only by a half-suppressed consciousness of art's failure to take man soaring above his mortal limitations. It is, finally, the matter upon which the widely-recognized theoretical fuzziness of the Preface rides. However sincere Conrad is in his romantic aspirations, this statement so often taken as a testimony to his optimism and a celebration of art is actually the product of despair. For all its questing after the Beautiful and the True, the romanticism of the Preface in the Wordsworthian sense of that term rests upon a foundation of outdated clichés and platitudes rescued from a century of progressive skepticism. For Conrad, the end of man's journey is death—the shadowy companion of the Wordsworthian death, which is a metaphor for the attainment of a visionary ideal—a death that in Conrad bears witness to the fate of that ideal. Conrad's encounter with Wordsworth reveals a universe consisting only of rocks and stones and trees.

The comparisons I have been making between Wordsworth and Conrad should help us better to understand the relationship between Conrad's private conflicts and the expression of these conflicts in his fiction (something in recent years appropriated to psychoanalytical criticism[33]). Especially, the presiding myth of an uncorrupted past, of a journey back to sources, of a paradise lost, is carried over to Conrad's fiction. Writing in his autobiography, *A Personal Record*, Conrad comments upon the significance to his writing of his life at sea:

> Having matured in the surroundings and under the special conditions of sea life, I have a special piety toward that form of my past; for its impressions were vivid, its appeal direct, its demands such as could be responded to with the natural elation of youth and strength equal to the call. There was nothing in them to perplex a young conscience. . . . No wonder, then, that in my two exclusively sea books—"The Nigger of the 'Narcissus,'" and "The Mirror of the Sea" (and in a few short sea stories like "Youth" and "Typhoon")—I have tried with an almost filial regard to render the vibration of life in the great world of waters, in the hearts of the simple men who have for ages traversed its solitudes, and also that something sentient which seems to dwell in ships—the creatures of their hands and the objects of their care. (VI, xvi–xvii)

Here Conrad talks about his seafaring years with reference to childhood, youth, simplicity, and to the naturalness, clarity, and directness of appeal in a life infused with "that something sentient," when he felt in perfect harmony with his environment. Though the correspondence is not exact, the stance the attitudes, the metaphors of this passage are fundamentally Wordsworthian—the mature man talking about his naive but heroic youth, when freedom from self-consciousness and his simplicity in experience meant that the world was united and life was like a pastoral paradise.

In his Preface to *The Shadow Line* (a fictional account of his first command) Conrad remarks, again with echoes of Wordsworth, "The effect of perspective in memory is to make things loom large because the essentials stand out isolated from their surroundings of insignificant daily facts which have naturally faded out of one's mind" (XVII, ix). And in his Preface to *The Shorter Tales of Joseph Conrad*, he refers to another autobiographical story, appropriately called "Youth," as "emotions remembered in tranquility."[34] The association of Wordsworthian metaphors with Conrad's accounts of his own life is especially significant in his autobiographical novels. For although Conrad would come to hate his reputation as a seaman-turned-novelist, he began his professional writing at the same time that he ended his professional seamanship; and the kinds of changes that this transition required lent themselves to definition in Wordsworthian terms. When Conrad quit the sea, he imagined that the unity of his youthful, sentient, heroic world was destroyed. Suddenly his activities were no longer ordered according to the ancient customs of seamanship; no longer would his place as an individual be defined so clearly in relation to other people and to his environment. Suddenly it seemed that he had to search within himself to discover what is "permanently enduring," reenacting the Wordsworthian journey to self-discovery at a time when romanticism was nearly dead; and suddenly the demands of art and not seamanship would require an education into a complex and sophisticated world. Quitting the sea after twenty years was like a new initiation into adulthood, and leaving a profession that aboard sailing vessels hadn't changed much since the fifteenth century was like stepping all at once into the modern world. In the transition of one moment of his life, therefore, Conrad seemed to have given himself a personal, historical, and literary past—and at the same time to have cut himself off from all three.

It is no wonder, then, that Conrad spent much of his career, particularly in the beginning and at the end, trying to redefine himself in a way that corresponds to Wordsworth's effort to recapture a mythical past. What replaces Wordsworth's childhood in Conrad is his sea years, which continued to fulfill his need for moral order and self-identity. "It may be my sea training acting upon a natural disposition to keep good hold on the one thing really mine," he says, "but the fact is that I have a positive horror of losing even for one moving moment that full possession of myself which is the first condition of good service. And I have carried my notion of good service from my earlier into my later existence" (*A Personal Record*, VI, xix). And on another occasion, paying tribute to the seaman's fidelity to his work, Conrad writes also about the artist, saying that "the fidelity to right practice . . . makes the great craftsman" ("Tradition," from *Notes on Life and Letters*, III, 94). The seaman's world, half-mythologized and celebrated elegiacally, becomes a point of reference, a measure of values, a platform of moral and artistic stability for Conrad. That world, like that of the child in Wordsworth, is the closest expression of Conrad's ideals; and the seaman's life is the metaphorical condition to which Conrad aspires.[35]

But Conrad's replacement for Wordsworth's childhood order leads him to a crucial variation upon the art of the poet. The seamen's ethics of fidelity and service do, in several ways, provide him with a link between his careers as a seaman and as a novelist. They legitimize his decision to become a writer, order his difficult transition from one profession to another and serve as the basis for an attempt to state generally and theoretically the purposes of his art. But they also drastically simplify the responsibilities of an artist toward his material. One example of this simplification occurs in Conrad's tribute to Frederick Marryat and James Fenimore Cooper, which appeared in an 1898 issue of *Outlook* and was reprinted in *Notes on Life and Letters* as "Tales of the Sea":

> Marryat is really a writer of the Service. What sets him apart is his fidelity. His pen serves his country as well as did his professional skill and his renowned courage. . . . His adventures are enthralling; the rapidity of his action fascinates; his method is often crude, his sentimentality, obviously incidental, is often factitious. His greatness is undeniable. (p. 54)

While Conrad implies that Marryat is an engaging though sometimes ungainly spinner of adventure yearns, his evaluation of his predecessor ultimately seems to rest upon other than strictly literary standards. Writing fiction and serving in the Navy are analogous activities in the previous passage, and for Conrad the "fidelity" and "service" of Captain Marryat seem to excuse a literary style that is often "crude" and "factitious." Marryat's fidelity "sets him apart"—apart from other novelists, but also apart from certain demands of literary decorum made by critics (the implicit enemy) who value "method" and craftsmanship rather than the ethics of the naval service. If Marryat's "greatness is undeniable," it is because this greatness is judged more upon ethical than artistic considerations; and if Conrad excuses Marryat's crudeness, it is because of the fundamental moral rightness of his work.

In the passage on Marryat, fidelity is both praised and practiced by Conrad as if he were still walking the decks of a ship. Conrad looks upon Marryat more as a brother seaman than as a writer, and thus defined, their relationship justifies and requires some sacrifice of literary judgment; and literary judgment here would seem to carry the same anathema as scientific judgment in the Preface. Marryat's characters, Conrad says, "do not belong to life; they belong exclusively to the Service. And yet they live; there is truth in them" (p. 54). "Art" is no longer like life when it is more like seamanship; but that doesn't matter, as long as the proper ideals are upheld. Fidelity becomes the scale by which a novelist's work is measured: fidelity to right practice is the credo of the craftsman; fidelity to human community is the doctrine of the artist; and the sacrifice of worldly judgment to the celebration of what Conrad calls the seamen's "primitive virtues" is easily transferred to a theory of art. Marryat's devotion to the values of the Service is analogous to the artist's devotion to that part of man's imagination that unites the human community, and Marryat, by way of that analogy, becomes a kind of idyllic model of the artist devoted to "truth."

All this, of course, seriously qualifies conventional critical opinion concerning Conrad's realism: his fidelity to his experiences, his promise "to make you see." Earlier I emphasized that "seeing" for Conrad means much more than the rendering of accurate images of life. Now, however, I would also insist that it can mean much less. What is really disastrous for Conrad's critical theories and for the worst of his fiction (which he himself called "fairy tales") is the persistent simplifying impulse behind his romantic sense of "vision" in art. Even the theories of the 1897 Preface are organized in a general way by the critical sensibility evident in the tribute to Marryat. Consider, for instance, the choice Conrad demands between fidelity to science and fidelity to feeling and art. Conrad does not deny the truths of science; he despises them and asks for a respite from them in a moment of artistic forgetfulness: "a sigh, a smile — and the return to eternal rest." More interesting yet is Conrad's comparison between the artist and a laborer in the fields, whom more intelligent and sophisticated people look upon from a distance with momentary wonder. Performing his tasks alone, in an odd pantomime of peculiar gestures sometimes with no apparent motive or objective, the laborer is a curiosity among men. Sometimes, if we are in "a brotherly frame of mind," we may "understand his object . . . [and] forgive his failure," for "after all, the fellow has tried, and perhaps he had not the strength — and perhaps he had not the knowledge. We forgive, go on our way — and forget." This laborer may in some ways remind us of Wordsworth's solitary reaper and his leech gatherer,[36] whom the poet admires for their more than human presence and for their closeness to nature and the fundamental truths of life. But Conrad's laborer does not reach the heroic stature of the leech gatherer; he is no "huge stone. . . . Couched on the bald top of an eminence." Moreover, in his isolation from men, this pastoral laborer seems an oddity, and considering his Wordsworthian prototype, an anachronism rather than a model of superhuman endurance.

Conrad must decide what to make of a diminished thing, and his solution is essential to our understanding of his heroic fiction. The very act of making an explicit analogy between the artist and the laborer in the fields suggests that, unlike Wordsworth, who is inspired by the pastoral artist to a higher and sublime art, Conrad sees his own role as that of the simple laborer — noble, futile, and depending upon your capacity for sympathy, either tragic or pathetic. Because he believes man's reunion with the universe to be a myth, he elegiacally celebrates a life made simple by the loss of time — and the loss of self-consciousness; he actually aspires himself to become the simple laborer, to obliterate time and death in a moment of forgetfulness by a self-willed ignorance rather than by a spiritual transcendence. Conrad, to be more exact, not only admires a writer like Marryat, who belongs to a simpler and more unified world, he wants to return to that world himself—to become a character within his own pastoral myth.

Before we may understand the romantic darkness at the end of Conrad's journey, we must first appreciate the tensions inherent within his romanticism. At the essence of Conrad's heroic vision is a conflict between his aspirations to a Wordsworthian paradise and the imaginative compromises of his pastoral myth. During the development of his career, Conrad learned to examine this conflict with a rigorous critical scrutiny that in part distinguishes his heroic journey from that of Wordsworth. He came to understand that the source of his dialectical vision is not an opposition between realism and romanticism but the proximity between mysticism and solipsism, between romantic paradise and romantic self-destruction—the equally untenable counterparts of romanticism itself. The pressure towards the resolution of the heroic journey, therefore, gradually reveals the fundamental instability of the journey and the fact that if paradise exists within the mind only, it does not exist at all. It is only an index of his despair, finally, that Conrad over a period of years increasingly and knowingly submitted to the sentimentality of both a heroic ethic and an aesthetic doctrine based upon fidelity to a fabricated world.

In this chapter I have tried to characterize two strains of heroic literature in the nineteenth century and to suggest, as a working hypothesis, that we may begin thinking about Conrad both at the end and in the convergence of these traditions. But rather than using these traditions simply to locate precedents or to draw parallels to Conrad, I have preferred to think of them more as a field of energy to which Conrad belongs and through which the conflicts within his heroic imagination become at once private and historical in their scope. In this way we may begin to understand that the voice speaking to him in Conrad's fiction identifies its personal struggles with the destiny of an entire era.

The heroic journey Conrad makes is simultaneously an incursion into the mind and an effort to return to the past. It is a journey to get at the source of things, to rediscover a primal state,[37] a timeless mythical community, perhaps even a mystical unity between man and the universe.[38] In some ways this endeavor is similar to those in several of the adventure writers I have discussed, especially those whose journeys set out to reclaim the values of an ideal and passing way of life. But unlike Conrad, these writers are fundamentally social in their visions: even their pastoral forms of society provide them with models of human community that bear the crude characteristics of a social world. Their cultural equipment, their institutional values, are central to their heroic enterprise. For Conrad, on the other hand, everything that equips the heroic journey—the externals of culture, the constructs of language, the temporally progressive plot of the journey itself—serves only to further distance his hero from an unimaginable ideal. Such forms and constructs in Conrad, as in Wordsworth, are contrivances of a fallen world, and by their very nature intervene between the hero and his objective. (Among the adventure writers I discussed, only Crane shares a vaguely similar stance. But Crane remains an ironist and a deflator of myths only, not a romantic in the Wordsworthian sense of the term.) Conrad, we must understand, seeks a human community that is not simply nonhistorical, as in Cooper and Kipling's images of a pastoral past, but one which is prehistorical as well. It exists (if it may be said to exist) not in a frozen moment of time, but outside of time altogether.

Hence, the special demands of Conrad's journey further link him to the imagination of Wordsworth. Like Wordsworth, Conrad will come to realize that it is necessary in some sense to divest himself of the tools and instruments of culture in order to continue beyond and beneath the cultural world. Like Wordsworth, Conrad at times appeals to a "vision" that attempts to see into the source of things. And like Wordsworth, Conrad thinks of art as an "image of a better time." But for Wordsworth, art seems at times to embody the powers of a divine realm. Even when it mediates between him and these powers, it assumes a transcendent sublime. Poised between the natural world and the divine, Wordsworth may thus have his "intimations" of immortality. Conrad, on the other hand, refuses at last to discard the idea of a journey, the metaphor of descent, penetration, and restoration. He is, in a sense, too devoted to language, to the journey, to a diminished vision that attempts to accomplish what he and Wordsworth each in his own way understands language cannot. What makes Conrad a heroic writer is his redefinition of Wordsworthian heroism—his insistence that the journey as a journey must be carried out to its end, and his dedication to the pursuit of a transcendent ideal that he knows full well he has not the means to achieve.

Consequently, the character of the "darkness" in Conrad is considerably altered from that of its prototype. Where Wordsworth "sees" a mystical eternity, Conrad "sees" either the illusions of a fallen world or an abyss left without the light of Wordsworth's mysticism. For Conrad, this abyss is something like the emptiness of the sea in Dana—a dimensionless nature which threatens to subsume the consciousness of man. (In contrast, I rely upon David Ferry's remark on Wordsworth that "'abyss' is a word he uses many times to suggest the hiding place of ultimate truths, and rarely uses

. . . so far as I know, in a pejorative sense."[39]) The darkness for Conrad is the destination of the journey that fails; it marks the end of all human endeavor, the furthest extension of the human imagination. Such, of course, is the material for tragedy, and indeed Conrad's journey becomes a metaphor not only for the act of writing in general but also for the course of his own writing as well. Conrad will share the destiny of his language and plots, a destiny that spells their imaginative destruction.

The story of Conrad's heroic journey is a remarkable one, and one that needs telling, for the formulations I have just offered in themselves do not do justice to the incredible energy Conrad expends in the process of his struggle. In the following four chapters I hope to document this process, to examine its failures, and to account for Conrad's strategies — all in different ways unsuccessful — for recovering his lost ideal. I hope to show how the arena for heroic endeavor in Conrad becomes diminished in size during a twelve year period in his career, beginning with the dissolution of the heroic community in *The Nigger of the "Narcissus"* and proceeding to the existential failures of Marlow in "Heart of Darkness" and Jim in *Lord Jim*. I will then examine the fantastic and weird "success" of the captain in "The Secret Sharer" and explain why such a success nonetheless precludes Conrad's efforts to unite mankind and to recover a lost ideal. Finally, my last chapter will offer both the conclusions and the extensions of my argument. In it, I will try to evaluate Conrad's literary career in terms of his adventure stories and to suggest ways in which we may compare him to his predecessors and contemporaries in the novel.

To begin with, then, is *The Nigger of the "Narcissus"* — Conrad's first step beyond the pale.

2

The Nigger of the "Narcissus":
A Paradise Lost

Whatever else we may say about *The Nigger of the "Narcissus,"* without doubt it is a novel of fine dramatic moments: the moment when James Wait baffles Mr. Baker with his cry of "Wait!" at the first muster of the crew (XXIII, 17), and the moment shortly thereafter when he declares portentously, "I belong to the ship" (p. 18); the moment during the storm when the ship heels over and when "the topsail sheet parted, the end of the heavy chain racketed aloft, and sparks of red fire streamed down through the flying sprays" (p. 59); the moment of near-mutiny, when Donkin flings an iron belaying pin at Captain Allistoun; and the triumphant reassertions of order, when the ship rights herself, when the captain humiliates Donkin, when Singleton "steered with care" (p. 19).

The novel becomes a gallery for such pictures of sea life that are often drawn in similes and regarded from a distance by a sensitive, aesthetic eye. The men become "like figures cut out of sheet tin" (p. 3), ships "like strange and monumental structures abandoned by men" (p. 14), the homebound *Narcissus* "like a great tired bird speeding to its nest" (p. 161). The story begins with a marvelous series of fast-action vignettes describing forecastle life at the sailors' call-back, as Conrad alertly scans the scene in raffish, exotic, and picturesque sketches of the crew boasting, quarreling, joking, swearing. Surely these scenes fulfill the imagistic sense of Conrad's promise "to make you *see*."

Yet, ironically, the novel Conrad wrote to commemorate his past is often criticized for its inconsistent point of view. The narrator, presumably a crew member telling the story in retrospect, focuses steadily upon the ship and its crew, but the angle of his vision constantly changes. He is on deck, in the heavens, and inside the mind of a previously inscrutable James Wait, all at will. He shifts from first to third person whenever he pleases. And he feels nothing is amiss when he turns from descriptive narrative to make the

Narcissus a platform for his rhapsodic oratory over the virtues of a life at sea.

Nevertheless, as often as these inconsistencies are pointed out, they are usually given very little attention. Albert Guerard brushes them aside, saying that for the most part "the changes in point of view are made unobtrusively and with pleasing insouciance."[1] Frederick Karl is more critical, charging "that Conrad was lazy in his conception, or at least was not seriously concerned with the logic of the narration."[2] But both men see the problem as essentially technical and as not interfering with the vision of the novel in a larger sense.

The problem with most interpretations of *The Nigger of the "Narcissus,"* however, is precisely that the novel is viewed usually from a distance, using the literary lenses of myth and allegory to clarify its vision. Conrad himself has done much to instruct critical opinion in this regard. In a late piece called "Stephen Crane," for instance, he tells us that Crane "appreciated my effort to present a group of men held together by a common loyalty and a common perplexity in a struggle not with human enemies, but with the hostile conditions testing their faithfulness to the conditions of their own calling."[3] As if taking his cue from Conrad, Morton Dauwen Zabel writes, "Conrad is doing more than writing a tribute to his old brothers of the days of sail. He is doing what all tellers of the tales of ships have done, from Homer in the *Odyssey* or the satirists of the *Narrenschiff* and *Ship of Fools* to Cooper, Dana, and Melville. He is making the *Narcissus* and her crew a world, an image of humanity on its hazardous voyage into the elements, the future, the unknown."[4] However, fancying the *Narcissus* as the "microcosm of mankind"[5] and extolling the pictorial and symbolic virtues of the novel often serve to gloss over the most important conflicts in the novel and tend to distort the myth that emerges at the end. There are conflicts among the narrator's attitudes toward the crew, among the kinds of irony and comedy he adopts, among various literary stylizations, and, perhaps most interestingly, between storytelling and picture-making, which produce the most subtle tensions in "point of view." The plot of the story itself seems to take two different directions. As Albert Guerard notes, there is a disparity within the structure of the novel between the story of Jimmy's relationship with the crew and the story of the crew's triumph over the elements. But even Guerard ends by affirming the novel's coherence, judging it a triumph of structure and style: "This structural problem, and even Conrad's solution of it can be simply stated . . . . The problem was simply to avoid writing two distinct short novels, one optimistic and the other pessimistic . . . . What Conrad does. . .is. . .to focus attention upon the ship . . . . Thus the object that unifies the two stories is the *Narcissus* herself . . . . In mere outline the matter is as simple as that. But there are novelists who in all their calculating careers never achieve such a triumphant simplicity and rightness of structure."[6]

The assertiveness of such interpretations, with their emphasis upon the triumph and completeness of the voyage, and their enthusiasm over the readymade scheme of voyage-as-plot, ignore the imaginative twists and turns, the indecisiveness, the occasionally strained rhetoric, and the confusions of purpose within a superficially coherent structure.[7] It is rarely suggested that the inconsistency in point of view is more than a technical confusion, that it represents the mechanics of larger, subtler, and more profound tensions within the novel. Actually, if there is a consistency of vision in the *The Nigger of the "Narcissus,"* it is one that the official stances and perspectives of the narrator are intended to avoid. It is a vision that divides the narrator's fidelity to "thought" from his fidelity to "feeling," to use the terms of the 1897 Preface, and results in a rhetoric just as tentative and defensive as that of the Conrad who styled himself the romantic he could never quite be.

It is easy to skim Conrad's statement about Wait in his 1914 preface, which refers to him as "merely the centre of the ship's collective psychology and the pivot of the action" (p. ix). Guerard's response is a bewildered but delighted "Merely!" which pronounces that word as if to accentuate a puzzling verbal slip or a careless oversight.[8] But the preface gives us no reason to read this statement ironically, and the novel itself is full of such unacknowledged ambiguities in tone and attitude. Consider, for instance, the narrator's comment on Singleton's reading of Bulwer-Lytton's *Pelham*:

> The popularity of Bulwer-Lytton in the forecastles of southern-going ships is a wonderful and bizarre phenomenon. What ideas do his polished and so curiously insincere sentences awaken in the simple minds of the big children who people those dark and wandering places of the earth? What meaning can their rough, inexperienced souls find in the elegant verbiage of his pages? What excitement? — what forgetfulness? — what appeasement? Mystery! Is it the charm of the impossible? Or are those beings who exist beyond the pale of life stirred by his tales as by an enigmatical disclosure of a resplendent world that exists within that border of dirt and hunger, of misery and dissipation, that comes down on all sides to the water's edge of the incorruptible ocean, and is the only thing they know of life, the only thing they see of surrounding land — those lifelong prisoners of the sea? Mystery! (pp. 6–7)

"Life" is introduced in this passage as the world of a corrupted society, and *Pelham* as a contrived and artificial version of that world. Singleton seems to be a naive old sailor reading fiction as if it were reality, understanding the evils of society only in comic book form. The passage throughout makes possible an ironic distance from which the narrator could comment on *Pelham*, on society, on bad literature, and on the sailors' naiveté and ignorance of these things. But what the narrator wants even more is to express his love of Singleton, to declare his fidelity to the seamen's world for its freedom from social taint and corruption. It is here the difficulty begins, for although the narrator starts as a bemused literary critic, marveling at Singleton's fascination for the "curiously insincere sentences," he gradually seems to condone and even participate in this fascination himself. His own language, that is, betrays a love of tawdry stylizations and sweeping rhetorical gestures, and the descriptions of a "resplendent world," are increasingly less ironical than self-indulgent, seeming to take pleasure in evoking the bizarre images ascribed to the author of *Pelham*. By the end of the passage we don't know whether to pity, admire, or deprecate the seamen for being "prisoners of the sea," for the critical voice that begins to dictate an ironical response to Singleton would rather abandon the opportunity for detached commentary for a more tender, playful reaction to the old sailor's literary tastes. The narrator in this instance prefers to congratulate the seamen rather than to criticize them, even when they engage in the follies of conjured emotions. Despite a certain fun in such a narrative perspective and tone, there is, I think, something disturbing about the rather casual treatment of this and similar incidents. The narrator seems too willing to ignore that the sailors' love of Bulwer-Lytton is more complex than his careless and charming questions at the end of the passage imply. The sailors seem just a bit too gullible to be merely naive, too attracted to the "charm of the impossible" and "that border of dirt and hunger" to be quite innocent, too infatuated with artificial deceptions to be the heroes of a heroic allegory, despite the insistence of both Conrad and many of his critics that they are.

The incident with *Pelham* becomes the occasion for the narrator's rhapsodical tribute to the sailors, and thus questions about the crew's psychology, gullibility, and credulity (all suggested by the passage) enter the novel only on the edges of stylization. The crew are "tainted" in a sense from the beginning of the novel, and in the early pages Conrad is already both observant and insistent enough upon a "fidelity" to observation and judgment to portray the seamen's world as a burlesque theater of society — comically racy, fractious, and self-absorbed. But Conrad's concern to a large extent is to maintain other kinds of integrity — in sentiment and in a certain literary structure — in praising the heroic community, despite his awareness that this community seems, at first in only frivolous ways, to violate its own heroic ideals. If, in other words, the comedy of the narrator's critical language may continue to be endearing rather than scathing, scenes like this will be part of the innocent charm of life aboard the *Narcissus*. Framing the sailors' world with a benignly comic perspective and freezing the dramatic action with images and "pictures" of the voyage, as he so often does, permits the narrator to smile while he gently chides the seamen for their foolishness. But if the effect of such comic withdrawal is to allow the sailors to be foolish with impunity and to remain pictures rather than dramatic characters, the novel risks a failure to explore the more complicated social and psychological vision it seems at times to attempt.

Conrad's acute observations of life on the ship often give way to his persistent need to declaim instead of narrate in order to glamorize and perfect the allegory of the voyage.[9] When this happens, Conrad's scrutiny of the crew from a distance results not in descriptive narrative but in a rather strained pomp:

> The passage had begun, and the ship, a fragment detached from the earth, went on lonely and swift like a small planet. Round her the abysses of sky and sea met in an unattainable frontier. A great circular solitude moved with her, ever changing and ever the same, always monotonous and always imposing. Now and then another wandering white speck, burdened with life, appeared far off — disappeared; intent on its own destiny. The sun looked upon her all day, and every morning rose with a burning round stare of undying curiosity. She had her own future; she was alive with the lives of those who trod her decks; like that earth which had given her up to the sea, she had an intolerable load of regrets and hopes. On her lived timid truth and audacious lies; and, like the earth, she was unconscious, fair to see — and condemned by men to an ignoble fate. The august loneliness of her path lent dignity to the sordid inspiration of her pilgrimage. She drove foaming southward, as if guided by the courage of a high endeavor. The smiling greatness of the sea dwarfed the extent of time. The days raced after one another, brilliant and quick like flashes of a lighthouse, and the nights, eventful and short, resembled fleeting dreams. (pp. 29-30)

Much about this passage is magnificent: the Olympian perspective, the sweeping periods of the sentences, and the descriptions of the great motions of nature. At the same time, the writing slips all too easily into stagey, artificial writing that makes its case with forced, attenuated rhetoric. The copious use of simile too dutifully insists upon the *Narcissus* as a moral microcosm, a "small planet" inhabited by melodramatic emotions and moral abstractions (in the stylized dichotomy between "timid truth" and "audacious lies"). The metaphors are ground out, almost machine-like, with fanciful touches like "another wandering white speck, burdened with life" that seem (in the alliteration of the "w's" for instance) to be more concerned with the way the language sounds than with the dramatic action of the voyage. The seamen, finally, are too obviously noble (they "trod" instead of "walked" the decks), and nature is too easily Arcadian and cooperative with their activities (the sea smiles and the sun is curious). Despite its ambitions, the rhetoric in this passage strains the limits of heroic language in the novel. The narrator removes himself from the crew, casts them in artificial terms, and turns a dramatic event into a rhetorical occasion. All the ship is doing here is sailing through a sea of words from one rhetorical space to another.

Unfortunately, the escape from social and psychological conflict aboard ship becomes at last an exercise in platitude and cliché.

The neatest and best parts of the heroic language in the novel bear some relationship to the artifices of the previous passage but remain direct and unpretentious, relying upon a narrative which describes, rather than on a description that takes the place of narrative. Often this language is weighted by nautical terms. For example,

> "The carpenter had driven in the last wedge of the main-hatch battens, and, throwing down his maul, had wiped his face with great deliberation, just on the stroke of five. The decks had been swept, the windlass oiled and made ready to heave up the anchor; the big towrope lay in long bights along one side of the main deck, with one end carried up and hung over the bows, in readiness for the tug" (pp. 3–4).

This is not, of course, part of the famous storm sequence in this novel, and yet it sets the tone for the heroic scenes later on. The professional terms in this passage seem to harmonize with the somber and picturesque movements of the carpenter to celebrate the nobility of pure, uncomplicated endeavor. The technical language not only provides a way of talking about the hardships of the voyage but also emphasizes that simple, routine, good seamanship is important to the success of the venture. Because of the need for good seamanship, this technical language is given further moral ramifications in a passage such as this one: "The *Narcissus* was one of that perfect brood. Less perfect than many, perhaps, but she was ours, and consequently, incomparable. We were proud of her . . . . She was exacting. She wanted care in loading and handling, and no one knew exactly how much care would be enough. Such are the imperfections of mere men!" (pp. 50–51) The problems of the heroic community here are implicitly and simply defined. In order to sail from Bombay to London, the crew of the *Narcissus* must be excellent sailors and more, they must live up to the demands of their professional pride which all morally good sailors possess. The values of community are determined by a code of ethics, sentimental but impersonal, because it dictates human relationships according to a prescribed and predictable form. The dramatic conflicts in this world are not among men, but between men and the sea.

Like the description of the ship as a microcosm, this impersonal code of ethics provides a literary style through which dramatic conflicts within the novel are shaped and controlled and social and psychological problems avoided. Connected with these stylizations, the descriptions in the storm scenes recall traditional ordeals in literary and maritime mythology. These scenes are rendered in vividly Gothic terms ("Shrieks passed through the air," "Outside the night moaned and sobbed," and "Hung-up suits of oil-

skins swung in and out. . .like reckless ghosts of decapitated seamen dancing in a tempest"), reminiscent of "The Rime of the Ancient Mariner" and
perhaps some archaic fables of the sea. Though represented as severe, the
hardships of a world thus defined have something comforting about them.
"Most seamen remember in their life one or two such nights" (p. 54), the
narrator reminds us. Literary tradition and maritime experience are wedded
in the ancient ordeal of men against the sea. Nature is threatening, and yet
in a way as cooperative with the affairs of the seamen as it was when the sea
smiled and the sun was curious at the beginning of the voyage.

The storm scenes are justly famous for their vividness and immediacy,
and the traditional literary context in which the drama is set serves to
magnify and elevate the trials of the *Narcissus* to splendidly mythical proportions. But these scenes still belong to a world of myth and not to a world
of men. It is, in fact, to the narrator's best interest to distinguish the seamen
from the rest of mankind, to remove them into a world of artifice: "The
true peace of God begins at any spot a thousand miles from the nearest
land; and when He sends there the messengers of His might it is not in
terrible wrath against crime, presumption, and folly, but paternally, to
chasten simple hearts—ignorant hearts that know nothing of life, and beat
undisturbed by envy or greed" (p. 31). Not only does this passage reassure
us with the promise of ordeal and redemption, but it also sets up fundamentally pastoral distinctions between sailors and men of the land. The relatively simple codes of behavior, the traditional demands of seamanship and
heroic virtue, are contrasted with the more complex (though also stylized)
trials of a duplicitous, morally fallen world of the land. The simple life of
the seamen provides Conrad with an idealized community and a model for
heroic endeavor. The seamen are not like landsmen. They are not strictly
speaking representative of mankind. They are, rather, figures in a prefallen
world, acting within the conventions of a pastoral myth. And it is important
to understand that our reading of *The Nigger of the "Narcissus"* as an
heroic allegory depends in large part upon the narrator's sustaining the
pastoral perspectives and maintaining the distinctions between seamen and
landsmen evident in the previous passage. The integrity of the heroic community depends upon its lack of complexity and duplicity, its absence of
"crime, presumption, and folly." It requires, in short, the control of an
impersonal scheme of human relationships to replace the changing, complicating, psychological terms of real social experience—it even depends upon
a caricatured antipastoral society that may be easily distinguished from the
seamen, that may be defined by formula so that the subtleties of "the ship's
collective psychology," to recall the 1914 preface, may still be qualified by a
"merely."

At first, the characterizations of the crew fit nicely into the scheme of heroic allegory. They represent types of sailors: the patriarchal "Old Singleton," the inexperienced "young Charlie," the sentimental and irascible Irishman, "Belfast," and Podmore, the foolish but zealously dedicated cook. One of the most interesting, and misinterpreted, seamen is the filthy and pugnacious Donkin, who is often considered by critics to be a lesser version of James Wait. It is true that Donkin and Wait enjoy a curiously symbiotic relationship with one another. Wait actually loves Donkin's abuse, and Donkin seems to draw inspiration for his political agitation from Wait. Both are described as objects of "universal charity," and each seems to be a master of guile and deceit. Yet Donkin's deceit is typecast, predictable, manageable, and unquestionably a by-product of a corrupt society, while Wait is full of paradoxes and contradictions. As the following delightfully comic description will indicate, Donkin's character is quite consistent with the pastoral formulas that the narrator must maintain to preserve the identity of the heroic community. Donkin reinforces the schematized distinctions between landsmen and seamen; he becomes a transplanted landsman rendered harmless by a brilliantly comic style:

He stood with arms akimbo, a little fellow with white eyelashes. He looked as if he had known all the degradations and all the furies. He looked as if he had been cuffed, kicked, rolled in the mud; he looked as if he had been scratched, spat upon, pelted with unmentionable filth. . .and he smiled with a sense of security at the faces around. His ears were bending down under the weight of his battered hard hat. The torn tails of his black coat flapped in fringes about the calves of his legs. He unbuttoned the only two buttons that remained and everyone saw he had no shirt under it. It was his deserved misfortune that those rags which nobody could possibly be supposed to own looked as if they had been stolen. His neck was long and thin; his eyelids were red; rare hairs hung about his jaws; his shoulders were peaked and drooped like the broken wings of a bird; all his left side was caked with mud which showed that he had lately slept in a wet ditch. He had saved his inefficient carcass from violent destruction by running away from an American ship where, in a moment of forgetful folly, he had dared to engage himself; and he had knocked about for a fortnight ashore in the native quarter, cadging for drinks, starving, sleeping on rubbish heaps, wandering in sunshine; a startling visitor from a world of nightmares. He stood repulsive and smiling in the sudden silence. This clean white forecastle was his refuge; the place where he could be lazy; where he could wallow, and lie and eat—and curse the food he ate; where he could display his talents for shirking work, for cheating, for cadging; where he could find surely someone to bully—and where he would be paid for doing all this. They all knew him. Is there a spot on earth where such a man is unknown, an ominous survival testifying to the eternal fitness of lies and impudence? (pp. 9-10)

This passage is among the best in the book. Once Conrad gets started, he can't resist heaping a whole dictionary of degradations and moral tags upon Donkin, who, standing "with arms akimbo" in the forecastle, is amusingly at the mercy of the narrator's vituperation. The passage is both descriptive and dramatic: the participles present Donkin physically acting out the narrator's description of him, and the rhythms and sounds of the sentences themselves create a dramatic, crescendo effect, as in a theatrical declamation. The syntactical variations, the changes of tone from the pathos of "the broken wings of a bird" to the bitter irony of "he smiled with a sense of security," to the burlesque of "pelted with unmentionable filth" and "cadging for drinks, sleeping on rubbish heaps, wandering in sunshine" — these characteristics, and the dramatic finale of the rhetorical question, when the narrator steps out of the description to phrase the moral issue in terms made comically obvious by the scene, contribute to our sense of Donkin as a figure to be loathed and laughed at, and even loved in a sense, for the opportunity he gives us to despise him. In all, the passage casts Donkin in a theatrical, Dickensian style that makes him more comic than disgusting, less lethal and more the object of our pleasurable disapproval.[10]

Although he is not metaphorically a part of the heroic world, Donkin is actually just as necessary to the moral allegory of the novel as Singleton is. He is everything Conrad's ideal hero is not — he is filthy, lazy, loquacious, subversive. And yet he is only a caricature of a moral recreant, a figure who helps accent the abstract differences between the pastoral and the antipastoral worlds that the voyage itself is officially intended to underline. Indeed, his presence in the novel lines up the terms of the opposition between the sea and the land in such a way as the Bulwer-Lytton passage uncomfortably did not. Donkin may thus be subsumed rather easily under a variety of standard difficulties that the heroic community must overcome in order to maintain its integrity. The narrator notes that the crew "all knew him," and because they do they disrespect him and vilify him, while Baker beats and subdues him. Of course Donkin's presence does remind us of how susceptible the heroic-pastoral community is to incursions from its caricatured social counterpart, and this susceptibility should not be underplayed. But when Donkin makes his greatest bid, with initial success, to exploit the confusion Jimmy causes by attempting to turn that confusion into mutiny, his rebelliousness is almost licensed by the opportunity it gives the captain to reassert his authority over the ship and the crew their moral solidarity — to defeat, however tenuously, the world of political anarchism with which Donkin is associated.

What the novel crucially turns upon is the development of the crew's relationship with James Wait. So long as Wait remains in the background, the human flaws of the crew may be affectionately rendered and included without much strain within an essentially idyllic world. In Wait's emergence as a dramatic force in the novel, however, the heroic-pastoral world is reordered in ways that undermine its place in the scheme of the heroic allegory. This happens slowly and even comically at first: after Belfast steals a pie for Jimmy, "The *Narcissus* was still a peaceful ship, but mutual confidence was shaken" (p. 38). Shaken confidence, however, is a serious matter in Conrad's heroic imagination, because the perpetuation of the heroic ethic depends upon the conventionality of the risks and the predictability of the crew's responses.

Although Wait is not of the sailors' world, he is not, strictly speaking, of the "social" world either. Indeed, his presence in the novel is felt most strongly in his resistance to definition. It is in his breach with conventionality that the sailors' problems really begin. While the crew have encountered Donkin's "type" before, they are confused by Jimmy, and their responses to him waver among admiration, pity, distrust, hate, and compassion, and occasionally result in disagreements over how he should be treated. Even more interestingly, the narrator, whose stake in the story depends upon the consistency of his heroic vision, seems himself to participate in the crew's bewilderment. With similarly various and uncertain reactions, he describes Jimmy at one point as "calm, cool, towering, superb," while immediately thereafter attributes to him "a head powerful and misshapen and a tormented and flattened face—a face pathetic and brutal: the tragic, the mysterious, the repulsive mask of a nigger's soul."[11] Even in this introduction of Wait, in the profusion of irreconcilable adjectives (he is sordid and heroic, pathetic, tragic, and repulsive) it is clear only that it will be impossible to fit him into any moral pattern suggested by the "men against the sea" myth. It is here that "the centre of the ship's psychology and the pivot of the action" begins to challenge the formulas of heroic allegory, for, among other things, Jimmy requires of the crew a complex and obliquely "human" responsiveness that disrupts the impersonal and artificial terms under which an allegory in this novel must operate.

Critics who want to read *The Nigger of the "Narcissus"* as an allegory of the triumph of good over evil usually have difficulty fitting Jimmy in their symbolical formulas. Albert Guerard, for example, first remarks that Jimmy "comes in some sense to represent our human 'blackness,'"[12] then cautions that "our task is not to discover what Wait precisely 'means' but to observe a human relationship."[13] The second remark is more promising than the first, but Guerard still circles around a notion of symbolism that becomes all the more confusing for the openness he knows he must maintain: "What this something is—more specific than a 'blackness'—is likely to vary with each new reader."[14] This seems to me question-begging and a hedging with critical terminology that cannot cope with the material it tries to explicate. It may indicate, too, that Jimmy resists the definitions of critics no less than those of the crew, and that in the very act of defining him or assuming he can be defined we are prone to reduction and simplification.

The dishonesty of definition among the crew is amply demonstrated in their failures to resist Jimmy's fraud and manipulation and to decide, more fundamentally, what he is inventing and what he is not. At first the crew believe he is a sham ("He coughed often, but the most prejudiced person could perceive that, mostly, he coughed when it suited his purposes," p. 44), and Jimmy himself confesses to Donkin at one point that he's merely "out of sorts," and that he's done this sort of thing on a ship before. Yet this confession does not really deny that Jimmy is sick, just as Singleton's terse comment that Jimmy will die (certainly—all men die!) does nothing to clarify the ambiguities about him, at least in the minds of the crew. To us, it may appear that Jimmy is suffering in the late stages of tuberculosis, but that is rather beside the point. The narrator's own refusal to "diagnose" Jimmy's illness in itself implies that the problems of interpretation are not medical but social, moral, and psychological instead. If we may point to where the sailors "go wrong," it is in their acting upon assumptions about Jimmy's health that privately they distrust. When Jimmy claims he is sick, they try to accommodate his desires, bringing him food, speaking in low voices not to disturb him, humoring him as if they are playing a game of pretending he is really sick while suspecting him of fraud. Ironically, when he insists he is getting better, the crew come to believe he is in fact sick and dying. But once again they agree to a kind of game, humoring him, pretending they believe he will recover—until he does die, and everyone (except Singleton) is shocked. Social order upon the ship had actually come to rely upon Jimmy; but this "order," of course, is an ironical one. In a way reminiscent of the heroic community Henry Fleming is accepted into after receiving his false badge of courage, the heroic community aboard the *Narcissus* has actually subscribed to a public lie. Here, however, the crew all know it.

It has been noted by several critics that in the dramatic development of the novel, Jimmy's function is to bring out the "humanity" of the crew. He is a "catalyst," as one critic puts it, of the crew's "progressive demoralization,"[15] which in the novel is identified with their humanization. The crew's previously endearing foibles and idiosyncrasies are accented and expanded in the sailor's reactions to Jimmy. Donkin's laziness and rebelliousness, Belfast's sentimentality, Singleton's naiveté, and the cook's religious fervor all take a bizarre turn as the novel progresses. Often, as with Podmore and Belfast, the sailors become absurd parodies of themselves. Even Singleton's Wordsworthian silence (which may recall that of the leech gatherer) is at one point suspected by the crew to be a sign of senility rather than unspoken wisdom. Their suspicions of their patriarch may, of course, be written off as evidence of their demoralization, but quite aside from their perspectives Singleton is, in fact, just as inept and egotistically inflated as they are in their "understanding" of Jimmy. Each crew member assumes Jimmy may be defined according to his own presuppositions; but it is Jimmy, who is predisposed to nothing for very long, who controls the moral "order" aboard ship.

What underlies this new order is Conrad's imagination of social chaos. What accompanies it and what gives it expression and temporary form in the changing mythology of the voyage, are a new set of allegorical terms in which Jimmy is cast in the role of a Satan:

> He was demoralizing. Through him we were becoming highly humanized, tender, complex, excessively decadent: we understood all his repulsions, shrinkings, evasions, delusions — as though we had been overcivilized and rotten, and without any knowledge of the meaning of life. We had the air of being initiated in some infamous mysteries; we had the profound grimaces of conspirators, exchanged meaning glances, significant short words. We were inexpressibly vile and very much pleased with ourselves. We lied with gravity, with emotion, with unction, as if performing some moral trick with a view to an eternal reward. We made a chorus of affirmation to his wildest assertions, as though he had been a millionaire, a politician, or a reformer — and we a crowd of ambitious lubbers. (p. 139)

The simple bonds of heroic community are now replaced by the "decadent," "overcivilized," and "rotten" exchanges of a duplicitous, fallen society. Jimmy's relationship to the crew is described in terms of commercial and political relationships, "as though he had been a millionaire, a politician, or a reformer — and we a crowd of ambitious lubbers." The crew have become like men of the land, but their fall from their pastoral world is described on the scale of Adam and Eve's fall from the Garden of Eden: their "humanizing" experience implies that the seamen will have to cope with the subtleties of social relationships predicated upon dissembling, manipulating, and game-playing among people, in much the same way that the seduction passages in *Paradise Lost* show Adam and Eve engaging in similarly subtle, "human," and decadent deceptions.[16] The crew, furthermore, begin to sound like the "chorus" of fallen angels in the Miltonic hell, subject to a moral trickster in the form of a chameleon-like demagogue promising eternal reward. Thus the "humanity" of the crew is a curse, and from that curse necessarily result all the fastness and sham that the narrator attributes to the society of the fallen world. In order to find the "meaning of life" that the narrator refers to in this passage, the sailors would have to remain isolated from what we ordinarily think of as life — from human, dramatic, social relationships, and of course from what the narrator renders as the antipastoral life in the Bulwer-Lytton and other passages.

The entire novel is full of other suggestive echoes of *Paradise Lost.* The sailors' corruption is evidenced, for instance, partly by their loss of simple words (p. 134) and the acquisition of a worldly vocabulary. Elsewhere, at the end of chapter 2, the narrator says of Jimmy, "Invulnerable in his promises of speedy corruption he trampled on our self-respect. . . . Had we been a miserable gang of wretched immortals, unhallowed alike by hope and fear, he could not have lorded it over us with a more pitiless assertion of sublime privalege" (p. 47). If the myth of the Fall of Man does not inform the entire structure of the novel, it increasingly pervades the sensibility of the narrator as he describes the corruption of the crew. In fact, despite his other vacillations, Conrad is remarkably consistent in his sense that, underlying the rhetorical and moral orders of the novel is the drama of the steady decomposition of the crew.

Yet the *Paradise Lost* myth, like the lesser mythical structures of the novel, does not gain ultimate ascendency over the inconsistencies in perspective the narrator continually demonstrates. And I am not at all sure Conrad deserves criticism for this structural failure, because often it represents a kind of integrity that does not allow for a merely rhetorical imagination. Just how subtly and integrally *The Nigger of the "Narcissus"* is a novel of conflicting perspectives and shifting points of view is evident in the close proximity in Conrad's imagination between pastoral allegory and social satire and between Conrad's vision of the heroic ideal and his perception of social chaos. As the letters quoted in chapter 1 indicate, the ideal and the fallen worlds are really versions of each other; both offer illusions of order, both are masks of an underlying chaos. Jimmy is not so radically antipastoral as one might think. Unlike Donkin, who is clearly so, Jimmy appeals to the best instincts of the seamen: loyalty, self-sacrifice, the union of comrades in the brotherhood of the sea. He is a shrewd manipulator, sure enough, but in curious and surprising ways he seems to uphold a version of the very order that Donkin obviously tries to destroy. It would be a more accurate assessment of Jimmy to say that rather than fracturing the order of the sailors' world, he supplants the captain and the ship as symbols of that order; he appropriates for himself the veneration of the crew on the same terms that they venerated the ship earlier in the novel. He is a satanic figure and an antihero in that sense, but he corrupts by an ironical fulfillment rather than by a simple subversion of the crew's heroic inclinations.

In the scene where the crew extricate Jimmy from the shambles of his cabin during the storm, the narrator comments,

We had so far saved him; and it had become a personal matter between us and the sea. We meant to stick to him. Had we (by some incredible hypothesis) undergone similar toil and trouble for an empty cask, that cask would have become as precious to us as Jimmy was. More precious, in fact, because we would have had no reason to hate the cask. And we hated Jimmy Wait (p. 72).

The revealing point here, which other critics have noted but have not, I think, fully appreciated, is that the seamen have translated the problem of dealing with Jimmy into "a personal matter between us and the sea." For the very reason that Jimmy appeals to the seamen's code of ethics, the sailors are forced to include their relationship with him within their official duties, treating him as fidelity to professional standards requires. But, because we know such ethics are limited to a world where ordeals can be expressed only in terms of heroic-pastoral conventions, the crew's actions are placed here in an ironic perspective. Jimmy is too "subtle" and "complex" to belong to the seamen's community, and the seamen lack both the judgment and the moral guidelines necessary for dealing with his complexity. Hating him as an alien to their way of life and yet treating him as a brother seaman simply perpetuates his tyranny, and what's more important, transforms the heroic code of ethics into a grim parody of itself. By this time in the novel, professional conduct merely comes to rationalize an irrational loyalty to Jimmy, pathetically destroying its integrity in the very actions that try to preserve it.

The crew consequently can remain heroic only during the storm scenes, and even then only when they overcome their human fears of the sea and when they ignore Jimmy, reducing their problems to those of seamanship. Of course at the same time they are "heroic" we are conscious of their isolation from more complex experience that these heroic standards of conduct impose upon the crew; and it is with this new perspective on heroism that we are made to see the delusions that are necessary in dividing human experience into pastoral and antipastoral, the delusions that are at the heart of the heroic world. Captain Allistoun is actually aware in some sense of the necessity of pretense in the preservation of order on the ship. In a conscious evasion of James Wait, he denies that Wait presents any problem at all: "This head wind is my problem . . . head wind! all the rest is nothing" (p. 126). Confiding to Creighton, the second mate, his sympathy for the man he realizes is dying, the captain tells Jimmy nonetheless, "You have been shamming sick. . . . Why, anybody can see that " (p. 120). Allistoun seems to understand that the moral universe of the *Narcissus* must consist of opposites: rights and wrongs, truths and falsehoods; and he is keen enough to perceive that Jimmy does not fit into this scheme. He knows that Wait is sick and shamming sick at the same time, and he knows that he must evade Wait's duplicity. Yet he wants to be compassionate and act humanely with him. Thus, in a brilliant stroke of irony, Conrad makes Allistoun himself into a conspirator who confides to Creighton a sympathy he cannot make public and who announces to the crew a judgment he does not entirely believe. To maintain the ship's order and to act compassionately, Allistoun himself is caught up in the irreconcilable conflict between the heroic-pastoral and the human worlds. And although he upholds the facade of the stern and rigid seaman, he has become humanized along with the rest of the sailors, and thus his orders to Jimmy prolong the very duplicity that he helplessly tries to suppress.

It is part of Conrad's deeply felt vision of loss in this novel that every conventional reassertion of order aboard the ship is underlain by evidence of the steady degeneration of that order. Chapter 3 ends with the triumphant victory of the ship over the sea and the storm and the simple, poised, ennobling image of Singleton at the wheel. Yet in chapter 4, Singleton collapses in the forecastle, for the first time aware of his mortality, while Donkin is nearly successful in perpetrating a mutiny, and Jimmy's performances continue to divide the crew from their officers. At the end of that chapter, the next great triumphant moment occurs, when the captain reasserts his authority over Donkin and regains the respect of the crew. But chapter 5 begins with that Miltonic description of the fallen sailors, who have become "excessively decadent." The order and the allegory of the heroic voyage and the triumphs of seamanship are thus only tentative triumphs over chaos. The paradise of the *Narcissus* is in fact in surreptitious anarchy throughout.[17]

The crew's entire experience with Jimmy from the first muster of the crew until near the end of voyage depicts a progressive disintegration of order aboard ship which is caused not only by Jimmy, but largely by the inherent limitations and failures of the sailors to deal with complex social, psychological, and moral events. In a sense the sailors "fall" not because they do change but because they don't — because they do not respond differently to a different kind of problem, a new set of demands; and because their "lies" to themselves are, in a way, efforts to preserve the values of loyalty, fidelity, and heroic community in a world where these values are no longer relevant. The sailors have become victims of Jimmy's game-playing, but they are also unwitting victims of their own "games" of heroic conduct.

Finally, as the novel takes shape — or rather, as it loses shape — the issues of the voyage take a last turn towards the most pervasive "myth" of the story. The crew are not simply — are, in a way, not at all — the sources of their downfall. The "hateful accomplice" (p. 41) of both Jimmy and the crew is death. All along the most consistent imagery of the novel has been that of death: "The double row of berths yawned black, like graves tenanted by uneasy corpses" (p. 22); "a black mist emanated from him; a subtle and dismal influence; a something cold and gloomy that floated out and settled on all the faces like a mourning veil" (p. 34); "Hung-up suits of oilskin . . . like reckless ghosts of decapitated seamen dancing in a tempest" (p. 54). The examples are plentiful and the implications far-reaching. For if the allegorical terms of the novel ever become consolidated, they depict a movement towards death; Jimmy's death, the disbanding and forecasted death of the crew, and the end of the ship's voyage, when the narrator says, "She had ceased to live."

The novel becomes exactly as Conrad often described it, a tribute to the seamen of the past. But more accurately, this heroic past seems to exist only as a fiction: from the very first the heroic world is contained within various self-delusions. To find a true and perfect heroism, the narrator must talk about a mythical community of seamen that is given no dramatic place in the novel, that exists out of time entirely and only in a kind of museum of the imagination:

> They were the everlasting children of the mysterious sea. Their successors are the grown-up children of a discontented earth. They are less naughty, but less innocent; less profane, but perhaps also less believing; and if they have learned how to speak they have also learned how to whine. But the others were strong and mute; they were effaced, bowed and enduring, like stone caryatides that hold up in the night the lighted halls of a resplendent and glorious edifice. They are gone now — and it does not matter. . . . Except, perhaps to the few of those who believed the truth, confessed the faith — or loved the men. (p. 25)

These are not the sailors of the *Narcissus* that the narrator is speaking about. They are the sailors of Singleton's generation, strictly speaking; but more exactly, they are the creatures of an imaginary world. They are described as emblematic pictures: "effaced, bowed and enduring," and voiceless. These "children of the sea" are indeed subject to more than the game-playing of someone like Jimmy Wait or to the follies aboard the *Narcissus*, but to reality itself — to society, time, change, and consciousness of death. Believing the "truth" in this passage must depend upon a kind of religious faith that disregards the "truth" of the public and temporal world. And thus the heroic sailors can exist only in an imaginary world, which the narrator preserves by turning them into "stone caryatids," where they may be frozen in an inanimate state that, in a way, doesn't even pretend to real life. Conrad's encomia are reserved not for people but for things: (to recall some earlier examples) men "like figures cut out of sheet tin," ships "like strange and monumental structures abandoned by men" and sailors "like stone caryatids" — as if all are artifacts of a dead world. Here Conrad's resistance to dramatic development, to plot, to storytelling, in favor of image-making, becomes most obvious. Anything that speaks to time, change, and human relationships do not belong to Conrad's imagination of the heroic. The voyage itself can only lead to the end of the heroic world.

Singleton, who is the least affected by Jimmy, is also the least "human" of the crew: "Singleton lived untouched by human emotions. Taciturn and unsmiling, he breathed amongst us — in that alone resembling the rest of the crowd" (p. 140). Yet, another testimony to the pervasive vision of the novel, to Conrad's sense of loss, is the way that even Singleton, the remaining talisman of the mythical heroic world, becomes dramatically and metaphorically framed in images of death, in a description that seems to remind us of the largest perspective of the novel: "And, beyond the light, Singleton stood in the smoke, monumental, indistinct, with his head touching the beam; like a statue of heroic size in the gloom of a crypt" (p. 129). All the poignancy and poise of the novel exists in passages such as this one. Even when resisting the novel's movement toward death, Conrad still sketches his pictures with a distinctly symbolical integrity that saves his story from bathos. The pictures themselves remind us of what the crew is coming to, of how increasingly depressing and out of touch with the heroic world the novel has become in relation to the pastoral language early in the story.

Toward the end of the novel, James Wait declines in stature. His private fears, his self-delusions, and his sexual egotism are examined by an omniscient narrator and dramatized in a couple of dialogues with Donkin. The Jimmy of the last chapter is defeated, and like the sailors, the victim of time and death. The decline in his "symbolic" presence is sometimes seen, with some justification, as a flaw in the novel.[18] But if so, it is a failure in a larger and more interesting way than is generally recognized. For Jimmy, domineering and insouciant, the specter of change, is in the end no Satan, no symbol of Evil, but a pathetic and disturbing reminder of the emptiness that pervades the moral fiber of the seaman's community. If Jimmy's decline does damage the mythical impact of the story, it is because the novel itself tends to deflate such myths as the narrator's vision of the heroic community gives way to his unpremeditated consciousness of the social world.

Near the end of the voyage, even the *Paradise Lost* myth is reduced to sentimentality; the fallen angels have become dispirited men, and nostalgia mingled with dismay takes over where symbolism has played itself out:

> Jimmy's death, after all, came as a tremendous surprise. We did not know till then how much faith we had put in his delusions. We had taken his chances of life so much at his own valuation that his death, like the death of an old belief, shook the foundations of our society. A common bond was gone; the strong, effective and respectable bond of a sentimental lie (p. 155).

Point of view is still at issue here. In allowing words like "deception," "delusion," and "lie" to enter his critical vocabulary, expressing his chagrin over the crew's easy commerce between naiveté and ignorance, the narrator almost completes the identification between the heroic and the social worlds: only the most tentative distinctions remain. But the narrator does his best to maintain them. The "death of an old belief" is used only as a simile, as if the narrator merely suggests and then disowns the implications that such an old belief has died; moreover, he makes it seem as if that old belief was the sailors' faith in Jimmy, whereas it is evident to us that ultimately their beliefs in the heroic community are also at stake. Finally his disgust over the "delusions" of a "sentimental lie" still tends to blame Jimmy more than the crew, as if a loyalty to him were any more "sentimental" than the loyalty to the ship and had been. The narrator's criticisms of the sailors are laced with tender and wistful regrets, and he is, even in his severest moments, rueful in his condemnations of their conduct.

Conrad as narrator senses more than he says. And because of that knowledge, and indeed, because of some fundamental consistency in his vision, he is nearly forced out of his affectionate ironics to more devastating ones. But from that turn in perspective, he ultimately withdraws. It seems that both his evaluations of the crew's failures and his effort to redeem the sailors' world require him to abandon his critical perspectives to praise the sailors in elegiac terms:

> Good-bye, brothers! You were a good crowd. As good a crowd as ever fisted with wild cries the beating canvas of a heavy foresail; or tossing aloft, invisible in the night, gave back yell for yell to a westerly gale. (p. 173)

It is a moving and generous tribute that the narrator offers here. But this tribute in a way represents a failing in his own integrity. Rather than a commentator or a critic, he has become an elegist, a kind of pastoral poet singing the praises of a mythical and imaginary past. In the end, Conrad cannot and will not reconcile the detachment of an ironist with the emotional involvement of a participant. And therein lies the final conflict in point of view. The superbly critical eye and the subtly ironical voice that begin to emerge at various points in the novel finally give way to Conrad's desire to relive his past, to retreat into nostalgia and sentimentality and into a world of his own making. This retreat, as I suggested earlier, is actually forecast in the prefaces to the novel, and Conrad does allow us an ironic perspective that he does not permit himself. Rather than expressing his fidelity to the standards of judgment associated with the temporal, mutable world of science that he alludes to in the 1897 Preface, Conrad remains faithful to his ideal of human community and to his own feelings. In the end, he is sentimental toward Jimmy. In each case, that tinge of dishonesty in the surrender to shibboleths is counterpoised by a very humane sympathy.

Jimmy is far more interesting and complicated a character because he is the object of this sympathy, too. Although he is almost always described as a symbol of evil, or some such thing, his "blackness" does not lend itself to such allegorical readings. It is interesting and revealing that Conrad, to his friends and his reading public, always spoke of this character affectionately. He tyrannizes over the crew, and both they and Conrad hate him and love him for it. In his duplicity, Jimmy fools even himself; in his tyranny, he caters to the illusions of brotherhood that Conrad himself wants to sustain. Jimmy is the shadow of an imaginary past and a complex reminder that the seamen's world is an attractive, self-deluding, sentimental sham. In him, Conrad's imagination of the heroic community slides into his imagination of the fallen social world.

In *The Nigger of the "Narcissus"* autobiography and history come together for Conrad in a myth of a paradise lost, a myth Conrad seems to recognize as an illusion, as a fictive way of expressing the loss of an ideal. Milton's conception of the fall, Wordsworth's idea of self-consciousness and the consciousness of death, combined with a sense of history as disintegrating order, all contribute to Conrad's imagination of the modern world. *The Nigger of the "Narcissus"* is Conrad's farewell to the past and the only time among his greatest works that he deals extensively with an heroic community in its resistance to history and society and the modern world. In finally evaluating this tale, we would probably agree that it is not a story that leaves us thinking about its failures. In it Conrad's nostalgia does become elevated to mythical terms, his sense of personal loss to a myth of historical loss. And if he does finally sacrifice judgment for feeling, we must give him credit for having warned us of his choice—indeed, for allowing us to witness that choice in such complex reversals and subtle turns. *The Nigger of the "Narcissus"* is the first and last time Conrad with such unabashed fervor, despite an implicit awareness of futility, pronounced his allegiance to a world which in his imagination he celebrated as his own.

3

"Heart of Darkness":
Beyond the Heroic

In a letter written shortly after the publication of *The Nigger of the "Narcissus,"* Conrad assured his friend R. B. Cunninghame Graham that Singleton's heroism depended directly upon his lack of "education" and the absence of self-consciousness. He described Singleton as a figure we might compare to Wordsworth's leech gatherer, "in perfect accord with his life . . . simple and great like an elemental force . . . [because] he does not think."[1] This letter makes explicit what *The Nigger of the "Narcissus"* finally seems to imply: that the crew's corruption should be seen as the development of their self-consciousness and that the myth of a lost heroic community is an historical extension of a personal myth of lost innocence. As in Milton and Wordsworth, corruption for Conrad is an inevitable function of man's rational, mortal mind. And thus the crew's betrayal of their heroic community should not be seen as a result of any simple or willfull defection from their code of ethics; its source, rather, is their humanity itself: their awareness of death, their consciousness of themselves, and their knowledge that the object of their fidelity, James Wait, is a sham. It is important to reaffirm that the crew's public code of ethics remains essentially intact throughout most of the story. What does change is the crew's relationship to that code of ethics, for once each man develops a private self-consciousness, he has already by definition violated the unity of the group. Fidelity to the group under these conditions is more than a self-delusion; therefore, it is a self-conscious and communal lie.

It follows that the journey that would sustain this "heroic world" must itself be seen in a different light. During the course of the story the official values of the seamen's ordeal are not demonstrated and reinforced by the journey but subtly parodied and destroyed by it instead. Rather then a dramatic encounter between men and the sea and an allegory about a triumph over human corruption, the voyage may be seen as an historical movement away from a timeless pastoral ideal. Yet, to complicate matters, it is difficult to point to a precise moment in the novel when the crew's paradise is in fact lost, for their humanity (and therefore their corruption), latent and submerged, seems to exist from the start. Their heroic "perfection," in other words, is apparent only when they follow the appropriate procedures under the controlled circumstances of a "sea story"; while their encounter with James Wait eventually suggests that heroism must involve more than just following the right rules. The seamen's ethics by the end of *The Nigger of the "Narcissus"* are exposed as a mere counterfeit of heroic conduct; despite all that appears noble about it, the seamen's community is never more than a fallen version of an assumed but unrealized heroic ideal. One may think of the allegorical journey itself as a kind of moral prescription that is subverted by Conrad's imagination of social relationships and historical change.

If paradise has indeed been irrecoverably lost, heroic action must now take the form of confronting whatever has replaced it. In "Heart of Darkness," Conrad is still unwilling to abandon the idea of a journey, but the tactics of that journey must be considerably changed. Conrad must direct that journey beyond the self-deluding endeavors of a human community, both inward and beneath human consciousness and back through time to some condition that predates history, which in its entirety is now seen as a process of corruption and change. Hence, in the beginning of "Heart of Darkness," there are several important developments in Conrad's imagination of the heroic ordeal. The first is that he isolates a knowledgeable, self-conscious narrator among an audience within the modern world and defines his moral perspectives according to both. The second is that he becomes explicitly concerned with the journey as a metaphysical and a verbal strategy — as a way to recover truth and to give some rhetorical shape to the process of discovering it. The third development is that he makes it the stated purpose of his journey to pursue a moral and ontological inquiry into human history, and simultaneously into the human mind, that takes him back to a condition that precedes that of the fallen world. In "Heart of Darkness" there is no sense of a prelapsarian paradise. There is no presumption of a Wordsworthian state of innocence. "Heart of Darkness" does return us to the kind of Wordsworthian universe we have glimpsed in Book VI of *The Prelude* and Book I of *The Recluse*, but here the intimations of divinity are replaced by the shadows of a demonic darkness. This is a story written in the twilight of romanticism; its landscape is the legacy of the nineteenth century. Yet its darkness is not answerable to man's desire for immortality, but rather to his capacity for psychic horror, which it finally overwhelms. The romantic promise of divinity in "Heart of Darkness" becomes an apocalyptic union between the self and the darkness, a plunge into self-destruction. This journey is a grim business from the start.[2]

The focus of all these developments is one of the most remarkable characters of modern fiction, Marlow. The voice of the first narrator serves largely to introduce Marlow and to direct out attention to him as a narrator. It is a voice that is distinct from that of Marlow, one that will virtually disappear as Marlow begins to talk. It is a voice that sounds significantly like the one in *The Nigger of the "Narcissus"* that is no longer of use to Conrad in the journey he is about to undertake: "The *Nellie*, a cruising yawl, swung to her anchor without a flutter of the sails, and was at rest. The flood had made, the wind was nearly calm, and being bound down the river, the only thing for it was to come to and wait for the turn of the tide. . . . The air was dark above Gravesend, and farther back still seemed condensed into a mournful gloom brooding motionless over the biggest, and the greatest, town on earth" (XXVI, 45). This voice, somber, romantic, and gloomily picturesque, echoes the descriptions of the *Narcissus* at berth in Bombay. But as it gives way to Marlow's narration, we learn that the "sailors" of this story are Marlow's listening audience, the professional men aboard the *Nellie*. As the first narrator says, they had all "followed the sea, " but they are identified now only by their roles in the urban, commercial world: the Lawyer, the Accountant, the Director of Companies — the modern descendents, one might say, of the crew of the *Narcissus*. Marlow himself, we are told, still follows the sea but "did not represent his class" (p. 48). He serves as a mediator, it seems, between the pastoral world of seamen and the modern world to which his audience belongs. Within this precarious and often ambivalent position, Marlow's moral perspectives are formed.

Marlow's role as a storyteller is presented among the first of his ambivalent perspectives, as he seems to be an intermediary between what is familiar and comprehensible and what is obscure or unknown. "The yarns of seamen have a direct simplicity," the first narrator says, "the whole meaning of which lies within the shell of a cracked nut." But Marlow was not typical (if his propensity to spin yarns is excepted), and to him the meaning of an episode was not inside like a kernal but outside, enveloping the tale which brought it out only as a glow brings out a haze, in the likeness of one of these misty halos that sometimes are made visible by the spectral illumination of moonshine" (p. 48). Just as Wordsworth did a century earlier in *The Recluse*, Conrad claims that the journey Marlow makes and the story he tells will add a new dimension to our conception of heroism. And, according to its Wordsworthian prototype, this journey will include a moral and ontological descent into the darkness of the self to discover that which is eternal and true. But also like Wordsworth, Conrad implies that such a journey can be begun only through conventional means, if not according to an internalized version of the Miltonic epic, as in Wordsworth, then according to a version of a seaman's yarn whose outcome will be indirect, confusing, perhaps irresolute according to the usual standards. Indeed, as James Guetti suggests in *The Limits of Metaphor*,[3] there seems to be a paradox involved: the first narrator's analogy to the nut implies that meaning for Marlow will somehow exist beyond the moral and narrative frameworks of his adventure; while Marlow's own way of talking about his story seems to claim that some kind of meaning is nonetheless to be found at the "center" of the tale, which in terms of the drama of the story is located at the Inner Station, at the climax of Marlow's journey ("It was the farthest point of navigation and the culminating point of my experience," he says of his meeting with Kurtz, p. 51). Marlow's commitment to find some meaning for his experience, in other words, includes at least a tentative commitment to an imaginative order, for his way of talking about his physical journey has an explicit metaphorical structure to it: the concept of a journey provides a conventional vocabulary to evoke the discovery of some unconventional and esoteric truth revealed only within the "heart of darkness." In terms that remind us of both Milton and Wordsworth, Marlow suggests that his journey into the darkness "seemed to throw a kind of light" (p. 51).

As in Bunyan and, in a similar vein, Cooper, the physical terms of the heroic journey provide a vocabulary for Marlow that defines what might be called a moral geography, a field of action for the heroic protagonist. When, for example, Marlow early in the voyage describes the river "whose banks were rotting into mud, whose waters, thickened into slime, invaded the contorted mangroves, that seemed to writhe at us in the extremity of an impotent despair" (p. 62), the physical aspects of the jungle seem to be laden with a symbolic significance. The words "invaded," "contorted," "rotting," and "writhe" all carry connotations of moral degeneracy. Moreover, descriptions of the European machinery exported to exploit the wilderness for its economic resources are full of moral irony:

> I came upon a boiler wallowing in the grass, then found a path leading up the hill. It turned aside for the boulders, and also for an undersized railway-truck lying there on its back with its wheels in the air. One was off. The thing looked as dead as the carcass of some animal. I came upon more pieces of decaying machinery, a stack of rusty nails. To the left a clump of trees made a shady spot, where dark things seemed to stir feebly. I blinked, the path was steep. A horn tooted to the right, and I saw the black people run. A heavy and dull detonation shook the ground, a puff of smoke came out of the cliff, and that was all. No change appeared on the face of the rock. They were building a railway. The cliff was not in the way or anything; but this objectless blasting was all the work going on. (pp. 63–64)

Passages like this one coupled with the descriptions of the rotting river bank suggest that the wilderness is a place of corruption, a symbolical landscape, a garbage dump for the emblems of Western culture, which are imagined here like a dying species of some primitive beast, "wallowing in the grass . . . dead as the carcass of some animal."

But the wilderness, in fact, does not become a symbol for the wreckage of civilization, although such effects are scattered, like the boiler and the railway truck, in various places throughout the story. More important to the previous description, and for the development of the journey, is the image of the man dynamiting the cliff with no measurable effect and no apparent purpose. The wilderness in these instances seems to resist the incursions of civilization without any visible change.

Marlow, of course, is trying to make an incursion of his own, which, although of a different kind from that of the other Europeans, subtly identifies him with them. In fact, while he is ironical about the equipment of the men dynamiting the cliff, similar ironies elsewhere are occasionally qualified by a certain admiration and incredulous awe. He remarks of the company's comical chief accountant, who kept his collar starched, his hair brushed, his boots varnished, "like a hairdresser's dummy," "That's backbone" (p. 68). And he jokes much later that Kurtz's Russian friend, with his book, his rifle, and his cartridges, seemed "excellently well equipped for a renewed encounter with the wilderness" (p. 140). If Marlow ultimately sees these men as absurd figures whose physical equipment would be of no use to him in his own struggles, he nonetheless anticipates meeting Kurtz in similar terms, "equipped with moral ideas of some sort" (p. 88). The idea of "equipment," in other words (and here we may recall Dana's idea of "equipment") seems essential to making the journey into the darkness, whether one thinks of that journey as a physical or a moral ordeal.

For Marlow, equipping oneself seems essentially a moral affair, and the challenges of the wilderness for him are primarily to his ability to make moral judgments, to find meaning in the darkness. Often he is able to do so. When he privately castigates the members of the Eldorado Expedition, for example, he compares them to "sordid buccaneers," and "burglars," and implicitly to a band of thieves in an urban slum (pp. 87–88). Their lack of any apparent moral purpose clearly does not deter Marlow from placing them in a conventional moral order in which right and wrong may be easily defined. They are thieves, burglars, and social derelicts, and Marlow sees them as perversions of civilized man. Elsewhere, under even more difficult circumstances, Marlow continues to prove his ability to call upon a moral order which provides him with a language to talk about his experiences in the wilderness. "It takes a man all his inborn strength to fight hunger properly," Marlow says. "It's really easier to face bereavement, dishonour, and the perdition of one's soul—than this kind of prolonged hunger" (p. 105). The word "properly" here seems to mean both "effectively" and "rightly" and combines a sense of social morality with a notion of "inborn strength" that implies man's inner resources are anchored to the professed values of his culture. Even when faced with the problem of starvation, Marlow would seem to say, man may still count it as an extension of his more familiar moral crises. And as in those crises, one may react either "properly" or "improperly." Thus Marlow's comments about starvation like his attack on the Eldorado Expedition, take the form of an ironical commentary. His criticisms of the company people in general assume no great problem for Marlow's moral imagination. Their hypocrisy is merely hypocrisy, merely moral duplicity, and Marlow can see through it sarcastically, bitterly.

But if Marlow's equipment for survival consists largely of such an ability to make moral judgments, his journey into the wilderness gradually divests him of the very means that would allow him to proceed further. The savages are so baffling to Marlow because, unlike him, they "still belonged to the beginnings of time—had no inherited experience to teach them" (p. 123), and therefore it is difficult to find a moral context within which they may be judged. The voyage, moreover, becomes so dangerous because it "was like travelling back to the earliest beginnings of the world . . . till you thought yourself bewitched and cut off for ever from everything you had known once—somewhere—far away—in another existence perhaps" (pp. 92-93). The journey up the river, in other words, yields Marlow only a series of progressively radical cultural dislocations, taking him to a region where he cannot draw upon a familiar moral order to make sense out of what he sees.

For a while, Marlow seems ready to meet such a challenge, to transcend the conventional means for making such a journey: "What was there after all . . . but truth—truth stripped of its cloak of time . . . [man] must meet that truth with his own inborn stuff—with his own inborn strength. Principles won't do. Acquisitions, clothes, pretty rags—rags that would fly off at the first good shake. No; you want a deliberate belief" (pp. 96-97). This passage may be taken as a virtual rejection of all versions of the equipment of the Russian and the clothing of the company accountant; such are "acquisitions, clothes, pretty rags," useless in the wilderness Marlow wants to explore. More importantly, this statement bears a direct relation to the tradition of heroic adventure tales that I characterized in chapter 1 and represents Conrad's most explicit and self-conscious break with his forbears in heroic literature. The duck trousers and checked shirts of Dana, the red badge of Henry Fleming, the "castle" of Robinson Crusoe, and the winter shelter of Roswell Gardiner all, like the uniforms of the company people, specifically and repeatedly identify clothing and equipment with self-identity and ideological order. Marlow has traversed the boundless seas of Dana and Cooper and dares to continue. "Truth," after all, is what Marlow bargains for, and he still expects that the journey to the heart of darkness may yet be made.

Nevertheless, it is finally in this attempt to transcend the limits of civilized man that Marlow finds he may proceed no further. His search for the truth of his experience now becomes increasingly associated with the idea of redemption from the wilderness and all that the wilderness may imply. The idea is first stated relatively early in the journey, as Marlow begins to realize that the wilderness evades his conventional moral judgments:

> I went to work the next day, turning, so to speak, my back on that station. In that way only it seemed to me I could keep my hold on the redeeming facts of life. Still, one must look about sometimes; and then I saw this station, these men strolling aimlessly about in the sunshine of the yard. I asked myself sometimes what it all meant. They wandered here and there with their absurd long staves in their hands, like a lot of faithless pilgrims bewitched inside a rotten fence. The word "ivory" rang in the air, was whispered, and sighed. You would think they were praying to it. A taint of imbecile rapacity blew through it all, like a whiff from some corpse. By Jove! I've never seen anything so unreal in my life. And outside, the silent wilderness struck me as something invincible, like evil or truth, waiting patiently for the passing away of this fantastic invasion. (pp. 75–76)

If the company people are "absurd" and "unreal," and Marlow needs to be "redeemed" from them, the wilderness is even more disturbing, because in the wilderness there is "something invincible, like evil or truth," from which Marlow also needs to be redeemed. It is most of all in response to this evil or truth — some bleak version of Wordsworth's abyss — that Marlow finds himself in the previous passage staking off boundaries in his imagination, in a way that recalls the walls built by Robinson Crusoe, between himself and "the silent wilderness." Whatever the wilderness contains, it is still "outside" the camp and beyond Marlow's understanding.

Some time after Marlow leaves the Central Station on the final leg of his journey, he comes across a book in a hut located along the river. The book, a manual of seamanship, will be among the Russian's "equipment" that Marlow jokes about later. At the time he discovers it, though, Marlow speaks about it with a warm and reverential irony:

> It was an extraordinary find. Its title was, *An Inquiry into some Points of Seamanship,* by a man Towser, Towson — some such name — Master in his Majesty's Navy. . . . Within, Towson or Towser was inquiring earnestly into the breaking strain of ships' chains and tackle, and other such matters. Not a very enthralling book; but at the first glance you could see there a singleness of intention, an honest concern for the right way of going to work, which made these humble pages, thought out so many years ago, luminous with another than a professional light. The simple old sailor, with his talk of chains and

purchases, made me forget the jungle and the pilgrims in a delicious sensation of having come upon something unmistakably real. (p. 99)

Marlow is wonderfully poised in this passage in the way he balances his perspectives on the book. Unlike the narrator in *The Nigger of the "Narcissus,"* he does not have to sacrifice either feeling or judgment: he is critical yet tender, amused yet respectful, sentimental without being maudlin. Yet, he does unquestionably relegate this book to the moral order of pastoral seamen, where the problem of survival is a subject for technical inquiry.

It is important to note, therefore, that Marlow, in his need for moral equipment, seemingly turns to something like Towson's approach to making a voyage: "I don't like work," he says, "—no man does—but I like what is in the work,—the chance to find yourself. Your own reality—for yourself, not for others—what no other man can ever know. They can only see the mere show, and never can tell what it really means" (p. 85). If Marlow believes at this point that he has found that "inner truth" he is searching for, it appears that he sees the problem just a few pages later with the same perspective he had on Towson:

I had to keep a lookout for the signs of dead wood we could cut up in the night for the next day's steaming. When you have to attend to things of that sort, to the mere incidents of the surface, the reality—the reality, I tell you—fades. The inner truth is hidden— luckily, luckily. (p. 93)

At last Marlow's penetration into the wilderness has become practically as futile as the dynamiting of the cliff early in the story.

The journey, of course, does continue, but its object is importantly different from what it previously appeared to be. In a way it becomes better defined, but at the same time more indirect with relationship to the wilderness: "I became aware that that was exactly what I had been looking forward to—a talk with Kurtz" (p. 113). Rather than a meeting with evil or truth, Marlow looks forward to hearing the language of Kurtz, as if he were a prophet of some sort: "The man presented himself as a voice . . . was his ability to talk" (p. 113). Indeed, Marlow, who himself is introduced in the story as a kind of prophet with extraordinary verbal facility, imagines Kurtz primarily as a man of words, a supposition borne out by what others say of him. The Russian, for example, tells Marlow that Kurtz had often discoursed of love and poetry, and the journalist near the end of the story claims that Kurtz had "electrified large meetings" (p. 154). Moreover, Kurtz, who appears to come from an ubiquitous European background, seems to Marlow the representative of an entire civilization: "All Europe contributed to the making of Kurtz" (p. 117). And, we might imagine, all of Europe's languages. What Marlow has done, it appears to me, is to reduce all his own strategies and all his equipment to the idea that his redemption ultimately relies upon some articulated belief with which to oppose the wilderness, and that only through verbal contact with Kurtz, a master of languages, will this belief be made possible.

What happens, however, is that when Marlow finally encounters Kurtz and discovers that he is indeed a master of many languages—and many ways of talking—he learns also that Kurtz remains committed to none of them. Marlow is amazed by Kurtz's report to the International Society for the Suppression of Savage Customs, filled as it is with the profession of lofty ideals and an imperialistic, missionary earnestness. But contained at the bottom of the last page, "evidently written much later," Marlow reads the words, "Exterminate all the brutes!" (p. 118). He learns, too, that Kurtz speaks the native languages, that he has presided at their bizarre ceremonies, that he raids the country for ivory, that he had ordered the attack on Marlow's boat. Marlow comes to believe that who or what Kurtz is can never be established. Near the end of the story, he phrases the problem this way:

> . . . to this day I am unable to say what was Kurtz's profession, whether he had any— which was the greatest of his talents. I had taken him for a painter who wrote for the papers, or else for a journalist who could paint—but even [his] cousin. . .could not tell me what he had been—exactly. He was a universal genius. (pp. 153-54)

This kind of talk on Marlow's part does not, as James Guetti argues, suggest that Marlow sees Kurtz as a "fallen man" in any simple way.[4] He is exasperated by Kurtz's willfulness, but to him Kurtz is not a hypocrite or charlatan. He is, rather, an "extremist," who "could get himself to believe anything—anything" (p. 154). He is like the other company people only in the way that James Wait is like Donkin: we cannot simply say he is corrupted, for the essence of his "corruption" is to resist all definitions. He has "kicked himself loose of the earth" (p. 144) with an egocentricity that is both outrageous and sublime.

Although in a conventional sense, Marlow has at his disposal practically the same verbal resources as Kurtz has, Kurtz's use of language seems to differ from that of Marlow in that he uses language as a weapon to dominate, while Marlow uses it as a shield to protect himself. Marlow seems to exist for us and for himself only as he is able to define, distinguish, evaluate, and pass judgments. His moral being, in other words, relies directly upon his verbal implements—his humor, his irony, his ability to satirize those whom he disapproves of. Without these to locate himself, he is lost in the darkness of the wilderness. Kurtz, in comparison, seems to exercise the powers of some nonverbal "inner self" (full of "monstrous passions," p. 144) that are not defined by culture or history. Language for him is an instrument that gives expression to his desire to gain ultimate ascendency over others, and it appears to be his greatest weapon in his struggle with the wilderness, too.

But in this verbal weaponry is also Kurtz's vulnerability, for, as we have seen, the wilderness seems to fend off or absorb the inventions of men. Throughout the story we have learned to associate the wilderness with some universal and abstract principle. We know only that it is immense, invisible, silent, and apparently invulnerable; and that whatever it is symbolically, its meaning seems to exist beyond the definitions of language, culture, and history and beneath man's consciousness of himself. It is, in short, a romantic darkness, different from Wordsworth's abysses only in that its horrors are more fully realized, being more relentlessly pursued. Marlow, like Wordsworth, gives us adequate reason to believe that if a man is sensitive and courageous enough he will realize that the darkness of this wilderness resides within us all. But it seems that Kurtz alone dares to confront this darkness directly, to attempt to fill its silence with his words. In pressing this encounter, however, he opposes infinite powers, and his ordeal is thus described as if he has possessed himself of "an impenetrable darkness" (p. 149), as if he has taken on some universal demon in a struggle for the mastery of his soul ("Oh, but I will wring your heart yet! he cried at the invisible wilderness," p. 148), and "He struggled with himself, too . . . . I saw the inconceivable mystery of a soul that knew no restraint, no faith, and no fear, yet struggling blindly with itself" (p. 145). In the end, he fails, and his defeat by the wilderness is marked by his cry, "The horror! The horror" (p. 149), which is the last and incomprehensible whisper of a man who had been a genius with words.

For Marlow, these are the last words that could possibly have any meaning, and so he grasps at them as if they provide the belief he is looking for: "He had summed up—he had judged. 'The horror!' He was a remarkable man. After all, this was the expression of some sort of belief; it had candour, it had conviction, it has a vibrating note of revolt in its whisper, it had the appalling face of a glimpsed truth—the strange commingling of desire and hate" (p. 151). Yet what Kurtz had summed up, how and what he judges, is left unsaid. Kurtz has appeared to us in a series of paradoxes as incomprehensible as the wilderness itself. There appears nothing to "sum up," and nothing even to judge, for both Kurtz and the wilderness partake of one another, both are "hollow at the core" (p. 131). And while Marlow suggests that "the horror" is "some sort of belief," he himself becomes increasingly unsure of whether "belief" is the right word. That cry simply had the ingredients of a belief (candor, conviction, etc.), simply, in other words, resembled a belief. Whatever it was, though, the "vibrating note of revolt" hardly sounds contrite (as some interpretations would claim), and the violence of Kurtz's voice does not sound confessional or even self-deprecating. We might say only that Kurtz and Marlow both have failed: Kurtz to dominate the wilderness and Marlow to find a way to protect himself against its implications of universal obliteration, other than withdrawal. Hence, he withdraws.

Marlow's retreat from the ultimate confrontation with the darkness carries implications for the heroic journey and heroism in general:

> Droll thing life is — that mysterious arrangement of merciless logic for a futile purpose. The most you can hope from it is some knowledge of yourself — that comes too late — a crop of unextinguishable regrets. I have wrestled with death. It is the most unexciting contest you can imagine. It takes place in an impalpable greyness, with nothing underfoot, with nothing around, without spectators, without clamour, without glory, without the great desire of victory, without the great fear of defeat, in a sickly atmosphere of tepid scepticism, without much belief in your own right, and still less in that of your adversary. If such is the form of ultimate wisdom, then life is a greater riddle than some of us think it to be. I was within a hair's breadth of the last opportunity for pronouncement and I found with humiliation that probably I would have nothing to say. (pp. 150–51)

Marlow seemingly goes far enough to reject the traditional trappings of heroism: the glamor, the spectacle, the glory, even the fear of death. But in his allusions to Kurtz's (shall we say?) existential death, Marlow still speaks in a way that simultaneously rejects and clings to the remnants of a conventional heroic vocabulary, where the word "adversary" (which ironically is very muddled in this context) still has some palpable meaning. Beyond a "sickly atmosphere of tepid scepticism," Marlow's heroic imagination stops. And while he languishes in his failures, he affirms that Kurtz had carried out the heroic journey beyond its comprehensible end. While Marlow returns to Europe armed with the rhetoric of a heroic nihilism, Kurtz follows the implications of his aspirations to universality and disappears into the unknown. With both admiration for Kurtz's heroism and a mixture of relief and guilt over his own escape, Marlow confesses that Kurtz "had made that last stride, he had stepped over the edge, while I had been permitted to draw back my hesitating foot" (p. 151).

"Heart of Darkness" becomes the central tale among Conrad's adventure stories, for it represents the farthest extension of his heroic journeys into the regions of the unknown. It marks the end of the tradition of adventure tales that I defined in chapter 1 and the failure of Conrad's romantic search for a universal truth. Clearly this journey becomes the inversion of similar past endeavors in Wordsworth when its fulfillment implies self-annihilation. But at the same time, for this very reason, it is also the farthest extension of the Wordsworthian quest, whose end Wordsworth contemplated in moments of transcendence from a bleak and shadowy distance. In "Heart of Darkness" Conrad begins with the idea of the heroic journey and ends by scurrying back in terror to a civilization he views as both a refuge for the cowardly and a demesne of lunatics. Because the idea of heroism must undergo several transformations during the course of this story, it is necessary to define more exactly the heroism displayed by Marlow as he enters and then emerges from the wilderness and to discuss its relationship to Conrad's imagination of man.

In a traditional sense, certainly, Marlow is no coward. He is clever, industrious, inventive; he is cool under the pressures of physical danger; and he reacts with poise and determination in defending his boat and humanely scattering his attackers. Though frightened by the savages, he is sufficiently equipped, morally and psychologically, to handle himself heroically in a conventional sense. He even makes statements unthinkably daring to a traditional hero like Robinson Crusoe. Commenting on the savages at one point, for example, he says:

> They howled and leaped, and spun, and made horrid faces; but what thrilled you was just the thought of their humanity—like yours—the thought of your remote kinship with this wild and passionate uproar. Ugly. Yes, it was ugly enough; but it you were man enough you would admit to yourself that there was in you just the faintest trace of a response to the terrible frankness of that noise, a dim suspicion of there being a meaning in it which you—you so remote from the night of first ages—could comprehend. (p. 96)

This is just one example of Marlow's wonderful capacity for both sympathy and resilience. But ultimately this capacity relies upon a system of defense Marlow often exhibits when confronted with danger. At one point, he comments ironically about the cannibals, when their leader expresses a special interest in the savages along the river bank, "I would no doubt have been properly horrified, had it not occurred to me that he and his chaps must be very hungry" (p. 103). Marlow here may be mocking his own sense of "propriety" ("It takes a man all his inborn strength to fight hunger properly"), but in doing so, he also takes refuge in the cannibals' moral logic, as he sees it, because, while founded upon different (and at this point, humorously justifiable) premises from his own ideology, it is logical nonetheless. In fact, their moral logic may resemble ours, if we are honest enough to see the connections: if you are hungry, you must eat; if you are accustomed to eating men, you crave human flesh. There is more sense to this reasoning than there is to the mindless plotting of the company people. What really distinguishes between Marlow's reaction to the savages and the fear of the wilderness is the way he can extend the logic of his imagination but cannot contradict it. His mind is large enough to accommodate the rationale behind cannibalism, because he can make connections between it and his own way of thinking. But he cannot handle the strain of paradox, the horror that "the earth seemed unearthly" (p. 96), the inability to make any imaginative contact with his experience whatsoever.

Next to the fear of such an imaginative failure, Marlow welcomes the usual horrors, "the usual sense of commonplace, deadly danger, the possibility of a sudden onslaught and massacre. . .which pacified me, in fact, so much, that I did not raise alarm" (p. 141). These are dangers he can picture, can create images about in his imagination; and such image-making, as in the metaphors of light and darkness in the following passage, are essential to him. Commenting upon the human skulls surrounding the hut of Kurtz, Marlow says: "After all, that was only a savage sight, while I seemed at one bound to have been transported into some lightless region of subtle horrors, where pure, uncomplicated savagery was a positive relief, being something that had a right to exist—obviously—in the sunshine" (p. 132). This statement does not, of course, imply that Marlow is not upset by "pure, uncomplicated savagery," but that his heroism is large enough to reinforce him against his fears. It is Marlow's conscious mind, his marvelous ability to see connections, to make distinctions, to assimilate alien ideas (all of which link him with Dana) which is his most impressive quality. But this rationality, this ability to "[keep his] head pretty well" (p. 145), as he says of himself in contrast to Kurtz, is also like the rationality of Crusoe and his fictional descendents: it is used, in effect, as a verbal and psychological defense against fear. Marlow's irony, like the irony and sarcasm he directs against the company people, allows him to define, order, and evaluate his experiences—so long as he is not dealing with the wilderness itself.

Marlow's achievement as a heroic figure is perhaps best measured by the way that he, unlike Dana, Gardiner, and Fleming, is not simply a voyager but a "wanderer," an observer, a cultural commentator whose sense of himself is born out of a highly sophisticated moral consciousness that may at times distance itself from and bear witness to the culture that formed it. But because Marlow's imagination seems to rely upon his ability to make analogies between what is familiar to him and what is unknown, in understanding what happens to him in "Heart of Darkness," we might appeal to the general logical precept that all analogies ultimately break down. Marlow is able to compare the natives' drums to Christian church bells (p. 71), their demonstrations and dances to "an enthusiastic outbreak in a madhouse" (p. 96). But the wilderness is more than the savages—it is the darkness that Marlow constantly invokes, the darkness within which the devices of analogy fail. And because Marlow's entire cultural experience is inadequate as a vehicle for further analogies, we might say that both Marlow's language and his culture share the same fate. Together they represent the limitations of man's consciousness and rationality and the irrelevance of morality in the darkness that is beyond the inventions of man.

If Marlow is going to continue to live as a moral being, he must, once again, shelter himself from the wilderness within the limitations of order and coherence made possible by his conscious mind. It is a kind of willful self-delusion that permits him to escape Kurtz's fate. As in *The Nigger of the "Narcissus,"* language is associated with artifice and deception, with a contrived order. It is the counterfeit of some unrealized truth that would assert "life" against the apparent chaos of the wilderness. In "Heart of Darkness," as in *The Nigger*, the idea of a "lie" has a special meaning to it: "There is a taint of death, a flavour of mortality in lies," Marlow says, "—which is exactly what I hate and detest in the world—what I want to forget" (p. 82). After these two stories, there is only one way to read this statement so that its association between mortality and lies will make sense. All things human are lies—culture, morality, social order—because they are evasions of the darkness. The idea is explicitly stated in one of the letters I quoted in chapter 1, "Our refuge is in stupidity, in drunkenness of all kinds, in lies, in beliefs, in murder, thieving, reforming, in negation, in contempt—each man according to the promptings of his own particular devil." After "Heart of Darkness" it should be clearer why this catalogue of human activities is so varied and so inclusive: it is a condemnation of mortality itself. Yet, if man wants to escape lies, as Marlow wants to, he must follow Kurtz into self-obliteration. Without lies, human life is impossible; the order which is essential to it could not exist. Hence Marlow by the end of the tale must live with the knowledge that he too has to be a liar in order to survive.

The effect of Marlow's newfound wisdom upon his relationship to other people is something like that in Swift when Gulliver returns to England. Perhaps the best index to the changes in Marlow is the way his relationship develops to his peers, the members of his listening audience, in the increasing antagonism he feels towards them. His narrative asides begin as appeals for his audience's sympathy: "Do you see him? Do you see the story? Do you see anything? It seems to me I am trying to tell you a dream—making a vain attempt, because . . . No, it is impossible. We live as we dream—alone" (p. 82). Later these interruptions become more pointed, defensive, vindictive, as he compares his listeners to circus performers "on your respective tight-ropes for—what is it? half-a-crown a tumble" (p. 94), to which some insulted listener answers, "Try to be civil, Marlow." Marlow's immediate apology is colored with ironic indulgence, qualified mainly by including himself among the performers: "I beg your pardon. I forgot the heartache which makes up the rest of your price . . . You do your tricks very well. And I didn't do so badly either" (p. 94). But the full measure of Marlow's disgust with himself, his listeners, and his entire society is unleashed in portrayals of society late in the novel that are shockingly warped if we are to compare them to his relatively harmless Dickensian caricatures earlier:

> You can't understand. How could you? — with solid pavement under your feet, surrounded by kind neighbors ready to cheer you or to fall on you, stepping delicately between the butcher and the policeman, in the holy terror of scandal and gallows and lunatic asylums — how can you imagine what particular region of the first ages a man's untrammelled feet may take him into by the way of solitude — utter solitude without a policeman — by the way of silence — utter silence, where no warning voice of a kind neighbour can be heard whispering of public opinion? (p. 116)

The condemnation here is for both society's sordidness and for its vulgar comforts. It is an ugly picture to be sure, with its depiction of public gossip, institutionalized insanity, gruesome executions — a life that has its own risks and precariousness, its own horrors, a life in which even one's friends no more than "whisper" their warnings before they too may turn on one. This is a society that seems to prey upon itself. But — and this too is part of the condemnation — it is also a society that is perversely reassuring. At least one knows something about the risks, at least there are ways of deciding who one is and what one may expect. As long as one "steps delicately" enough, one may evade the gallows and the asylums where the Gullivers or the Marlows are more likely to end up. The price for social order is paid in honesty, courage, and some lingering notion of human decency.

"Heart of Darkness" perhaps should have ended on this note, for the vision the previous passage presents is consistent with the one developed throughout the story. Yet the story ends somewhat differently, with a twist on the idea of Marlow's humanity that also grows out of the movement in the story. The last scene in the book, the interview with Kurtz's Intended, may seem a kind of sentimental footnote. The woman is a saint, her suffering is more pathetic than tragic, Marlow's kindness is in a sense another failure of his integrity, and Conrad himself seems to be reaching into his fantasies for ideal figures to shine amidst the ruins. But I find myself touched by this scene more than I am touched by Conrad's tribute at the end of *The Nigger of the "Narcissus,"* and I am not embarrassed about it here. The ironies of the scene are so blunt, yet so powerful. Marlow imaginatively brings the wilderness with him to the interview in a sequence that is cinematic in its flashbacks, juxtapositions, and superimpositions of sounds and images from the Congo: images of deepening darkness, sounds of the river, the drums, and the savages; and, as the pale, suffering woman extends her hands to greet Marlow, the image and voice of Kurtz himself crying, "The horror! the horror!" The wilderness pervades Marlow's being as he now knows it pervades the souls of all mankind, beneath the surface. As he offers his sympathy by endorsing the woman's platitudes ("His end. . .was in every way worthy of his life" p. 161), he writhes in their irony and hates himself for his lies. But then, in a wonderfully benign, generous, even tragic gesture on his part, Marlow admits that "My anger subsided before a feeling of infinite pity." And for the very fact that he does recoil from the lie he tells her ("The last word he pronounced was—your name."), he does not console himself by his consolation of the woman. He is able, instead, to temper his fear, his irony, his contempt for the weakness of mortals who need such lies with a marvelously moving assertion of life. Perhaps cowardly in one sense, this concession to humanity nevertheless is itself a kind of triumph.

There will henceforth be a difference in Conrad's fiction between what he lives with and what he lives by. Over truth he has chosen humanity— sadly, generously, knowingly. This is not heroism, it is sentimentality—but here, at least, it is so poignant, so fine.

4

Lord Jim:
Romance and the Public World

Since the novel first appeared in 1900, *Lord Jim* has been frequently criticized as a short story gotten out of hand. For the fact, if not the evaluation, there is considerable evidence. Originally, Conrad planned only a relatively modest tale of 20,000–30,000 words, anticipating serialization in two issues of *Blackwood's Edinburgh Magazine*.[1] But the story ran for fourteen installments between October 1899 and November 1900; and *Blackwood's* records are full of indications that Conrad had no idea the story would become as long as it did and little notion during the writing and submitting of a few chapters, and even a few pages, at a time, exactly where he was going with it.[2] The novel is constantly experimenting with its materials. It rejuvenates itself several times after episodic climaxes. It changes its direction and redefines its terms more than once, especially after the first eighteen chapters. In trying to resolve both the plot and the moral issues of the novel simultaneously, Conrad, for over 200 pages, did not know where to stop. But in establishing these opinions, this chapter will not criticize the novel's lack of structure. Rather, I hope to explore the sources and implications of Conrad's indecisiveness and to inquire further into this product of an imagination withdrawing to a simpler kind of romanticism as it attempts to rescue some concept of heroism from Marlow's failures in "Heart of Darkness."

A brief summation of the fourteen installments of *Lord Jim* in *Blackwood's* will give us a crude map of Conrad's winding strategy as he worked his way, *ad hoc*, through problems I will hereafter discuss in greater detail:

1. Chapters I-IV: A kind of prologue introducing Jim.
2. Chapter V: Marlow's narrative begins.
3. VI-VII.
4. VIII-IX.
5. X-XI.

6. XII-XIII: Marlow's interview with the French lieutenant. Conrad promises David Meldrum of *Blackwood's* a rapid conclusion.
7. XIV-XVI: Chapter XI contains Marlow's interview with Chester and Chapter XV his sudden resolution that Jim must "withdraw" ("he had no place where he could—what shall I say?—where he could withdraw. That's it! Withdraw—be alone with his loneliness"). Chapter XVI forecasts Jim's "Arcadian happiness." Conrad seems to be orienting himself for a conclusion shortly to follow.
8. XVII-XX: Marlow's interview with Stein in Chapter XX. Stein's dictum, "In the destructive element immerse."
9. XXI-XXIII: Stein and Marlow place Jim on Patusan. Marlow proclaims in Chapter XXI that Jim "did not go out, not at all. On the contrary, he came on wonderfully." Chapters XXII and XXIII sketch the world of Patusan. A relieved Marlow declares, "My heart was freed from that dull resentment which had existed side by side with interest in his fate."
10. XXIV-XXVII: Marlow tells of his visit to Patusan two years later. Jim recounts his adventures in brief comments and allusions. Marlow remarks, "Jim the leader was a captive in every sense. The land, the people, the friendship, the love, were like the jealous guardians of his body." Marlow seems disturbed that in the midst of success Jim has sacrificed rather than redeemed his inner life through his position on Patusan. And Marlow knows that privately Jim is still troubled.
11. XXVIII-XXX: Jewel is introduced. The "love story" begins. "Romance had singled Jim for its own," Marlow says (p. 282), "—and that was the true part of the story . . . . "
12. XXXI-XXXV: Jewel worries that Marlow will take Jim back with him. The narrative sputters. In Chapter XXXIV Marlow's listeners become impatient. Marlow apologizes, "I suppose I must have fallen into a sentimental mood; I only know that I stood there long enough for the sense of utter solitude to get hold of me so completely that all I had lately seen, all I had heard, and the very human speech itself, seemed to have passed away out of existence. . .as though I had been the last of mankind (p. 323)." Marlow's failures to find a "way out" for Jim end in his shadowy, dark romantic images. Marlow invokes his mantra, "He is one of us," a couple of times, and leaves Jim on Patusan in the enveloping darkness.
13. XXXVI-XL: The "epilogue." Marlow's audience breaks up, seemingly unimpressed except for one man. Marlow writes to this man two years later, telling him of Jim's fate. The Brown affair begins.

14. XLI-XLV: The Brown affair concluded. Marlow ends with an elegy to Jim.

Broadly speaking, the tone of *Lord Jim* differs from that of "Heart of Darkness" (which is rightly read, as Conrad intended, as a companion piece) by its rather more wistful perplexity and its less discriminating overlap of philosophical detachment and emotional engagement, of its sympathetic irony and its sentimental biases; and by a general willingness to allow Marlow's nostalgia to modify his intellectual concerns. Marlow in this novel acts as both a moral detective and a pastoral poet in relating a volume of stories, tales, and legends based upon characters who differ as widely as the French lieutenant, Chester, Brierly, Stein, Brown, and Jim himself, all of whom serve (at least in part) to provide either illustrations or interpretations of heroic actions and models for different types of courage. *Lord Jim*, which has provided some critics with a gold mine of Wordsworthian props and romantic conventions, is actually more distanced from Wordsworth than either of the tales discussed so far. Less tenacious and lower-keyed than "Heart of Darkness," *Lord Jim* in its meandering and yet poignant journey, reenacts the struggle between "thought" and "feeling" that Conrad first identified in the Preface to *The Nigger of the "Narcissus"*; as a consequence, this novel may be read simultaneously as a moral documentary and a collection of heroic fables in which Jim is the sentimental and philosophical center of a more general moral concern.

One way to focus upon the divisions in Marlow's role in *Lord Jim* is once again to observe his relationship to his listening audience, a relationship that is importantly more obtrusive and more central to the tale than that in "Heart of Darkness" — so much, in fact, that it serves as a mirror on Conrad's own consciousness of himself as a storyteller. The listeners, we may note, are probably very much like the ones Conrad might imagine reading the story in *Blackwood's*. They are comprised apparently of a small group of professional men who seem only sympathetic enough to allow Marlow the role of group entertainer. We may assume this audience's values to be commercial, nationalistic, and perhaps colonialistic, and thus the men may be described as practical and rather affluent gentlemen, smoking their cigars and relaxing on an unnamed host's verandah in a chummy, clubbish atmosphere. In all, they are ideal products of late Victorian culture. As in "Heart of Darkness," Marlow is a part of his audience's world and yet both his sentimentality and his seemingly esoteric moral consciousness tend to isolate him in personal reflections which his listeners frequently do not seem to understand. Partly because this novel, unlike "Heart of Darkness," rarely loses touch with its group of listeners, we will become especially aware, as the story develops, of the division between Marlow's responsibilities to this

Victorian world and his sympathies towards a world created largely out of his personal and sentimental imagination.

The opposition between these two moral contexts is first laid out, in a slightly different form, in chapter 4, when Jim appears before the court of inquiry and Conrad provides us with still another audience, one that is within the story Marlow tells: that of the men witnessing the trial. Although this second group, unlike the first, is comprised mainly of seamen, the values they represent are presumably the same. As representatives of conventional public values, the men at the inquiry will condemn Jim as a coward, while Marlow in telling the story to his listeners in effect reopens the case on appeal, becoming a kind of lawyer or, as I've called him, a moral detective. Marlow's case begins as a plea—polemical, declamatory, laudatory, insisting upon the universality of Jim's predicament, representing Jim as Everyman, or at least every Englishman:

> I watched the youngster there. I liked his appearance; I knew his appearance; he came from the right place; he was one of us. He stood there for all the parentage of his kind, for men and women by no means clever or amusing, but whose very existence is based upon honest faith, and upon the instinct of courage. I don't mean military courage, or civil courage, or any special kind of courage, I mean just that inborn ability to look temptations straight in the face—a readiness unintellectual enough, goodness knows, but without pose—a power of resistance, don't you see, ungracious if you like, but priceless—an unthinking and blessed stiffness before the outward and inward terrors, before the might of nature, and the seductive corruption of men—backed by a faith invulnerable to the strength of facts, to the contagion of example, to the solicitation of ideas. Hang ideas! They are tramps, vagabonds, knocking at the back-door of your mind, each taking a little of your substance, each carrying away some crumb of that belief in a few simple notions you must cling to if you want to live decently and would like to die easy! (XXI, p. 43)

If Marlow appeals to his audience's sympathy here, he is asking more of them than may at first be apparent. In fact, the most obvious and critically accepted reading of passages such as this one make Marlow's case a bit too simple. Jim, as Marlow will so often tell his listeners, is "one of us." His commonness, simplicity, faith and endurance make him special, because in those qualities he is true to an old English folk tradition of moral pluck and stiff upper lips. Yet it is curious that Marlow's acclaim of this tradition is so pervaded by an attack upon "the strength of facts," the "contagion of examples," the "solicitation of ideas," and the "seductive corruption of men." At this point in my argument, it should be clear in what moral context Marlow's metaphors characterizing the court of inquiry and its social values should be read. The suggestions of lewdness, criminality, sloth, and disease, and the evocations of a corrupt humanity in a filthy urban slum, all remind us of Donkin, of the Eldorado Expedition, of the description in "Heart of Darkness" of society as a lunatic asylum. But the recipients of Marlow's disgust here are not people but *ideas*: it is not the Eldorado Expedition that are parasitical "tramps, vagabonds, knocking at the back-door of your mind." Similarly, Marlow talks of English folk history as a social condition just as the narrator of *The Nigger of the "Narcissus"* spoke of the crew as a microcosm of mankind: both carry the same subtle identification between an ideal society and a state of mind. Pastoral man, here placed in an English cottage, is a myth no less than he was aboard the *Narcissus*, and civilized man the cannibal ("taking a little of your substance. . .carrying away some crumb of that belief") no less than in "Heart of Darkness." But ultimately the enemy (as expressed also in the letters quoted in chapter 1) is consciousness and all its attendant evils: in Conrad, as in Wordsworth, man thinks himself into the fall.

So the relationship between Marlow and his audience is actually a more delicate and problematical affair than it might at first seem. Marlow, after all, is both conscious and self-conscious and in some ways very much a part of a fallen world. If he is different from his audience, this difference is a result of his discovery of the limitations of consciousness as it manifests itself in science, in systematized morality, in a historically constituted society, and in this instance in "military courage, or civil courage, or any special kind of courage." The problem for Marlow is that he must still confront this society—both in refuting the court's judgment and in persuading his audience that Jim's case is worth reexamining—often on their terms, as a man of ideas appealing to men whose culture depends upon ideas, and as a man who detests society and yet appeals to a social ideal.

And so he argues: Jim's cowardice, if such it was, is a morally ambiguous and venial act. The *Patna's* bulkhead was apparently going, a squall was approaching, there were not nearly enough lifeboats for the eight hundred pilgrims, Jim's associates were crude and obviously remiss in their duties, and Jim was not so much afraid as he was confused by the emergency. Jim's leap from the ship, like Henry Fleming's cowardice in *The Red Badge of Courage*, is committed in one impulsive moment in the temporary absence of all restraints, indeed, in a moral vacuum. Would we have acted differently? Marlow seems to ask. Don't we see something of Jim in ourselves? And can't we find in our heroic tradition room for a person decent by nature who has practically fallen victim to circumstance? Marlow insists that there is a kind of courage in Jim's "facing it out as he does, knowing very well that if he went away nobody would trouble to run after him" (p. 67).

Yet Marlow himself is not certain how he may judge Jim, for Marlow's ideal cultural hero would not have jumped from the *Patna*. "I would have trusted the deck to that youngster on the strength of a single glance," Marlow says, "and gone to sleep with both eyes—and, by Jove! it wouldn't have been safe" (p. 45). And later: "I was aggrieved against him, as though he had cheated me — me! of a splendid opportunity to keep up the illusion of my beginnings, as though he had robbed our common life of the last spark of its glamour" (p. 131). Not only are corrupt public models of heroism called into question by Jim's case but Marlow's cultural ideal as well, making his position as defender of Jim all the more difficult. The examination of heroism in *Lord Jim* takes on a private dimension for Marlow, and he now must question his own assumptions about the heroic self.

Marlow's efforts to redeem Jim and satisfy his own need for heroic models begin with an attack upon "official morality" through the character of Brierly. Brierly is presented to us in chapter 6 as a man afraid of nothing and a man who, despite his obnoxious egotism, is also "one of us." His courage, that is, may be defined not so differently from Marlow's idea of the traditional Englishman — indeed, there is no other way to define it. He is the captain of "the crack ship of the Blue Star line," and he has a perfect record: never makes a mistake, never causes an accident, has rescued ships, saved lives at sea. He has, in other words, proven himself a hero within the same moral context in which Jim has proven himself a coward. And yet, Jim's case affects him in an unexpected way. Marlow tells us that while Brierly is trying Jim's case, he also opened up his own for private inquiry. And, as Marlow says, "the verdict must have been unmitigated guilt," for he jumped overboard to his death barely a week after the inquiry.

Conrad does not care enough about Brierly to make him much more than a stage prop in this novel. But the story of Brierly initiates Marlow's efforts to do more than attack conventional heroic standards by distinguishing between a public heroism and some undefined, existential, and private heroism that he thinks Jim may achieve. Brierly is a hero in a way that Jim is not; but Jim may be a hero in a way that Brierly is not. It is upon such an assumption that Marlow is willing to pursue Jim's case further. For both Jim and Marlow, the heroic journey has begun.

Most of the questions Marlow asks about heroism are asked fairly early in the novel. It is his interview in chapter 13 with the French lieutenant who spent thirty hours aboard the foundering *Patna* ("It was judged proper," he remarks to Marlow, p. 141) that forms the dramatic center of Marlow's contention that courage is normally and insufficiently defined by public standards and that there must be some kind of heroism beyond the confines of culture. In this dialogue, the almost oracular sobriety of the lieutenant is played off against Marlow's random and parenthetical French quotations, giving the reader an effect something like cinematic dubbing, making him aware of the dramatic interplay between the speaker and the translator. The exchange becomes comic (particularly in view of the awkwardness of the linguistic peculiarities of the translation), for the French phrases parody the translated pronouncements. And yet the lieutenant is as compelling a figure as Coleridge's ancient mariner. He carries the authority of a wisdom that seems to be of the ages, something like Tolstoy's Kutuzov in his world weary irony. The lieutenant's words sound almost like decrees, but we approve of them, because of their understatement and modesty, their generosity and tact, and because these characteristics combined with the lieutenant's comic qualities make him seem so human, so endearing:

> "One is always afraid. One may talk but . . . . " He put down the glass awkwardly . . . . The fear, the fear — look you — it is always there . . . . " (p.146)
>
>   *   *   *
>
> "Yes! yes! One talks, one talks; this is all very fine; but at the end of the reckoning one is no cleverer than the next man — and no more brave . . . . " (p. 146)
>
>   *   *   *
>
> "Man is a born coward (*L'homme est né poltron*). It is a difficulty — *parbleu*! It would be too easy otherwise. But habit — habit — necessity — do you see? — the eye of others — *voilà*. One puts up with it. And then the example of others who are no better than yourself, and yet make good countenance . . . . "
>
> His voice ceased.
> "That young man — you will observe — had none of these inducements — at least at the moment," I remarked . . . . His right hand went up, and he swayed forward. "Allow me . . . . I contended that one may get on knowing very well that one's courage does not come of itself (*ne vient pas tout seul*). There's nothing much in that to get upset about. One truth the more ought not to make life impossible . . . . But the honour — the honour, monsieur . . . . The honour . . . that is real — that is! And what life may be worth when" . . . he got on his feet with a ponderous impetuosity, as a startled ox might scramble up from the grass . . . "when that honour is gone — *ah ça par exemple* — I can offer no opinion. I can offer no opinion — because — monsieur — I know nothing of it." (pp. 147-48)

As compelling a figure as he is, the lieutenant reveals little that Marlow doesn't already know: that heroism is a social convention, born out of "habit — necessity. . .the eyes of others . . . . And then the example of others to. . .[to] make good countenance." This definition seems to confirm Marlow's contempt for the artifices which comprise conventional ideas of heroism (the "contagion of example" and special kinds of courage he condemns in the first passage quoted in this chapter). But the lieutenant is not finished, as he corrects the drift of Marlow's thought ("Allow me . . . . I contended") and asserts that indeed "one's courage does not come of itself," but "that is nothing to get upset about." It is when man loses his "honour" that the real problem begins. What happens when "the honour" is gone the lieutenant doesn't say, brushing off further inquiry: "This, monsieur, is too fine for me — much above me — I don't think about it." Marlow learns no more from his transient companion, but he knows that he has hit upon the problem that he too has sensed all along ("Hang the fellow! he had pricked the bubble . . . . I sat down again alone and discouraged" pp. 148–49). Heroism in *Lord Jim* is invented in the eyes of society, as it had been in *The Red Badge of Courage*. But unlike *The Red Badge*, *Lord Jim* begins to suggest that only in such public heroism is man able to find his own private sense of worth—a notion that is closer to Marlow's work ethic in "Heart of Darkness" than anything in Crane, the idea of finding one's inner self in what others see as "the mere show." Marlow's sense of heroism, in other words, is still tied to some notion of participation in cultural endeavors and to the idea that a true hero, whose heroism may become a very private affair, can exist only within a community of men. Whatever "honour" is (one's private sense of moral worth, we would assume), it is not dependent upon mere courage. Jim is courageous at the trial, but to be a hero in *Lord Jim* depends upon some wedding of the self and a cultural ideal.

The failure of the lieutenant to offer some definition of heroism for a man disgraced and banished from his society returns him to the annals of military heroism from which he came, while Marlow is led into the murky realm of the isolated self and the problem of man's existential worth. It is something that Marlow will balk at, talk around and evade for much of the novel. For the time being his strategy is to seek answers to the questions raised in the first part of the novel by looking for heroic models which in some way defy conventions. The comedy of "little Bob Stanton's" mock chivalric death and the testimony of the two helmsmen of the *Patna* at the inquest provide two anecdotes about heroism that is unconventional partly because it is so amusing. Unfortunately, Stanton is finally just a funny character in a sailor's yarn and the helmsmen (who did not leave the ship because no one told them to) are seen simply as well-trained coolies. Later, in another encounter, Marlow meets the audacious and irreverent Chester, who calls the mate's certificate that Jim loses "a mere bit of ass's skin," adding "that never made a man. You must see things exactly as they are—if you don't, you may just as well give in at once. You will never do anything in this world" (p. 161). Chester's cynicism and materialism don't exclude "courage," but they do redefine it. He dies in a reckless enterprise designed to profit from (appropriately enough) a guano island, untouched because of its treacherous location. Chester's assertion that Jim is good for nothing but lording it over an island full of bird excrement ironically implies his acceptance of the court's "official morality" ostracizing Jim, and amusingly becomes a way of deprecating himself for his own pursuit of that enterprise. Chester's contempt for the conventions of public morality does not really distinguish him from that public but rather confirms the notion that those conventions have placed him where he belongs. His courage is that of a scoundrel, and Marlow discusses him partly to present his audience with another bleak alternative (like Brierly's suicide) to blanket conformity to public standards.

Marlow, in other words, fails during the first part of the novel to find a way of talking about heroism that meets the special requirements suggested by Jim's case. All Marlow's "public" models of heroism, from Chester to the French lieutenant, are ultimately heroic in styles that issue from public conventions. Chester is a conventional rogue, and the lieutenant is a conventional military officer in the sense that his heroism is defined "by the book." The alternative to these public standards seems to be, if anything, the boyishly romantic and literary models of heroism that Jim subscribes to as a youth on the training ship. And then, too, there is still Marlow's image of the heroic common man. But neither public nor literary standards may in any simple way apply to Jim now.

Throughout the course of the *Patna* episode, the first eighteen chapters, Marlow plays an increasingly active role in the novel, both as a dramatic character managing the affairs of Jim and as a storyteller who becomes more and more a commentator. His dramatic involvement with Jim intensifies from the time he conveys Brierly's offer of escape to Jim, through the letters of introduction he writes to various ship chandlers, to his pivotal counsel with Stein in chapters 20 and 21. But as the novel approaches the end of the *Patna* episode, it is also clear that Marlow and Conrad both react uncomfortably to the strain of any impending failure to define a heroic ethic that supercedes the limited models offered by society. In November 1899, Conrad was forecasting that the novel would be completed shortly after chapter 13[3] — the one in which Marlow's frustrations with the French lieutenant are compounded by an emotional episode in which Jim, insulted and hurt by his purveyance of Brierly's escape money, turns his back on Marlow and leaves: "Absolutely running, with nowhere to go," and as Conrad sent off chapter 18 to *Blackwood's*, he wrote to David Meldrum: "I am driving on with the story and you may expect another Chap: shortly. And then the end! I do wish for the end."[4] But that was just as Stein was being introduced into the novel, and Marlow was beginning to say things about Jim like, "what I could never make up my mind about was whether his line of conduct amounted to shirking his ghost or to facing him out" (p. 197); and "I was concerned as to the way he would go out" (p. 223); and "At the moment I merely wished to achieve his disappearance" (p. 229); and "To tell this story is by no means so easy as it should be" (p. 275). Marlow's pleading of Jim's case and his helping Jim with new opportunities to express his heroic aspirations form the fictional components of Conrad's

own groping for ways to give shape and purpose to Jim's wanderings and to
create a heroic environment to replace the one no longer hospitable to Jim's
endeavors. But it is pretty certain that, approaching the Patusan episode,
Conrad did not anticipate what he was yet to do. When Marlow declares,
"My last words about Jim shall be few" (p. 225), he is barely halfway
through the novel.

During this time Marlow's relationship with his audience changes crucially as he becomes less sure of himself as a defender of Jim and as he
realizes he must turn away from public standards of heroism in following
Jim's destiny. A good index of these changes is in Marlow's use of the
phrase "one of us." While "one of us" in the first half of the novel tends to
accumulate a number of meanings (one of us seamen, us common people,
us Englishmen, us white men, and "us" mankind in general), Marlow's
continued use of the phrase ironically has the effect of distancing Jim from
the listeners. When Marlow in chapter 5 says that Jim "was outwardly so
typical of that good, stupid kind we like to feel marching right and left of us
in life," he is already beginning to distinguish Jim from his audience. Jim is
the kind of simple, reliable fellow who does the sweat and blood work of
more sophisticated, affluent, and implicitly less courageous people.
Marlow's mild sarcasm towards his audience is also a self-directed repri-
mand, delivered because Jim's struggles seem so much more meritorious
than any of his own. From these early reprimands, Marlow continues to
undercut any sense that "one of us" means "every man." "The point, however, is that of all mankind Jim had no dealings but with himself," Marlow
says, "and the question is whether at the last he had confessed to a faith
mightier than the laws of order and progress" (p. 339). Said late in the
novel, this statement seems to remind us that Marlow's audience is among
those who subscribe to a faith in the laws of order and progress, and that
Jim, in being exiled from his society, had to look elsewhere for his "opportunities."

More interesting perhaps is the way "one of us," which at first seems to
include Marlow with his audience, comes increasingly to isolate him from it.
The phrase begins to sound almost like a private incantation, appearing so
often in places where we expect Marlow to make a crucial judgment.
Instead of a clear judgment, we repeatedly hear, "I only know that he was
one of us." To recall an earlier remark, Marlow says, "I was aggrieved
against him, as though he had cheated me—me! of a splendid opportunity
to keep up the illusion of my beginnings . . . . " Jim cheats "me," not "us."
We are aware throughout the novel that Marlow's audience is skeptical of
his efforts to talk about Jim's specialness, that they are not really willing to
sympathize or even capable of the kind of sympathy Marlow desired ("He

paused again to wait for an encouraging remark perhaps, but nobody spoke; only the host, as if reluctantly performing a duty, murmured—'You are so subtle, Marlow'" p. 94). For Marlow, "one of us" will also mean "one of us romantics," to adopt Stein's term, and Marlow recognizes in himself a special romanticism—the "glamour of our common life," "the illusion of my beginnings," which he also sees in Jim. But Marlow's "illusion," actually belongs exclusively to himself, for as that previous quotation ("I was aggrieved against him") suggests, Jim himself seems to have his own ideas about the conditions of his redemption. "Our common life" does not seem to include Marlow's audience, who are too practical and urbane, but it doesn't include Jim either. Rather it describes the personal fiction that Marlow would like to sustain about his own past and his relationship with Jim.

Thus Marlow actually tries to appropriate the character of Jim for his own purposes, "I am telling you so much about my own instinctive feelings and bemused reflections because there remains so little to be told of him. He existed for me, and after all it is only through me that he exists for you" (p. 224). Marlow's gradual sympathetic identification with Jim is more intense than ever. But the issue hardly seems any more "What is heroism?" or "How can Marlow help Jim?" but whether or not Jim can be the hero that Marlow would like him to be. The answer to this question is preceded by an address to Marlow's audience that highlights his growing discontent over the public role he has had to play as a man of "ideas" and over his failure to establish imaginative contact with a group of respectable men from his society:

> I affirm that he had achieved greatness; but the thing would be dwarfed in the telling, or rather in the hearing. Frankly, it is not my words that I mistrust but your minds. I could be eloquent were I not afraid you fellows had starved your imaginations to feed your bodies. I do not mean to be offensive; it is respectable to have no illusions—and safe—and profitable—and dull. Yet you, too, in your time must have known the intensity of life, that light of glamour created in the shock of trifles, as amazing as the glow of sparks struck from a cold stone—and as short-lived, alas! (p. 225)

This passage marks a turning point in both the language and the shape of Marlow's narrative. Marlow here feels embarrassed about his affections for Jim, and he fills his apology for these sentiments with both an attack on the public imagination and an appeal to a common nostalgia for man's faded youth. Marlow's resistance to sentimentality is breaking down.

The major change in the novel is forecast as early as chapter 16, when Marlow remarks that Jim "captured much honour and an Arcadian happiness. . .in the bush." In a related move in chapter 22, Marlow, like the narrator of *The Nigger of the "Narcissus,"* turns history to his moral ends, contrasting heroic and antiheroic societies in rehearsing the deeds of the seventeenth century traders and contrasting those men to "us, their less tried successors." The heroic myth has returned to Conrad's writing along with the idea of history as degeneration. The problem then is to remove Jim from history, to place him in an environment free of the pressures of society and change, to send him back into "Arcadia." We are not observing the ordeals of existential heroism on Patusan, we are indulging in a literary romance. Marlow the moral detective is about to become Marlow the pastoral poet.

After chapter 19, it is Stein — significantly, the old romantic — who triggers a new series of episodes in the second half of the novel. Stein is surely one of Conrad's most enduring characters — comic, captivating, almost hypnotic in his mysterious intensity. The stories from Stein's youth told in chapter 20 are wonderfully colorful, full of the élan of boyish adventure tales and the comedy of the picaresque. In the account of his participation in a Malaysian tribal war, Stein is marvelously entertaining in relating the attempt on his life. Confronting several men lying in ambush for him, Stein pretends to be hit, and as his enemies emerge from their cover, he coolly shoots three of them before they realize they have been tricked. Then, as he surveys the bush for signs of further trouble, he suddenly becomes paralyzed with excitement: he sees a rare species of butterfly sitting on a heap of dirt. Forgetting his enemies, he follows and catches the insect with his felt hat and, wobbling with emotion, has to sit down on the ground for relief. The incident is as delightful as it is improbable; it is the stuff of storytelling, and Stein is the creation of a performing artist who, like Dickens, triumphs in the act of invention.

But the strength of Stein as a dramatic character, as the subject of romantic stories, is also the source of his weakness as a philosopher of heroism. Stein seems to have very little contact with the public world that Marlow sketches for us in the beginning of the novel, especially not with Marlow's audience. Stein is, rather, a storybook figure, "rich in generous enthusiasms, in friendship, love, war — in all the exalted elements of romance" (p. 217). He is not, it seems, educated in matters of the "world" as we have come to know it; and the matter of heroism for him is simply a given fact of his life. His courage is like "good digestion. . .completely unconscious of itself" (p. 203). Similarly, Stein's famous directive, "In the destructive element immerse" (p. 214) and his pronouncement that Jim is a romantic, dramatize Stein's own character more than they shed light on Jim's problem (Says Marlow: "When at last I broke the silence it was to express the opinion that no one could be more romantic than himself" p. 215). Even as he is seduced by Stein's pronouncements, Marlow questions the term "romantic"; "'But *is he*?' I queried" (p. 216). Stein says of course. Who can doubt it? And returns, at the end of his chapter to his butterflies, dwelling on his past, his romantic memories, adventures that mistily and wistfully fill the mind of an old man. Stein's butterfly collection seems to be the perfection of his romanticism: lovely, delicate nature made into artifice and preserved behind glass casing.

It is not surprising, then, that the style of Jim's heroism on Patusan is fraught with the conventions of literary romance. In many ways his achievements are reenactments of his youthful fantasies aboard the training ship early in the novel, and in that sense his heroism (at least for the time being) appears very much like Henry Fleming's in *The Red Badge of Courage*.[5] This is how his fantasies are described on the ship:

> On the lower deck in the babel of two hundred voices he would forget himself, and beforehand live in his mind the sea-life of light literature. He saw himself saving people from sinking ships, cutting away masts in a hurricane, swimming through a surf with a line; or as a lonely castaway, barefooted and half naked, walking on uncovered reefs in search of shellfish to stave off starvation. He confronted savages of tropical shores, quelled mutinies on the high seas, and in a small boat upon the ocean kept up the hearts of despairing men — always an example of devotion to duty and as unflinching as a hero in a book. (p. 6)

When Marlow comes to Patusan after two years of Jim's "reign" to find that Jim has become a legend, Jim's heroic exploits are described as follows:

> The conquest of love, honour, men's confidence — the pride of it, the power of it, are fit materials for a heroic tale; only our minds are struck by the externals of such a success, and to Jim's successes there were no externals. Thirty miles of forest shut it off from the sight of an indifferent world, and the noise of the white surf along the coast overpowered the voice of fame. (p. 226)

What is just as interesting as the recitation of the heroic trappings of Jim's success are Marlow's protestations that he is doing something other than telling a romantic tale. His talk about heroic lore as "external" is particularly deceptive, because the word really shifts in meaning from the beginning to the end of the statement. We think of it at first as implying "superficial" as opposed to private or personal, the mere emblems of heroism rather than the existential reality of it. But what the word "external" designates by the end of the passage is the public or "outside" world, as opposed to the "internal" world of the island. This metaphor, in other words, ostensibly suggests that Jim's heroism on Patusan is more real than romantic because it is an "inner" type of heroism. Yet this "inwardness" is achieved merely by retreating from the public eye. A seemingly moral and psychological distinction thus becomes merely a geographical and social division between the island and the outside world, and finally a type of literary division between the public and the heroic-pastoral worlds of the novel. Marlow's distinctions between the island and the outside world are seemingly a way for him to dodge the apparent fact that "the conquest of love, honour, men's confidences" and the vaguely classical, literary "voice of fame" are all he can talk about as being "heroic" in any meaningful way — and these of course *are* the fit materials for a heroic tale. After the end of the *Patna* affair, when the question of heroism becomes an academic cipher, the only way to observe Jim's heroism, with "official" standards denied him and existential standards nonexistent, is through heroic fantasy. And Marlow doesn't protest against fantasy as much as we might expect; he, as he claims of Jim, merely wants "some such truth or some such illusion — I don't care how you call it, there is so little difference, and the difference means so little" (p. 222). But the fact remains that Jim's heroism is not, after all, given an inner life; only his guilt and his failures are.

The particulars and the chronology of Jim's heroism on Patusan need only to be referred to and paraphrased by Marlow, not dramatically presented, for they are familiar to us already. When Marlow begins his tale of Jim's new adventures, only a casual reference is made to "the remnants of Sherif Ali's impregnable camp," less, I would suggest, as a technical variation upon narrative sequence as a concession to Marlow's need to pictorialize the Patusan episode for much the same reason the narrator of *The Nigger of the "Narcissus"* does the same: to take the episode out of both narrative and historical time. The details we learn more about some time later, but they too are both predictably romantic and sketchy "stills" of action that takes place in a world that resists movement and change. What we imagine to be Jim's most difficult problems — more difficult than storming a fortress — are barely important for Marlow to mention:

> When he arrived the Bugis community was in a most critical position. "They were all afraid," he said to me — "each man afraid for himself; while I could see as plain as possible that they must do something at once, if they did not want to go under one after another, what between the Rajah and that vagabond Sherif." But to see that was nothing. When he got his idea he had to drive it into reluctant minds, through the bulwarks of fear, of selfishness. He drove it in at last. And that was nothing. He had to devise the means. He devised them — an important plan; and his task was only half done. He had to inspire with his own confidence a lot of people who had hidden and absurd reasons to hang back; he had to conciliate imbecile jealousies, and argue away all sorts of senseless mistrusts. Without the weight of Doramin's authority and his son's fiery enthusiasm, he would have failed. (p. 261)

Heroism in the above description is anything but private or "inner," but it also seems to call for something other than the grand gestures of a romantic hero. The man Marlow is describing to us should draw his style from clever and ingenious political manipulation, and would have to be capable of using the emotions, placating the fears and jealousies, and inspiring the political consciousness of a divided state. Yet, can we really imagine Jim conciliating imbecile jealousies and arguing away all sorts of senseless mistrust? Have we any basis to imagine him inspiring confidence among a whole community? I doubt it. Jim ironically has to be removed from the public world in order to become a public hero. As Jim himself says, "I can't conceive of being able to live anywhere else" (p. 305). Marlow, I suspect, doesn't believe this kind of heroism satisfies the more sophisticated demands of the first half of the novel, and that such is not "true heroism" in either a public or an existential sense. But then, we must remember that true heroism is not at issue any more; it is whether or not Jim will go out in good form. But the only "form" left to Marlow is a literary one. Jim, whom Conrad endows with an insouciant acumen of his own, declares that the islanders "are like people in a book, aren't they?" (p. 260).

The novel's philosophical concerns consequently suffer greatly in the Patusan episode. Only rarely does Marlow sound like the Marlow of the earlier episode when dealing with moral issues; but once, in a rather unlikely situation, he sounds like the Marlow in "Heart of Darkness." Responding to the grief of Jewel fairly late in the novel, he says:

> It had the power to drive me out of my conception of existence, out of that shelter each of us makes for himself to creep under in moments of danger, as a tortoise withdraws within its shell. For a moment I had a view of a world that seemed to wear a vast and dismal aspect of disorder, while, in truth, thanks to our unwearied efforts, it is as sunny an arrangement of small conveniences as the mind of man can conceive. But still—it was only a moment: I went back into my shell directly. One *must*—don't you know?—though I seemed to have lost all my words in the chaos of dark thoughts I had contemplated for a second or two beyond the pale. These came back, too, very soon, for words also belong to the sheltering conception of light and order which is our refuge. (p. 313)

This passage practically represents a program for Marlow's ontology and epistemology in "Heart of Darkness": we save ourselves from chaos by withdrawing into the artificial structures of our institutions—everything from language to law to morality to selfhood. But for the very reason that such a statement seems appropriate to the moral climate of "Heart of Darkness" it seems oddly out of place at this point in *Lord Jim*. We have just heard Jewel's story of the death of her mother, at a time when they had been locked in a room together, Cornelius outside screaming, "Let me in! Let me in! Let me in!" and his wife crying "No! No!" while Jewel was shoving with all her might against the door. The woman's death, I imagine, hardly touches us, Jewel's grief only slightly. Only Marlow would dare say that "it had the power to drive me out of my conception of existence . . . . " It is unlikely that such a response is simply evidence of Conrad's difficulties in handling feminine psychology. With Kurtz's Intended, to cite a parallel situation, Marlow is tender, paternal, inwardly pained but never out of touch with the immediacy of the dramatic occasion, even when the "wilderness" encroaches upon it. Here, on the other hand, Marlow's reaction to Jewel seems to be a more generalized statement on a cumulative failure to "understand." Seemingly this passage represents a failure to coordinate the drama of the novel with its philosophical concerns. Perhaps, too, it is an effort to formulate a legitimate and honest despair at a point in the novel where the cost in emotional strain is not as high as elsewhere. In any case, it indicates the mixing of intentions and purposes that pervades the atmosphere of *Lord Jim*. "Feeling" and "thought" are still confused.

Roger Sale nicely assesses the situation I have been describing throughout the course of this chapter:

> Jim is wonderful, Jim is one of us, yet he jumped and as Marlow tries to fathom that fact he speaks in sentences as confused, as intelligently unable, as those of the speaker in *The Waste Land*. But Marlow never faces the implications of his confusion, Jim tries to deny he was ever confused at all, and Conrad himself seems not to know where to take his story after the first long dialogues between Jim and Marlow are over. Had Conrad pushed on. . .he might have created a modern hero, and he almost certainly would have written a better second half to his novel. Instead, by giving Jim a haven on Patusan where he can redeem himself at least in the terms of the boy's books that shaped his imagination in the first place, by letting Jim become a romantic hero, by giving Marlow a story he can tell mistily and comfortably, Conrad reverts to a distinctively nineteenth-century kind of romance and heroism, one we associate with Robert Louis Stevenson or perhaps Alexander Dumas.6

Although dealing with Conrad only incidentally in his "Afterword," Sale offers an excellent evaluation of what happens to *Lord Jim* after the *Patna* affair, and according to his standards justifiably denies the novel a place among the fiction of "modern heroism." But my purposes require a closer look at what happens within this novel, one that will make Conrad's position less easy to define. Marlow, as I have suggested, is not entirely comfortable, Conrad doesn't know how to push on, and Jim is a more elusive and restless character than we (and Marlow) might expect him to be. Jim's presence as a dramatic character is considerably diluted in Conrad's world of shadowy romance, and yet he is exasperatingly resistant to Marlow's arcadian designs. While Marlow would be happy to see his friend remain a storybook hero, for Jim, Patusan is not a romantic refuge but a place for some "opportunity" that is no more realized here than it is earlier in the novel. Unquestionably the romantic world of Patusan appeals to Jim, but it does not answer to his need to redeem himself; it does not blot out the memory of his past. If Jim earlier in the novel did not see his problem in the same theoretical terms as Marlow did, on Patusan he does not see it in Marlow's romantic terms. At one point Marlow confronts Jim with the crucial question: "'You have had your opportunity,' I pursued. 'Had I?' he said. 'Well yes. I suppose so. Yes. I have got back my confidence in myself—a good name—yet sometimes I wish . . . . No! I shall hold what I've got. Can't expect anything more.' He flung his arm out towards the sea. 'Not out there anyhow'" (p. 333). Jim's existence in the novel is still willed by Conrad, and it is difficult to be impressed by Jim's belief that he has gotten back his confidence and his good name. But he remains a haunting expression of Conrad's dissatisfaction with his literary formulations, with Marlow's romantic dreams. Jim's answer to Marlow is rather wistful, sad, inconclusive, and anticlimatic. Part of his mind, like part of Conrad's imagination, is still responsible to historical time, personal memories, and the public world; and dislike it though he does, Conrad's sense of reality still requires a social satisfaction. He may think society is a sham, but he never forgets that he is seeking public approval for Jim. Unlike Kurtz in "Heart of Darkness," Jim would appear to need a cultural context for his heroism, and Patusan is disturbingly unreal. The previous passage is about as close as Jim comes to saying that he is satisfied with his life on Patusan, and, for the sake of Conrad's integrity as a novelist, we have to be glad that he is somewhat less than convincing.

Jim's sense of resignation, or uneasiness about the fictions that are built up around him (by the islanders, by Marlow, by Conrad) protracts the inconclusiveness of the novel without further advancing the moral drama or the plot. There is an unsteadiness in the language of the Patusan episode, as it continuously forecasts a rapid conclusion to the novel, then turns around to express Conrad's worries over the conventions upon which this writing appears to rely. First Jim becomes the subject of local legends: he reenacts Stein's youthful deeds, complete with a "war-comrade," a native girl, and an assassination attempt. But chapter 27, which climaxes the account of the "legend," ends by asserting that Jim is a lonely and somewhat melancholy man. It is there that Marlow introduces the "love story," as he calls it, a story which reminds him of a "knight and maiden meeting to exchange vows amongst haunted ruins" (p. 312), seemingly an attempt to duplicate an English romance, but a story which he fidgets over, saying that to tell it is "by no means as easy as it should be—were the ordinary standpoint adequate" (p. 275). By the end of chapter 35, Marlow is picturing Jim as he sees him for the last time, receding into the darkness of Patusan, as the story ends—only to be picked up in an "epilogue" Marlow writes to one of the listeners two years later. This is the indecisiveness and experimentation I mentioned at the beginning of this chapter, Conrad's refusal to let his story go as his desire to remake Jim into a hero is still in conflict with his dissatisfaction over all the available, conventional means by which to do so. The result is that the novel stalls badly — until Conrad figures his way out of it with the Brown affair.

The last eighty pages of the book begin, as do the early chapters of the novel, with a polemical Marlow defending Jim, defending his story, and now announcing the motif of the last episode in Jim's life: "You must admit that it is romantic beyond the wildest dreams of his boyhood, and yet there is to my mind a sort of profound and terrifying logic in it" (p. 342). And on the next page: "Something of the sort had to happen. . .there is no disputing its logic." One is tempted to ask here what the source of this logic is and what exactly is the connection between such logic and the "romance" of the episode (it is romantic *yet* logical). If I am right that Marlow's earlier concern with the way Jim "would go out" may be read both as an expression of Marlow's sentimental concern for Jim and as Conrad's own way of commenting upon the problems he has in composing the novel, it would seem that chapter 36 signals Conrad's new strategy to resolve the moral issues simultaneously with the plot. And if Conrad has come up with a new strategy, it would seem that the logic of the plot in this episode is fairly clear. The encounter between Brown and Jim reenacts, in grotesque and stylized terms, most of Jim's struggles with the "outside" world, particularly his failure to be heroic according to public standards. He "betrays" the trust of the islanders, he "fails" in his responsibility for their safety. He is judged a traitor by Doramin and later a "hollow sham" by the dying Brown. But here, Jim is the victim of the conspiracy, here he suffers because of his faith in man, his belief in himself, and his courage to take action that he knows could have disastrous consequences. Brown in this episode is a specter from the public world, a symbol of its wretchedness, cynicism, and sanguinary exploitation of "that good and stupid kind" among which is Jim. Brown is a social pariah, an exile from civilization, and yet he is also the apparition of all that Marlow throughout the course of the novel has come to detest about the public world. The massacre of Dain Waris's party, Marlow says, is "a demonstration of some obscure and awful attribute of our nature which, I am afraid to say, is not so very far under the surface as we like to think" (p. 404). Brown is the assassin of all that is romantic, all that is ideal in human nature. If he seems too extreme, too perverted to symbolize the entire public world, it is because Conrad's resentment of that world erupts here in blind vengeance against his darkest vision of humanity. Brown represents the culmination of Conrad's disgust with the court of inquiry, the crew of the *Patna*, the public gossip, and the unsympathetic listening audience that Marlow derides and attacks in incredibly bitter terms. Brown, too, is "one of us."

What Conrad has done in the "logic" of his concluding episode is at once to vindicate Jim by discrediting the outside world and to explode the romantic world by destroying before the islanders the legend of the invulnerable Jim. Conrad redeems Jim from the *Patna* affair by creating an incident in which his disgrace may now be placed in quotation marks and in which the tyranny of the romantic world over Jim's life is lifted. Conrad in the end seems to sense that the romantic world did not do for Jim what he had wanted it to and that it had been built of fragile material in the first place. Jim, devoid of any public whatsoever (including, one might well imagine, the last of Marlow's listeners), is returned at the end to the sentimental imagination of Marlow, where he has been anyway since chapter 19. The price of this return is the last consequence of Conrad's "logic," for devoid of a field of moral endeavor, an environment for heroic conduct, Jim must die. "I have no life," says Jim, always intuitively right about himself, in response to Tamb' Itam's exhortations to fight instead of just die (p. 409). The environment which finally replaces Patusan is the one that increasingly pervades the latter half of the novel: the atmosphere of gloom and shadows, of the image Marlow evokes several times in the last one hundred pages of Jim (like Kurtz) receding into the darkness.

It is significant that Jim's death becomes his most grandiose, most misunderstood public act (more so than his endurance at the trial, more so than his leadership on the island), for Marlow can now claim that his heroism is of a special, private sort, one that the public may never be able to understand. Yet Marlow, too, may in the end fail to understand Jim. Early in the novel, we recall, the French lieutenant remarks to the effect that one must imagine a *public* heroism before one can be heroic. This observation must partly constitute the paradox of Jim's death. For neither Jim nor Marlow can imagine a heroic style beyond military codes, public exhibitions, and literary stylizations, all of which are discredited in the novel. Jim's "heroism" finds no expression: his death may be the opportunity he had hoped for; but in its ultimate silence, recalling in a more romantic atmosphere the horrible death of Kurtz, it is also what removes him from any definition or conception of heroic conduct. We cannot react to Jim's death by simply asserting that it accomplishes what his life had not.

Yet Marlow does, and his reaction is consistent with his character as it develops in the novel. Unwilling to abandon the sentimental belief that heroic identity is possible, he fashions Jim into a man whose heroism is achieved unheralded and misunderstood, in a voiceless and selfless world.

But in doing so, he has to turn his description of Jim into a conventional and lyrical elegy:

> And that's the end. He passes away under a cloud, inscrutable at heart, forgotten, unforgiven, and excessively romantic. Not in the wildest days of his boyish visions could he have seen the alluring shape of such extraordinary success! For it may very well be that in the short moment of his last proud and unflinching glance, he had beheld the fact of that opportunity which, like an Eastern bride, had come veiled to his side.

> But we can see him, an obscure conqueror of fame, tearing himself out of the arms of a jealous love at the sign, at the call of his exalted egoism. He goes away from a living woman to celebrate his pitiless wedding with a shadowy ideal of conduct. Is he satisfied—quite, now, I wonder? We ought to know. He is one of us—and have I not stood up once, like an evoked ghost, to answer for his eternal constancy? Was I so very wrong after all? Now he is no more, there are days when the reality of his existence comes to me with an immense, with an overwhelming force; and yet upon my honour there are moments, too, when he passes from my eyes like a disembodied spirit astray amongst the passions of this earth, ready to surrender faithfully to his own world of shades.

> Who knows? He is gone, inscrutable at heart, and the poor girl is leading a sort of soundless, inert life in Stein's house. Stein has aged greatly of late. He feels it himself, and says often that he is 'preparing to leave all this; preparing to leave. . .' while he waves his hand sadly at his butterflies. (pp. 416–17)

Heroism, we have seen, can be achieved, finally, in legends, in tales, and at last, only in elegies. Jim's "heroism" must be celebrated elegiacally or it cannot be celebrated at all. What strikes me about Marlow's final words is not simply how lovingly he speaks of Jim, but also how conventionally. Jim, as an "obscure conqueror of fame," would appear, from Marlow's elegy, to be an unsung hero in need of a bard; while the novel can only license such language with a sad irony. Marlow, I suspect, is at last made less complicated than we might suppose, while Conrad, too, though aware of the choice he's making, becomes once again the pastoral poet languishing over lost worlds of the imagination.

5

"The Secret Sharer": The Triumph of the Imagination

Viewed simply with regard to its timing in Conrad's career, "The Secret Sharer" appears an eccentricity. Written nine years after *Lord Jim*, during the decade of *Nostromo* and *The Secret Agent* and almost simultaneously with the completion of *Under Western Eyes*, it is an adventure tale surrounded by Conrad's great political novels — seemingly a story rescued from Conrad's past. A number of critics speculate upon the conception of this tale, which Albert Guerard rightly calls the "most frankly psychological of Conrad's shorter works."[1] One theory cites the recent split in the friendship between Conrad and Ford Madox Hueffer (during the summer of 1909), suggesting that "The Secret Sharer" is a symbolical reenactment of that traumatic separation.[2] In a more sentimental vein, there is the story about Conrad's meeting with Captain C. M. Harris, a Far Eastern shipmaster who, returning to England, decided to find out exactly "who [the] devil [had] been around taking notes."[3] On Conrad's own word, that visit led him to promise that his former acquaintances "shall have some more of the stories they like."[4]

It is true that Conrad wrote the story shortly before he suffered a severe and appalling mental breakdown which for three months found him delirious for much of the time, sometimes holding conversations with the characters in *Under Western Eyes*, other times raving in Polish, slipping into English only to recite sections of the Anglican burial mass.[5] Three months later, after his recovery, Conrad wrote to Hugh Clifford: "It seems I have been very ill. At the time I did not believe it, but now I begin to think that I must have been."[6] But what influence the Hueffer affair had upon these sensational events I am not prepared to say. And what effect it had upon "The Secret Sharer" I had best leave to those trained for such speculations, although I suspect the matter may be overworked for the service it renders psychoanalysis. Personally I prefer the Harris anecdote, even though it but touches upon the imagination of a man who in 1909, during a period which even at the time he recognized was "complicated by a terrible moral stress," had revived for the last time in his career the fiction of the heroic journey with anything like the concentrated energy of the earlier tales. Although "The Secret Sharer" does in several senses become the ghost of Conrad's past, it departs from the conventions of adventure fiction which broadly outline the intense and esoteric drama of the captain's heroic ordeal. The heroic journey in this story takes on the characteristics of a weird moral fable, a "doubles story," that defies most interpretive analysis, that maintains only the barest contact with the world of Marlow's England, with the demands of a critical audience. Conrad's sentimental and bizarre recovery of his heroic myth may indeed be seen only in relationship to a coalescence of many pressures he was reacting to at the time. In the remainder of this chapter I shall examine some of these pressures apparent in "The Secret Sharer" and gauge Conrad's response to them in light of the stories I have already discussed. I will show how in remaining true to his ideals Conrad extends his rebellion against the modern world, taking us into a grotesque and comic realm somewhere between fiction and fantasy, into a journey that twists and turns its way through the recesses of Conrad's heroic consciousness.

Compared with the heroic journeys of the earlier adventure tales, that of the captain in "The Secret Sharer" occupies a spatially diminished area, but at the same time one made larger by the captain and narrator. This is a change particularly worth noting because the worlds of the earlier novels are frequently evoked in the acts of inventing this one. Compare the following passage which I quoted earlier in my discussion of *The Nigger of the "Narcissus"* with a second one from "The Secret Sharer":

> The true peace of God begins at any spot a thousand miles from the nearest land; and when He sends there the messengers of His might it is not in terrible wrath against crime, presumption, and folly, but paternally, to chasten simple hears—ignorant hearts that know nothing of life, and beat undisturbed by envy or greed. (p. 31)

And from "The Secret Sharer":

> And suddenly I rejoiced in the great security of the sea as compared with the unrest of the land, in my choice of that untempted life presenting no disquieting problems, invested with an elementary moral beauty by the absolute straightforwardness of its appeal and by the singleness of its purpose. (XIX, p. 96)

These passages are roughly analogous in their pastoral characterizations of the sea and in their mapping of a field for heroic endeavor that takes man into literary artifice. But the similarity ends there. The pastoral world of *The Nigger of the "Narcissus"* is populated by little angels and spirits, the "messengers of God," who provide (at least tentatively) a framework for the trials of the *Narcissus* in the myth of men against the sea. In the latter passage, both the spirits and their celestial framework have disappeared. While "The Secret Sharer" assumes fundamentally similar moral values and draws upon a common literary tradition for its characterizations, the only inhabitant of this pastoral world is the captain. The crew of his ship are excluded, the angels of God do not exist, and the formulation of the moral universe is offered only on the authority of the man standing on the deck of his first command. In short, while the captain is indebted to a literary tradition, he appears responsible only to himself for adapting it to his private heroic world. He is not undergoing a trial prescribed by providential powers, even though the terms of his investiture are effectively the same.

A second comparison with *The Nigger of the "Narcissus"* reinforces these differences. First, from the earlier novel, part of the passage that speaks about the ship as a moral microcosm:

> The passage had begun, and the ship, a fragment detached from the earth, went on lonely and swift like a small planet. Round her the abysses of sky and sea met in an unattainable frontier. (p. 29)

And from "The Secret Sharer":

> She floated at the starting point of a long journey, very still in an immense stillness . . . . In this breathless pause at the threshold of a long passage we seemed to be measuring out fitness for a long and arduous enterprise, the appointed task of both our existences to be carried out, far from all human eyes, with only sky and sea for spectators and for judges. (p. 92)

Again the allegorical terms of each passage approximate those of the other. But again there are important differences in the sources and authorizations for such terms. The narrator of *The Nigger of the "Narcissus"* in this instance adopts a godlike perspective, speaking about passing ships as tiny white specks and the *Narcissus* as a "fragment detached from the earth." In these moments, the narrator may hardly be said to belong to the crew but rather to the convention of novelistic omniscience which justifies this point of view. In "The Secret Sharer," on the other hand, the godlike eye, which acknowledges a celestial audience, which proclaims the universe an arena for heroic ordeal, which takes the ordeal of initiation beyond the vision of the public world — this godlike eye belongs to the captain himself. While the passage from the earlier novel suggests a heroic trial within the context of external standards — those sanctioned by an omniscient narrator and imma- nent in a moral universe — there is in the latter story no distinction between the scheme of nature and the vision of the hero. The external standards for heroic conduct are invented from the stage the captain sets up for himself on the deck of the ship. He clearly imagines his own moral universe in which he both legislates and performs the heroic ordeal. Moreover, it is apparent that to the captain, the physical journey of the ship is no more real or in any substantial way different from the metaphorical ways in which he treats it.

The idea of the story as a stage performance is central to the dramatic and narrative situations of "The Secret Sharer." The captain sees his professional duty as a performance before a celestial audience personified as spectators and critics, or perhaps as jurists—the timeless, heroic, non-human counterpart of the variety of jurists, spectators, and critics in *Lord Jim*. Actually, the captain's consciousness of himself as a performer also defines two other audiences: the crew and the readers. At one point the captain decides, "I must show myself on deck," (p. 113) with a metaphor, "show," that both we and the captain may understand to carry a theatrical implication. Somewhat earlier he imagines himself and Leggatt being viewed by an audience which seemingly consists of both the crew and the readers: "He was not a bit like me, really," the captain says of Leggatt, "yet, as we stood leaning over my bed-place, whispering side by side, with our heads together and our backs to the door, anybody bold enough to open it stealthily would have been treated to the uncanny sight of a double captain busy talking in whispers with his other self" (p. 105). This remark is typical of the ambiguity the captain insists upon in describing his relationship to Leggatt (he was not at all like me, yet he was like me in every way), but typical too of the way he smoothly relocates the perspective upon the scene to a hypothetical audience ("anybody bold enough to open [the door]") eavesdropping upon his private world.

While the "audiences" in "The Secret Sharer" maintain a tenuous resemblance to those of the Marlow stories, the special conditions here remove the captain from the accountability Marlow was charged with. In this story, Conrad has abandoned his division between the narrator's fidelity to the heroic world and his responsibility to the "public." Self-conscious as he is, the captain never sees the necessity to justify to anyone the inventions of his heroic imagination. As a narrator, he is from the beginning removed from the social context in which Marlow appears, existing as the only voice and only as a voice in his storytelling, speaking from an unspecified time (apparently many years) after the event. We never see him through the eyes of a fictional public or with the perspective of a preliminary narrator. He appears, rather, only as a performer within and the inventor of his imaginative world. As a narrator he is only theoretically distinct from himself as an actor. Unlike Marlow, he is so engaged in the mind he describes and the incidents he relates that he never calls that mind or those incidents into question.

The captain's independence from the pressures of Marlow's storytelling suggests an interesting variation upon the earlier tales. The fact that the captain imagines and invents his audiences in "The Secret Sharer" may be seen as an extension of Marlow's attempts to persuade his. There is no point now in our charging that his heroic world is artificial or literary, as we might in *Lord Jim*; that his sense of the heroic is too esoteric, as Marlow's audiences seem to feel; or that his imagination of the universe is gratuitous as F. R. Leavis charges in his criticisms of "Heart of Darkness" — because all these things are made obviously true by the workings of the captain's mind. His sense of himself as "far from all human eyes" does not exclude an eavesdropping audience from the privilege of observing his performances; but it does insist upon a certain freedom from the morally judgmental eyes of Marlow's readers and listeners, who are given a more or less distinct and independent existence in the formal apparatus of those tales. Because the captain can call his own metaphorical shots, because, indeed, his metaphors and his morality reciprocally sustain each other, we are rather seduced into accepting the moral terms of his experience. His egocentricity, his projection of his inner life upon a universal stage, finds expression in his manipulations of his audiences: of the crew in the drama off the island of Koh-ring, and of us, too, in the understood proclamation of his right to legislate the procedures of his own trial. The captain, in short, tries not only to take possession of the ship but also to take possession of our imaginations. Although he lacks Marlow's contentiousness and is rather winningly confidential with his readers, he becomes in several senses the dictator of his own world.

As we have seen in the Marlow stories, the heroic imagination in "The Secret Sharer" is expressed in part by its antagonism to the public world. In *Lord Jim*, Jim struggles against the various images of himself created by the court of inquiry, by Chester, by the islanders, even by Marlow and Stein. Marlow's imagination, at the same time, is driven away from the social world as a result of its failure to justify itself according to the moral standards of his listeners. And in "Heart of Darkness," Kurtz, in his moral isolation, wrestles alone with the wilderness to create his identity out of a godlike will to dominate the moralities of civilization and to overcome the darkness of a metaphysical jungle. Along these lines, in "The Secret Sharer" the captain is driven further into himself, into his imagination, wondering "how far I should turn out faithful to that ideal conception of one's own personality every man sets up for himself secretly" (p. 94). Like the equation between Jim and mankind, however, the one between the captain and "every man" is never really made. Like Jim, the captain needs his own world in which to perform his deeds — a remote area that serves as a refuge from the sordid places of courts of inquiry and cowardly masters. But while in

Lord Jim the would-be hero is crowded out of the social world and onto an idyllic island, in "The Secret Sharer" the heroic world extends outward from the captain's mind, filling the universe with images of his own making, leaving no room for the encroachments of society or for a metaphysical abyss.

In such an atmosphere, the social world in "The Secret Sharer" becomes a peripheral annoyance compared to the public in *Lord Jim*. The crew of the ship represent a threat to the heroic world of the captain, but in an almost petty and pestiferous way. The chief mate's puzzle mentality appears to be a parody upon an unsentimental and narrowly analytical mind, and the mate himself is a caricature of a small-minded "fallen" man. Certainly he is a far cry from Baker of the *Narcissus*, being more at home in the cartoon world of *The Secret Agent* than aboard a ship in one of Conrad's adventure tales. The second mate and the steward are similarly dealt with: the mate's quivering lip becomes an emblem of an uncomprehending, cynical sneer; while the steward's meticulous efficiency is seen not as a virtue of his fidelity (as is Podmore's on the *Narcissus*) but as a collection of unctuous mannerisms and a product of a bothersome fussiness. Above all, "Archbold" (for the captain does not remember exactly his name), the captain's counterpart from the *Sephora*, is seen as a cowering functionary of a lackluster, antiheroic society (he keeps to schedules, is afraid of storms, and has a wife on board), a measure of the distance between a MacWhirr or an Allison and the seamen of the time "after the fall."

Still, in combination with the "spectator stars," the crew, in the mind of the captain, pose a threatening audience and jury and form a possibility of invasion into the captain's private heroic world. Shortly after the beginning of the story, the stars, rather than observing the captain, are described as "staring" at him, and the personified and private relationship with the ship (his "trusted friend") is broken by the "disturbing sounds" of footsteps and voices. The captain reads conspiracy even in the facial features of the chief mate, who approaches him "with an almost visible effect of collaboration on the part of his round eyes and frightful whiskers" (p. 94). He becomes a "stranger" to the ship and, as it were, to himself, as he fears he may be usurped from his position as the sole possessor of his command by the godlike presence in the world he has created in the privacy of his imagination.

When Leggatt becomes part of this tale, it is in a moral and psychological environment that requires for heroic conduct a reassertion of the ethics of heroism that were destroyed along with the pastoral world in *The Nigger of the "Narcissus"* and never regained in any convincing way in the Marlow stories. It is in the captain's relationship with Leggatt that the heroic community is revived. Through this partnership the captain may distinguish between a heroic community and everything that threatened such a community in *The Nigger of the "Narcissus"* and *Lord Jim*:

> The Sunday quietness of the ship was against us; the stillness of air and water around her was against us; the elements, the men were against us – everything was against us in our secret partnership; time itself – for this could not go on forever (p. 123).

The abundant and insistent parallels between Leggatt and the captain are probably the best known feature of this story. Not only do these parallels include a repeated physical identification between the two men, as if they were identical twins, but also an analogy between their social and moral predicaments. Both men are young, and both are graduates of Conway; both are officers who attempt to assert their command in the face of real or imagined opposition from petty or cowardly men. Leggatt is a social outcast, running from public judgment in a situation analogous to the lonely drama of the captain, in which the "judges" belong to both the social and a celestial world. Often there is a silent communion between the two men, each appealing to the other as if they each perfectly understood, "as if our experiences had been as identical as our clothes" (p. 102). As these two men line up against each other, almost all the struggles of Conrad's imagination of the heroic are neatly and formulaically reviewed: the lonely initiation into manhood; the journey into the self; the problem of creating a heroic self outside of a fallen contemporary society, and the effort to reclaim the heroic community of the past. The communal and the private ideals behind Conrad's heroic imagination find expression in the relationship between Leggatt and the captain such that it becomes the epicenter of all the moral and dramatic energies of the story. Leggatt in this way is both man and metaphor, both a dramatic character and an imaginative vehicle for the values of the heroic imagination.

Albert Guerard, in his commentary on Leggatt's role in "The Secret Sharer," cautions that "It would be improper to forget, while preoccupied with psychological symbolism, that Leggatt is substantial flesh and blood."[7] If I am right in all I've said about the captain's imagination, this otherwise level-headed attack on excessive symbolhunting is directed wide of the mark. Not only does it ask a definition of Leggatt that the story constantly resists, but it poses an alternative that both Conrad and his narrator ultimately ignore. In a story so intent upon establishing its own terms, the worst reading we could offer would defend those more familiar. If Leggatt is an avenging angel of Conrad's lost heroic world, it could stand to reason (the reason or rationale of the story, that is) that no one, besides the captain, ever "sees" him. When Captain Archbold of the *Sephora* comes aboard to meet his counterpart on the matter of Leggatt's escape, he tours the stateroom without detecting the murderer, who supposedly hides on the warning of Archbold's approach. In an even closer call, the steward goes into the captain's bathroom, where Leggatt is hiding, to hang a coat, but Leggatt escapes unseen: the explanation later given is that the steward put only his hand in the bathroom to hang up the coat. One of the characteristics of this story is that it is constantly creating incidents that raise the question of whether Leggatt "exists in the flesh." But beyond the energy expended in sustaining this ambiguity is the one indisputable fact that the world of the captain is dominated by a figure who for practical purposes is invisible to the rest of the crew, whose presence supplants the ship in the captain's fantasy of a personified and trusted friend, a figure whose spectral shadows seem to fill, beyond a mere physical existence, the captain's private world.

It is, of course, easy to see that, with this story's suggestion of an "alter-ego" for the captain, with the captain's seeming projections of guilt and paranoia into the character of Leggatt, with his repeated schizoid sense of himself as two people, "The Secret Sharer" confers psychological conditions on the world of heroic adventure that rarely if ever in Conrad's work suggest themselves to us in such clinical terms. The captain himself suspects he is nearly going mad, and in at least one specific instance confuses "inner" with "outer" realities, as he mistakes a knocking on the door with a knocking in his head. And then, too, we are offered the perspectives of his officers, who exchange knowing glances and tap their heads in gestures of amazed suspicion. But what strikes me as most interesting about these psychological overtones is not simply that the captain is mad, but rather the metaphorical identification between the captain's possible madness and the requirements of his heroic imagination. In that sense, the conditions of heroism in this story are connected to the conditions of Kurtz's heroism, whose godlike aspirations are identified with a kind of sublime madness. Still, the captain's madness in any mundane sense is somewhat beside the point. In a world where the metaphorical and the literal occupy the same plane of reality, heroism depends upon ignoring such distinctions — which the captain generally does.

But because the captain does refuse to sort out truth from artifice or madness from heroism, because he lacks the reflexive and self-questioning consciousness of Marlow, because he does seem to perform within an invented world, we as readers are permitted a perspective that in the end he neither possesses nor controls. The result is that the captain may be seen within a comic framework, but a framework which does not diminish him so much as it allows his freedom in one sense to become our freedom in another. Much of the fun of reading this story is not in trying to decide whether or not Leggatt exists but in observing how unable the captain is to consider such an issue. "Can it be," he asks himself in a way that characteristically neither confirms nor denies, "that he is not visible to other eyes than mine?" (p. 130). The fact that he is so incredulous over an obvious possibility implies that we may possess a freedom of imagination in observing his situation that he himself does not have. Yet he too is free — free to explore and dramatize his heroic imagination in a way that Marlow, with his dedication to the depressing truths of self-consciousness, could not. He is free even in his unselfconscious virtuosity in word play: "All's well so far," I whispered, "now you must vanish into the bath-room" (p. 114), he tells Leggatt. And later, when Archbold is in the stateroom, "My intelligent double had vanished. I had played my part" (p. 121). These represent just two instances in which "vanish" becomes a pun and in which the theatrical metaphor "played my part," comically enhances the captain's question-begging over Leggatt's physical existence.

The very fact that this story may be read in a literary context where heroic achievement takes the form of self-delusion (as that of Fleming in *The Red Badge* or the narrator in *The Nigger of the "Narcissus"*) alerts us to the possibilities and the limits of the captain's imagination. Yet the captain's unreliability as a narrator does not discredit his concept of heroism as the fantasies of Henry Fleming discredit his. That the captain is even more fantastic in his imagination than either Fleming or Jim — indeed, outrageously so — invites us to ask different questions about "The Secret Sharer." The question, "What is heroism?" is not necessary here; it becomes, rather, "Will the captain remain true to his vision of the heroic ideal and his imagination of the ideal self?" The weight of the drama correspondingly shifts from a quest for knowledge to a performance within an unquestioned code of ethics. And it is the performance, rather than the quest, that ultimately gives impetus to the drama.

In the relationship between the captain and Leggatt, the heroic imagination of Conrad is expressed in a fiction pretty close to fantasy. And this fantasy may be described as symbolic. Unfortunately, though, most interpretations of "The Secret Sharer" have made the story too tame, too Christian, too nineteenth-century. It is not a story about a young untried man whose ordeal facilitates his initiation into a social order and casts out the antisocial specter of his soul. The captain does become "initiated," but not into society, rather into an ideal. He is not ridding himself of demons but engineering a triumph of an abstract code of ethics which is asserted in the face of both social and universal opposition. Leggatt's act of murder is not crime but punishment against a fallen society; his escape is a flight from the modern world. The captain never doubts this, and Conrad himself was dismayed when a reviewer called Leggatt "a murderous ruffian."[8] The way Leggatt speaks of his "crime" would draw applause from Marlow and Jim: "You don't suppose I am afraid of what can be done to me? Prison or gallows or whatever they may please. But you don't see me coming back to explain such things to an old fellow in a wig and twelve respectable trades-men, do you? What can they know whether I am guilty or not — or of *what* I am guilty, either" (pp. 131-32). In the context of the Marlow tales, it should be clear what significance judges, courtroom, and gallows have in Conrad's imagination of society as a conglomeration of arbitrary, antiheroic laws. It is only in the captain's relationship with Leggatt that Conrad envisions a society founded upon other laws, upon the principles of fidelity and service. For the first time in his career, Conrad looks into the depths of his mind and does not find darkness. Instead, he finds the lost heroic community, a unity within one mind, a communion with himself.

The captain in "The Secret Sharer" has declared war upon society — and what's more, he wins. As the "journey" approaches its conclusion, the comedy and the drama of the captain swell to splendid proportions. As the crew stare in horrified silence, the ship, approaching the shoals of Koh-ring, drifts in the captain's imagination to "the gate of everlasting night" (p. 142), the "very gate of Erebus" (p. 140). (Is this so different from the mythical abyss in Wordsworth?) Images of eternity and of a timeless land and sea-scape magnify and celebrate the captain's initiation, not into the social world, but into a communion with the asocial, nonhuman world of the universe and with the ship, which once again becomes his "friend":

> And I was alone with her. Nothing! no one in the world should stand now between us, throwing a shadow on the way of silent knowledge and mute affection, the perfect communion of a seaman with his first command (p. 143).

We may hardly think the captain a bully or Leggatt a criminal in events which lead to such an affirmation of the heroic self.

Conrad, of course, has sacrificed the complexity of Marlow's relation-ship to the public world, as the "public" have become comparatively harm-less cartoon characters. And disarming as the captain is, unlike Jim, Marlow, and Kurtz, he remains free of complicating realizations about the nature of heroism. When he "changes," it is only within the framework of his initially stated code of ethics, and we have to react to his limitations with mixed feelings. In one sense, they allow the captain's heroism to be untested by the forces of society or the "wilderness" which had made the struggles of Marlow and Kurtz so awesome. But in another, Conrad has taken us into another realm of fiction. Having sustained the delicate ambiguities of Leggatt's existence, Conrad seems to have created an unresolved dialectical relationship between romance and the public world and has combined the external journey of nineteenth-century adventure fiction with the Wordsworthian inner journey into the self. The result is spontaneous and liberating.

Because we may read this story in the context of the earlier tales, Conrad's presence in "The Secret Sharer" is larger, and in a subtle, almost vapid way, more pervasive than that of the captain. There is a poignancy in the captain's reaction to Leggatt's decision to leave the ship, which takes us back to and at the same time beyond Conrad's elegiac celebrations of a lost paradise in the earlier novels. The captain protests that Leggatt must not leave; but Leggatt insists, with characteristic ellipses, that indeed he will, saying finally, "You have understood thoroughly. Didn't you?" For the captain, and in a crucial way for Conrad, this becomes a revelation: "I felt suddenly ashamed of myself. I may say truly that I understood — and my hesitation in letting that man swim away from my ship's side had been a mere sham sentiment, a sort of cowardice" (p. 132). The captain's confession of cowardice and profession of faith in his friendship with Leggatt gives the heroic ethic a kind of living, spiritual presence in his imagination of the hero in the modern world. It is a response that supersedes mere nostalgia. The captain will never "lose" Leggatt even in saying farewell to him; and he certainly will not try to hold on to him in a way that is melancholy or self-indulgently sentimental. Time, we recall from a passage I quoted earlier, is against their secret partnership, but the captain overcomes even the degeneration of time by the end of the story.

The last paragraph of "The Secret Sharer" also takes us beyond our earlier objections to Conrad's sentimentality and forced allegorizing, while he maintains his allegiance to the heroic ethic and sustains the parallels between Leggatt and the captain, asserting the triumph of the heroic self:

> Walking to the taffrail, I was in time to make out, on the very edge of a darkness thrown by a towering black mass like the very gateway of Erebus — yes, I was in time to catch an evanescent glimpse of my white hat left behind to mark the spot where the secret sharer of my cabin and of my thoughts, as though he were my second self, had lowered himself into the water to take his punishment: a free man, a proud swimmer striking out for a new destiny (p. 143).

Surely we must applaud the captain, as he indeed invites us to do throughout the story. Possibly it is the brilliance of focusing his sentimentality on the small white cap, rather than Leggatt himself, that saves the passage from the pathos of the conclusion of *The Nigger of the "Narcissus."* Rather than a madman, the captain sounds like a hero in triumph, and his triumph seems to justify and ameliorate his handling of the crew. The story in the end sounds so right, the sentiments so poised, that "The Secret Sharer" must indeed win us over to the heroic ethic that the Marlow tales had lost.

6

Conclusion:
"All the Past Was Gone"

The completion of "The Secret Sharer" at the end of 1909 marks the last important event in the chronicle of Conrad's adventure fiction; and along with *Under Western Eyes*, finished shortly thereafter, it represents the end of his great period of creativity that began with *The Nigger of the "Narcissus"* thirteen years before. With the exception of *The Shadow Line*, a trim, poised, and professional piece that modestly reiterates the theme of heroic initiation, and perhaps *Victory*, one of the most tightly constructed and evenly sustained of his longer novels, Conrad's later fiction consists of a series of lusterless and more or less conventional romances. Most accounts of this decline focus on Conrad's poor health, his desire to please a popular audience, and his inability to portray "normal" relationships between men and women. These explanations are in themselves inadequate, partly because they do not tell us much about the later Conrad that we do not already know about the author of "Heart of Darkness" and *Lord Jim*; and partly because the best explanation will issue from our understanding of what happens to the heroic journey itself. For this reason this chapter is about the end of the journey not only as a dramatic event in four stories, but also as a literary, biographical, and historical mode of thinking—as a metaphor for Conrad's writing and a model for the course of his career.

Throughout this book I have discussed the heroic journey as both a myth and a rhetorical process, each of which suffers a structural collapse after its inability to sustain the impossible demands Conrad makes upon it. The end of the journey as a heroic endeavor is unimaginable; and thus the end of the journey as a structural metaphor organizing the literary processes of these novels can only be a resolution of plot. Jim dies, the *Narcissus* returns to London, Marlow comes home from the Congo. But imaginatively, the fate of these stories is spelled out well before their last pages—it is written in their failures to fulfill the romantic promise of discovering a forgotten truth or of regaining a lost paradise. Verbally as well as mythically, these tales end in simplifications or diminutions of Conrad's heroic expectations.

In a larger and more general sense, I have shown that the heroic journey provides the grammar and vocabulary of a type of adventure story, practically a subgenre of the novel, which I described in chapter 1; and that the self-conscious voice we hear in Conrad's own heroic fiction speaks, therefore, not only in response to private conflicts and the internal demands of the heroic ordeal, but also to the literary, moral, and historical conditions that make that voice possible. In his struggle with a literary heritage, Conrad rejects the terms of the ideological resolutions in Dana, Cooper, Kipling, and Crane, while remaining trapped within the language and structures that give shape to their heroic imaginations. Hence, Conrad's journey can only take the course of progressively larger and more radical negations, until the very means by which he conducts his journey—his moral and verbal equipment—become tokens of imaginative failure. Taken as commentary upon the tradition of heroic fiction, Conrad effectively ends the style of thinking that gave form and impetus to romantic adventure fiction, while in one sense fulfilling the most extreme implications of such fiction in the universal obliteration of form, self, and imaginative order at the heart of a romantic darkness.

The nineteenth-century heroic adventure tale is itself a response to another tradition in the English novel: that of the social novel. Conrad, more than any of his predecessors in heroic fiction, explores and undermines the assumptions about literature and human experience that inform the great fiction of the nineteenth century. It is a critical commonplace that the English social novel of the nineteenth century is characterized by a kind of alliance between individuals and the places and institutions of England. According to such an argument, the characters of Austen and Eliot, the two great social novelists of that century, are indebted to the traditions of English society for their values and identities. Literary form itself often appears to rely in crucial ways upon the structure given to it by various social institutions. In Austen, for example, the problems of this fiction develop in terms of a character's education into society, with the resolutions of fictional tensions appearing in social terms—marriage, or the reassertion of the traditional, rural, domestic tranquility of the Garths in *Middlemarch*. The feelings, conflicts, and aspirations of the characters in these novels thus find expression within the order implied by the institutions of English culture, so that the best fiction throughout the century becomes a celebration of both the individual and the historical context within which the individual is formed.

But while the English novel had thus developed into a form of social literature—both in the range of its appeal and in its subject matter—Conrad adopts a fiction whose interest is in journeys and voyages moving away, both literally and symbolically, from the institutions of England and even away from Western civilization. In his narrative voice alone — one which is introspective and "private" — he seems to develop and refine a style noticeably different from the narrative styles of the parlor dramas, comedies of manners, and even the personal histories created within the social and moral frameworks of Victorian society. Often Conrad's narrators (as in *The Nigger of the "Narcissus"* and "The Secret Sharer") cannot be easily identified as people within that English society familiar with the details and subtleties of the language, customs, and habits of a Jane Austen or a George Eliot narrator; and when they are more so, as in the best of the Marlow stories, these narrators still are not able to speak to the late Victorian reader with the same familiar ease.

But if I am right about the concerns of both Conrad and his predecessors in adventure fiction, the nineteenth-century tale of heroic adventure in its most ambitious form attempts to identify no less than the social novel the destiny of the self with the fate of its culture. The important difference for the sake of my argument is that in this fiction not only the individual, but the entire culture, is put to a test, so that the moral fulfillment of the hero becomes the focus of a historical struggle, and the heroic journey turns into a culturally regenerative ordeal. Considering these larger intentions in the journeys of Dana, Cooper, and Kipling, it would not be stretching too far to suggest that this fiction sets out to defend a cultural order that in social fiction was simply assumed.

The journey to defend a social ideal runs into trouble, however, at least as early as Cooper in America. As I have argued in chapter 1, Cooper's purpose in writing *The Sea Lions* is in large part to answer the threat of chaos in America and to reassert the order of an ideal society. But this ideal really seems to exist outside of Cooper's more compelling imagination of historical deterioration, ultimately outside of the novel. Thus instead of cooperating with the movements of history, the journey (and therefore the plot, the structure) of *The Sea Lions* runs counter to the pressures of social change. It follows that plot in Cooper becomes a self-conscious invention of the novelist rather than a recapitulation of the processes that occur within the social world. For Cooper, the danger for such a plot is the realization of its artificiality and therefore the irrelevance to history of its allegorical design. This, as I have argued, is exactly what happens, and the results need only be summarized. Cooper's journey, if it is to succeed at all, must supplant his vision of historical corruption and the nothingness beyond history with a literary structure. To do this, however, he must compromise the heroic enterprise by turning to rhetorical devices for its fulfillment: not only to a repaired plot but also to the perfected, timeless, and pastoral images of a society Cooper knows is threatened by historical change. The heroic journey thus becomes a retreat into literary form.

The heroic journey in Conrad bears some important resemblances to the one in Cooper. It assumes that society once existed in a simpler, harmonious form and has since become corrupted, and its course is regressive, because it aspires to return to sources and archetypes, to models of social perfection. Part of the difference between Cooper and Conrad, however, is that in Conrad the journey as a rhetorical device is no more capable of "arriving" at the ideal society than the linear movement of history itself. To put it another way, while Cooper may still opt for literary versions of society to counteract his more compelling imagination of historical change, in Conrad's fiction history, rhetoric, and the heroic journey all occupy the same ontological status and all share the same fate. Each thrust into the past propels Conrad further into the future, more radically displacing him from his lost paradise. Thus, *The Nigger of the "Narcissus"* begins its heroic allegory by attempting to return to the world of the past and then celebrate, perhaps elegiacally, the virtues of that past. But the novel ends, instead, in the dissolution of the heroic world, the manifestation of the crew's latent corruption, the realization of death, and the linear movement of history away from a mythical ideal. The result is that the myth of the heroic community itself is exploded along with the idea that the crew of the *Narcissus* were anything other than fallen human beings in the first place. Later, in "Heart of Darkness," Conrad's journey to the source of things to recover some meaning in a primal human experience reveals at best that the savages are in some ways like us, but also that what Marlow is really looking for is inscrutable. It may be some truth; but such a truth is rendered as nothing at all, worse yet, as a darkness. For Conrad, we are forever cut off from the original and the ideal, from a social paradise, from the idea of paradise itself. It is significant to note that after the ultimate thrusts into the past and into the self fail in "Heart of Darkness," the journey in *Lord Jim* takes the form of an almost aimless wandering in both plot and in ideology, for "paradise" is nowhere to be found.

Conrad, like Cooper, seems to sense that heroic man can exist neither within nor without the context of a social world, and both seem to realize that where the real struggle begins is where the journey, with its sustaining ideology, ends. Cooper, of course, does not achieve the power and depth of Conrad's vision. He is unwilling (and, to be frank, unable) to pursue the heroic journey beyond its limits with Conrad's insistence and intensity and with his tremendous exertions of style. After such efforts Conrad himself exhausts the possibilities of language and plot in trying to give meaning to heroic experience and in attempting to recover his lost ideal. In that environment which is "beyond the heroic," as I have called it, heroic aspirations may be expressed only in the incalculable defiance of Kurtz. Whether or not Kurtz becomes a hero is a question that begs itself, because we no longer have the basis for such a definition. Yet, he becomes for Marlow, and I think for us, a "remarkable man"; for in his moment of outrageous rebellion against all restraints, we observe a character matched in the intensity and in the quality of his defiance only by Milton's Samson or Shakespeare's Lear. It is a rare moment in literature when such power is achieved: when Conrad, like Shakespeare and Milton in their own times, stands alone and bears witness to the last measure of human passion asserting itself against the ruin of civilization and the darkness beyond.

Undoubtedly other writers of adventure tales approach Conrad's moral position, if we are to state that position merely as a set of beliefs or intellectual stances. Stephen Crane fully dramatizes the moral barrenness of the public hero in nineteenth-century literature. The plot of heroic initiation, the bourgeois myth of manhood, even the idea of a heroic paradise lost, come together in Crane only to be parodied as cultural delusions. But in Crane's pessimism and nihilism, there is also a kind of safety. His answer to the end of heroism is to withdraw into a stony skepticism, so that the reader leaves his work, as Conrad himself seemed to sense, with an emptiness that makes one less impressed with the novel's ambitions as a whole.[1] The failures of heroism in *The Red Badge of Courage* are less poignant than they might have been, because those failures are assumed to exist, unchallenged, throughout the novel, and because history is cynically reduced to a mere set of stage props. Another and similar parallel to Conrad may be found in the late work of Robert Louis Stevenson, in a travel journal called *In the South Seas*, which Conrad admired.[2] Going to the South Seas for his health (with echoes of Dana), Stevenson finds a "fairyland" where the people are "as remote in thought and habit as Rob Roy or Barbarossa, the Apostles or Caesar." But Stevenson comes to discover that this romantic paradise, this idyllic prototype of European culture, is fraught with disease, hunger, overpopulation, and political strife, and the subversiveness of Western colonialism that is slowly destroying a once heroic race. While this disillusionment is expressed more deeply than Crane's, Stevenson's despair is analogously uncomplicated and final. There is no pressure applied against the vision of degeneration in the modern world, no hope of redemption, no effort to find a heroic ethic that may survive the demise of the old order. The power of Conrad's own despair is that he tries so hard to find a way out of it, even if that way leads deeper into the darkness and then back to the fallen world of man.

The greatness of Conrad's heroic tales is largely in the ambitions of their historical vision, which in truth is less in touch with society and public events than it is with a visionary's imagination of public events in stories, legends, poems. Conrad's is preeminently a literary rather than a social imagination. It is no coincidence that *The Nigger of the "Narcissus"* echoes Milton and "Heart of Darkness" implies a commentary upon Wordsworthian introspection, the descent into the mind. Although Conrad is not as obviously erudite as Joyce or Eliot, he seems to have absorbed a tradition in English poetry and rendered it in fiction: Milton's imagination of the fall of a human community, and Wordsworth's inner search for the sublime.[3] Conrad does not reenact the history of a society in the experience of his hero the way Defoe and Kipling do; rather he recapitulates a heroic tradition in English literature in which the range of heroic endeavor is diminished from a communal trial to the struggles of the isolated self. Unlike the journeys of conservative adventure fiction in the nineteenth century, those of Conrad at his best lead back to where they began with nothing discovered except that everything is lost, the least of which is that cultural order which Dana, Cooper, and Kipling try to defend. Perhaps, at last, the best testimony to Conrad's greatness and to the integrity of his vision is that he did not want to make this discovery, but that he did so in response to the demands that the pursuit of the journey made necessary. He instinctively seemed to know what he had to do next, where his journey must go.

To me, this instinctive and fundamental imaginative integrity accounts better than most other explanations for why Conrad, after establishing himself as a writer of adventure stories, suddenly began writing political novels, beginning with *Nostromo* (1904). Like Marlow, after "Heart of Darkness" Conrad had nowhere to take his heroic journey but back to the modern world; and like Marlow, he returned with a political vision that matured along with a growing despair over the fate of his heroic dreams. The worlds of *The Secret Agent* and *Under Western Eyes* are entirely inhospitable to heroic aspirations; and if there are heroes in *Nostromo*, they are, like Singleton and Jim on Patusan, framed in the rueful irony of a man who knows what the failures of his adventure stories imply.

One of the many ironies about Conrad's career is that the man who became the greatest political novelist in English literature was obsessed in these novels with a vision that grew out of his tales of romantic adventure. And while I will not presume to discuss these novels in detail in this study, our understanding of Conrad's heroic imagination is incomplete without some attention to the political ramifications of the earlier heroic tales in Conrad's later work. *The Secret Agent* is probably the most obvious case in point and in some ways is much closer to the adventure tales than it is to *Nostromo*. As Irving Howe argues in a fine chapter on Conrad in *Politics and the Novel, The Secret Agent* is something of a political cartoon in which Conrad simplifies his social consciousness in order to attack in society what he most fears. (Conrad himself subtitled the novel *A Simple Tale.*) Another way to look at the novel, though, is to see it as an extrapolation upon the fallen world of the adventure tales, the embodiment of Conrad's moral vision once the possibilities for an ideal world are destroyed. Thus the characters and the moral atmosphere of *The Secret Agent* are prefigured in Donkin, Chester, Brown, and the company people in "Heart of Darkness."

More interesting yet is the way this novel recalls the corrupted world of *The Nigger of the "Narcissus."* Although there is no allusion to a lost paradise in *The Secret Agent*, society in this novel, like the fallen crew of the *Narcissus*, manifests itself in the corrupted language of social relationships, one that echoes the language of the fallen Adam and Eve. As I argued in chapter 2, language itself seems to be an institution fundamental to the fallen world. Hence, the sailors who were once silent, noble, heroic, enduring, become cowardly, deceitful, complaining, and verbose. Cowardice and deceit in one sense are made possible in society by language — an attitude pervasive in Conrad's early letters (1895–1900) and reiterated in a somewhat different form in the ontology of "Heart of Darkness" and *Lord Jim*. Now, the extent to which *The Secret Agent* is about the anarchism of the modern world may best be realized in its sweeping satire of social and political vocabularies. All the "official" anarchists in the novel are, appropriately, propagandists who belong to a single revolutionary organization that is hopelessly chaotic, because each member has his own language for its political goals. Each man is identified by a revolutionary epithet, which seems to characterize metaphorically the kind of performance one might expect from him. Ossipon, the medical school flunkie called the "Doctor," believes that scientists will some day rule the world; Michaelis, the fat, slow-witted dreamer known as the "Apostle," is an economic determinist with utopian dreams ("Faith," "Hope," and "Charity" are the three sections of his book); and Yundt, "the Terror," turns out inflammatory tracts that dwell upon the violent destruction of the European social order. The maniacal Professor, called "the perfect anarchist," belongs to no organization at all but entertains his own private visions of the "perfect detonator," which he calls "a good definition" for his schemes of universal destruction.

Such moral and verbal discord is not, however, limited to these circles, as the identification between language and anarchy is extended. Vladimir, the diplomat from some unnamed "great Power" (Russia is the obvious though incidental allusion) hopes to terrorize the English with anarchistic outrages. His plan is to maneuver the government into repressive police action which would encourage a popular revolution. Scheming to blow up the Greenwich Observatory (symbolically dynamiting the first meridian), he instructs his undercover agent, Verloc, that "bombs are your means of expression," to perpetuate the propaganda of the deed. Still other characters contribute to what the Professor perceptively characterizes as "several kinds of logic" competing to order society. Chief Inspector Heat, assigned to the bombing case, is one of the best police officers in London because, as the narrator observes, he has the mind of a criminal. But he does not have the mind of an anarchist, and until he happens upon a conventional clue (a piece of Stevie's overcoat) his usual means of unraveling mysteries are thwarted. In another instance of a failure to define political events, the Assistant Commissioner and Sir Ethelred, a high government official, engage in a circuitous and hopelessly muddled "analysis" of the bombing, which shows Conrad at his best as a satirist of political jargon. Ethelred, who also bears a comic title (the "Great Presence"), is a fine parody of bureaucratic obtuseness whose ancient English lineage seems to contribute to his almost abstract existence in the novel, as if he has become absorbed into the institutions he is made to represent. And although the Assistant Commissioner fares better in the novel, eventually tracing the bombing plot to Vladimir, his astute political sense fails him in his efforts to understand the personal drama of Stevie and Verloc. Finally, Verloc, the comic focus of the novel's political intrigues (whose sign, humorously, is an equilateral triangle), works for all three of the political groups: for the anarchists, for Vladimir, and for Heat as a police informer. Verloc seems capable of mouthing all vocabularies with equal conviction. Because he is politically ubiquitous, we are never certain where his strongest allegiances lie — or whether he has any at all. He himself is a good definition of all the anarchism in *The Secret Agent*.

As the gloomily comic portraiture ranges into other areas of social life, Verloc's marriage is seen to be a domestic version of the political chaos in the novel. Winnie, Verloc's wife, jilts her romantic lover, the son of a local butcher, in order to marry Verloc, who she thinks will be able to provide for Stevie, her idiot brother. Unaware of Winnie's "bargain," as it is called, Verloc lives under the illusion that he is being "loved for himself" until Winnie murders him for his role in the death of her brother. But until then, the Verloc marriage is a comfortable and affectionate partnership that is based, nonetheless, upon each spouse's misunderstanding of the other. In this lack of real communication, the institution of middle class marriage, where private dreams are sacrificed for economic security and social convenience, becomes another area of social anarchy and another metaphor for the political world. At one point, in fact, the Assistant Commissioner speculates that the bombing incident may be but part of a "domestic drama" after all—which is, of course, but one other way to "define" the source of social conflict in the novel.

The satire of the middle class in *The Secret Agent* presents Conrad in his most extended and elaborate criticism of the English sensibility, which he often pokes fun at in the adventure tales, and which he occasionally attacks in Marlow's jabs at his listening audience. In this novel, Vladimir seems right when he charges that the the middle class is jaded in its sensibilities, deaf to its latent anarchy, unaware of the threatening world beyond its doorsteps. Verloc, who may be seen as a travesty of middle class values, is, in his indolent, self-absorbed moral flatulence, just as appalling as the Professor with his mad visions of universal destruction. Verloc is indeed a "humane man" and a "good husband" as the narrator ironically asserts; but his humanity and his generosity are limited by his inability to think or understand with any great feeling. Conrad notes that his affection for Stevie is, at best, that of a husband who quietly tolerates his wife's beloved cat; and when Stevie dies carrying the bomb to the Greenwich Observatory, Verloc's guilt is muffled by his gruff rationalizations to himself and his brusque condolences to Winnie. Yet Verloc is no monster: his desire for domestic peace and security and his business-like though lazy and phlegmatic approach to life are not a terrible distortion of a familiar type of morally uncommitted, self-serving "good citizen." And Conrad is not really ignoring his intrigues in the anarchist underground when he describes Verloc as "the defender of the social system," for such compromises of integrity and lack of fidelity to anything except self-preservation are the best insurance that society will never change. But if he is not a monster, his actions (or his inactions) are monstrous in their effects. In his commonplace ambitions, his shallow affection, and his lugubrious fears, he becomes a model of moral stagnation and deadening emotional insularity. While nominally active in all corners of his dismal society—as a husband, a shopowner, an embassy spy, and a police informer—he is both an instrument and a paragon of a degenerate form of humanity that Conrad implies is modern man.

Perhaps the only sympathetic character in *The Secret Agent* is the one person whose fate authenticates the disgust Conrad feels for his contemporary society. Stevie, whose compassion for mistreated horses and whose abhorrence of any word suggestive of violence, appears as an honest and pathetically touching protest to the impersonal and exploitative world that finally claims him. But then, even Stevie fails to develop into a spokesman for humanitarianism and becomes rather the testimony to the irrelevance and impotence of such benign instincts in an absurd world. It is a stroke of wicked humor that the only charitable character in the novel is an idiot.

Whatever his humane attributes, Stevie remains a comically weird oddity, "slight and short, with a thin neck, and the peaked shoulders raised slightly under the large semi-transparent ears" (p. 186), drawing his mad circles in what becomes another metaphor of hopeless anarchy.

If anarchy is less the subject of *Nostromo*, it is nonetheless part of an even more ambitious vision of social deterioration. While the range of Conrad's irony in *The Secret Agent* touches all corners of contemporary society, in *Nostromo* it swells to historical proportions, spanning several generations in the imaginary South American Republic of Costaguana. Moreover, with European capitalists, indigenous Spanish landowners, hidalgos, native Indians, and imported European laborers, Costaguana becomes a melting pot, a paradigm, and in the cryptic name itself (the Coast of Guano), a commentary on the entire Western world.

One may, like Irving Howe, anchor a discussion of *Nostromo* in an analysis of the history of Costaguana. In the process, we are bound to marvel at Conrad's acute understanding of social and political affairs, which is all the more remarkable because the adventure tales present us with a very different and mythical version of historical change. But a summary of that kind, as critically pertinent as it may be, really takes us away from the experience of reading the book. Actually, Costaguana's history is presented like a vast, panoramic painting with many small sketches that seem to blur rather than highlight the picture — or perhaps like a jigsaw puzzle in which added pieces expand rather than fill the dimensions of the entire scene. One tends to respond to *Nostromo* impressionistically. It is "opaque," as someone suggested, or "hollow," as F. R. Leavis said. The novel seems to defy plot, as the story is told piecemeal in what would ordinarily be called flashbacks and digressions, as the character studies refuse to settle upon any central figure, as the perspectives constantly multiply and rearrange the shades and colors of a fabric that seems infinitely variable and never complete. When we look at Costaguana through the astonishing array of panoramic images Conrad evokes, it often seems we are viewing it not through a lens but through a veil, sometimes exquisitely diaphanous, as in the lovely and sweeping descriptions of nature; sometimes murky and bleak, as in the allusions to the Republic's sordid political past; sometimes richly colorful, as in the little vignettes of regional life in the province of Sulaco. The series of character-narrators, moreover, places further screens between us and the "plot," which compound the effect of visual distance so often created by the omniscient narrator. Indeed, some of the most important events in *Nostromo* are narrated indirectly in the long letter of Decoud to his sister. Some of these happenings, such as the military revolt at Esmeralda, are barely summarized in this letter from information received in a telegraphist's dispatch. The most crucial military engagements of the revolution are narrated by the comic figure of Captain Mitchell, who conducts guided tours for rich visitors to the new republic near the end of the novel, while the omniscient narrator himself merely alludes to Nostromo's climactic ride to Cayta to recall the forces of General Barrios. Thus, in any number of stylistic effects, we are denied the full vision of the history we would expect the story to provide.

Most of the critical grumbling over *Nostromo* is directed against this constant pressuring away from the definite and the well defined. The common complaints are that Conrad's political sensitivities require "the protection of distance,"[4] or that Conrad is a stranger to the particulars of domestic life,[5] or even that "Conrad, at bottom, doesn't know what his attitude to his events and characters is."[6] This last criticism is the most intriguing, for it recalls the familiar Leavisite charges against "Heart of Darkness," and the link it establishes between the two novels is worth pursuing. What most annoys the Leavisite critic, I suspect, is that the historical vision of the novel is not articulated in strictly social and political terms. Indeed, politics and the history of public events seem to fade into the splendid and overwhelming natural geography of the country that bears some resemblance to the wilderness in "Heart of Darkness": the ghostly Golfo Placido, whose indomitable calms and shiftless winds defy for generations the sails of foreign shipping; the immense mountain, Higuerota, whose shadow delays the light of dawn from falling on the campo; the three Isabel Islands that the birds mysteriously avoid; and the "incorruptible" silver of the San Tomé Mountain. The atmosphere that pervades the novel is beautifully poetic but almost preternaturally weird, seeming to engulf the events of politics and history within a timeless world where the most enduring truths are left unsaid.

Needless to say, this is not an environment hospitable to a tea party or a walk in the garden, which makes the issue of whether or not Conrad could depict the details of domestic life as Jane Austen might beside the point. But more than that, such an environment suggests that the special power of *Nostromo* is precisely in that blankness or "hollowness" that Leavis talks about. However brilliantly the novel is conceived in style, in tone, and in the intricacies of its labyrinthine structure, the rhetorical perfection of *Nostromo* is subverted in a fundamental way. To describe or account for this subversion is, as most criticism of the novel indicates, not at all easy. It is only in a small way evident in the "ghosts" of the country's past that seem to accumulate in the present rather than fade into history: the haunting memories of the ruthless dictator Guzman Bento and his inquisitor, Father Beron; the apparitions of the legendary fortune hunters on the barren peninsula of

Azuera; and the shadows of the equestrian statue of Charles IV (and the history it represents), which, although dismantled, seems to survive spectrally in the "new" sculptures of Parrochetti. Partly, the country's timelessness and its atmosphere of shadowy presences are expressed in its local legends and popular myths, from which the narrator remains tacitly and respectfully aloof. But most of all this blankness is sensed in the feeling that behind all the schemes in the novel—either political or rhetorical (and both, as in *The Secret Agent*, are related through the double sense of "plot")—is the strange and timeless power of Nature that suggests, despite all finite resolutions, that in a fundamental way Costaguana does not change.

The power of nature to resist the schemes of men is perhaps best dramatized in the failures of many of the characters to exploit the silver of the San Tomé Mountain. The mine, as the narrator says, becomes the cornerstone of the social structure in Sulaco: "the San Tomé mine was to become an institution, a rallying point for everything in the province that needed order and stability to live" (IX, p. 110). Charles Gould, who holds the concession to the mine, is represented in the novel as the most powerful political force in the country, a man who can make or break governments. Courting his favor is a political necessity among all the factions in the province, and many, indeed, try to use the mine in the furtherance of their own ambitions. The American tycoon Holroyd invests in the mine as both a hobby and a mission, as he tries to establish a base for his Protestant religious crusades. The Englishman Sir John hopes for the backing of the Gould interests for the construction of the National Railway. In addition, the silver of the mine tantalizes the assortment of ambitious political rogues in Sulaco, especially the Montero brothers and the dull-minded Colonel Sotillo. Even the most apolitical characters, Monygham and Decoud, become directly concerned with the mine, as both, inspired by love, are drawn into counterrevolutionary intrigues. But as much as this plotting and scheming give shape to the social relationships in *Nostromo*, the preoccupation with silver seems the source not only of the political disorder but also of the isolation of each character from the others. Rather than gaining control of the mine, the major figures of Sulaco become enslaved to it. Their political plots become private obsessions which, in turn, become impersonal and dehumanizing, leaving only the inanimate silver "uncorrupted" and unchanged.

As the narrator grimly comments, "A man haunted by a fixed idea is insane" (p. 379), according to which Sulaco must be seen as a society consisting largely of madmen. This of course is not only the raving madness of a Sotillo dredging the harbor for days looking for a sunken treasure that is not there. It is also the calculating madness of the Monteros in their Napoleonic dreams, the sad, senile romanticism of Giorgio Viola, the decent, self-sacrificing nationalism of Avellanso, the slavish devotion of Monygham to Mrs. Gould, the suicidal despair of Decoud on the Golfo Placido, and the narcissistic self-betrayal of Nostromo when he exchanges his integrity for a cache of hidden silver. Ironically, the one man who might be thought to control the very mine that seems to possess everyone else has erected "a wall of silver-bricks" (p. 222) between himself and his wife. "Charles Gould was competent because he had no illusions" (p. 89), the narrator says in terms that remind us of Marlow's attack on the "laws of order and progress" in *Lord Jim* ("it is respectable to have no illusions—and safe—and profitable—and dull"). Charles Gould is the quintessence of material success. "Poor boy!" thinks Emily Gould in a moving and tragic moment, "He was perfect—perfect . . . but she would never have him to herself" (pp. 521-22).

In a sense, the characters in *Nostromo* are actually "political" in the most radical way, in that their deepest and most precious emotions finally exist only in the expression they give to them within the public roles they play. Not only the desire for power but also the desire for love becomes for Decoud, for Gould, for Monygham, for Nostromo, for every major character including the tragically lonely Emily, the property of national politics and the silver of the mine. Ironically, the foundation of the country's stability is the idol of its corruption, the focus of all the betrayals of self and of human community. At the end of the novel, when Costaguana is officially at peace, the signs of incipient revolution among the workers are merely surface ripples of the much larger currents in the novel. For although *Nostromo*, unlike *The Secret Agent*, is not explicitly about anarchy, its vision of social chaos is just as pervasive and even more profound.

We will best be able to dismiss the criticism that in *Nostromo* Conrad does not know what he is doing when we understand that *Nostromo* is as much about history as "Heart of Darkness" is about an African adventure. In *Nostromo*, history consists of manmade plots and material inventions, which in the context of a timeless Nature may be seen as falsifications of truth, even as illusions. As in the adventure tales, the only immutable presence in this novel is the geography of vast, empty space that absorbs the affairs of men into its austere silence. Conrad appealed to his best symbolic sense when he has Martin Decoud commit suicide on the motionless waters of the Placid Gulf. Decoud's more resilient predecessors include Crusoe and Dana, who were able to survive because they could conquer with the consciousness, because they fended off a nature that literally and symbolically threatened to swallow them up. But Decoud, the most cerebral character in *Nostromo* and seemingly the one who most depends upon society, language, and wit for his sense of self-identity, is for Conrad the ideal sacrifice to the infinite abyss. Personally, I think his death is played up too much in criticism; he is only the brief dramatic focus of what the whole novel is implying. Yet his suicide is a sharp reminder that, as in "Heart of Darkness," beyond the thin walls of consciousness, culture, and history, is total obliteration; it is the darkness that is beyond all human affairs.

The difference between the history of *Nostromo* and that of the adventure tales is the absence in this novel of the myth of a paradise lost.[7] In *Nostromo* history is a record of corruption which is never eradicated but which simply expresses itself in different forms. Material progress, as Marlow so often reminds us, is a veneer; but now there is no reminder that man was once heroic, that there was ever an historical time before the Fall. Only in the moral decline of Nostromo, it seems, do we see a remnant of Conrad's romanticism as it appeared in *The Nigger of the "Narcissus,"* for the only paradise destroyed in this novel is in the imagination of the *Capataz*. Ironically, of course, the heroic Nostromo was never more than a public image, a social instrument, "our man." And in his fall he simply trades his public service for a private and equally impersonal obsession with the silver. But like Singleton suddenly aware of his mortality or Jim shaken from his illusions, the poignancy of Nostromo's "fall" is in the shock of his self-consciousness, the awareness that he is subject to powers outside of himself. The only heroic paradise is ironically a state of mind; and it is in learning this truth that Nostromo is so appalled.

After *Nostromo*, there is perhaps less to say about the development of Conrad's political imagination than there is about the motions that run counter to the vision the earlier novels explored. When the best of the later novels logically extend the political implications of the earlier ones, the result is the physical and moral self-destruction of the hero; but Conrad, seemingly to preserve his own moral identity, increasingly gives way to artistic compromises that become stultifying and deleterious to the heroic imagination expressed in the adventure tales. *Under Western Eyes* (1911) and *Victory* (1915) are the novels that most strongly prefigure this imaginative paralysis suffered by Conrad late in his career.

This paralysis is actually evident in Conrad's fiction long before his "achievement" is complete. Certainly it is built into the structure of "Heart of Darkness." Nonetheless, comparing "Heart of Darkness" to the later novels shows just how well Conrad sustained the energy of his heroic vision even when the possibility for its fulfillment had been denied. The invention of Marlow as a narrator in these early tales made possible the pursuit of the heroic journey. Marlow was just the narrative device that Conrad needed to stabilize his fictional voice and to direct the course of that journey maintaining a sense of imaginative equilibrium and preventing the heroic ordeal from collapsing into chaos on one hand or mere rhetoric on the other. Some critics, however (Irving Howe especially), talk about this narrative device as a self-protective shield for Conrad, which in the Marlow tales is true enough but in an importantly qualified way. "Heart of Darkness" and *Lord Jim* are both stories about the process of storytelling; both create internal mirrors reflecting Conrad's private acts of imaginative invention. We often observe Marlow commenting upon his own credibility, planning his rhetorical strategies, worrying over how to render his feelings into words. We even see Jim in effect reminding Marlow that his fictional devices are not working as Marlow hoped they would. The effect of these internal mirrors, I think, is precisely consistent with Conrad's precarious vision in the adventure tales, because they isolate the devices of plot, style, metaphor, and sometimes even character, and identify them as fictional constructs in an atmosphere suffused with images of infinite darkness. In other words, the "mirror" techniques of the adventure tales express exactly Conrad's sense that all meaning is illusion, that all order is like that created in the authorial enterprise—in the invention of plots and fictions and artificial worlds.

In *Under Western Eyes*, however, the term "narrative shield" is much more accurate to describe the novel's fictional apparatus. In the Author's Note to the novel, Conrad justifies the invention of his narrator by invoking the need to "strike and sustain the note of scrupulous impartiality" (XXII, viii). But impartiality is hardly the issue. The "western eyes" that control the vision of the novel belong to an old, bland, socially impotent and imaginatively ossified professor of languages who translates the diary of Razumov into English. The fact that the narrator is a man whose business is "translation" and whose currency is words should in itself signify just how skeptical and disspirited Conrad has become. In reading Conrad, we are led to distrust words, which as Marlow says in *Lord Jim* "belong to that sheltering conception of light and order which is our refuge." What distinguishes the Conrad of the Marlow tales from the author of *Under Western Eyes* is that Conrad now refuses to venture into the darkness, beyond the pale, resigning himself to Marlow's failures in "Heart of Darkness" and *Lord Jim*. The official "philosophy" of *Under Western Eyes* is no different from that of the adventure tales. "Words," the narrator tells us, "are the great foes of reality" (p. 3). What is different in this novel, however, is that there is no imaginative resistance exerted against the skepticism of that idea; it is expressed, in other words, simply as a philosophy, merely as a subject for the professor's proselytizing. What's more, that the professor is self-critical and skeptical of his own enterprise does not deter him from pretending to some insight to which he is not, according to his own cautions, entitled. The "spirit of Russia," the great unknown in the novel, he "translates" into the word "cynicism." While such a verbal formula may remind us of Marlow's term "the horror" — and in some ways performs the same function — there is none of Marlow's tenacity, none of his tortured self-doubt in the professor's metaphor. His is not a last, desperate effort to avoid chaos but a willfull habit of mind. Aside from some early passages, in fact, the "spirit of Russia" is almost casually evoked in the novel; and there is no real attempt to explore it, as Marlow had journeyed into the darkness. The narrator of *Under Western Eyes*, it seems to me, is a paraphrase and simplification of Marlow in "Heart of Darkness."

Yet Conrad struggled as much with his vision of darkness in this book as he did in his adventure tales. Indeed, biographical testimony (cited in the previous chapter) suggests he did even more so. But *Under Western Eyes* is clearly symptomatic of an imaginative suppression, a denial of those areas of Conrad's mind where order disappears into chaos. "Life is a thing of form," says the professor in a statement that is likely to surprise readers of Conrad. "It has its plastic shape and a definite intellectual aspect. The most idealistic conceptions of love and forbearance must be clothed in flesh as it were before they can be made understandable" (p. 106). Here Conrad has adopted the very position he attacks in the Marlow tales; he has made his truce with the modern world; he has "translated" himself into a materialist.

Much could be said about the politics of *Under Western Eyes* that would contribute to my argument that anarchy is the pervasive motif in Conrad's social vision. But my discussions of *The Secret Agent* and *Nostromo* obviate a detailed elaboration upon such matters in *Under Western Eyes*. What interests me now is what seldom emerges from readings that assume the novel is "about" politics: that it is in fact about the destruction of the individual and the society that become political in any form. And, as Razumov's case suggests most emphatically, there is no choice involved. In one sense, Razumov becomes what other people see in him: for Haldin, he is a confidant; for the students at the university, a romantic conspirator; for Councilor Mikulin, a useful instrument for the secret police; and for the revolutionaries in Geneva, he is "one of us."[8] In a way, he is like Verloc, a tool for all political purposes. The difference here is that Razumov hates himself for becoming such a person and believes that he has "betrayed" himself, Haldin, Natalie, and even the revolutionaries whom he otherwise despises.

Razumov's guilt over these betrayals is often taken as evidence of Conrad's divided political allegiance or as a sign of some deep-seated Freudian trauma. But once again, without denying the value of these speculations, I think the most persuasive explanation here issues from the verbal associations, the dramatic repercussions, and the imaginative contexts of the novels themselves. Like the idea of a "lie," a "betrayal" in Conrad is almost a technical term and is used in a special sense. Like lies, betrayals are indigenous to the human condition, inevitable, really, as one becomes conscious of one's mortality. In *The Nigger of the "Narcissus"* it is not the crew's code of ethics that is betrayed (for the crew remain faithful to their brother seaman, Jimmy) but rather the idea that the seamen's world is timeless and "true." The sailors had no choice, in one sense, but to remain faithful to Jimmy, for had they betrayed him, they would have betrayed the ethical foundation of their heroic world as well. Of course, their fidelity to a sham places truth and betrayal in quotation marks; and as their dilemma is presented in the novel, either fidelity to the seaman's code of ethics or betrayal of Jimmy would amount to the destruction of the heroic world. Guilt in Conrad's fiction is inescapable. The heroic community is at best an imperfect imitation of paradise, so in remaining loyal to it, one betrays the idea of that heroic paradise. Yet, to betray the fallen community is to reenact the historical myth of the fall at a further remove from the ideal. Thus Jim in *Lord Jim* may feel guilty for betraying the code of ethics upheld by the court of inquiry. He knows the "facts" of the matter are more complicated than the court understands, and yet he seems to wish nevertheless that he could have been the romantic, professional, automatic hero that Brierly had become. Just as Marlow feels in "Heart of Darkness," human beings must remain faithful to *something*: "I did not betray Mr. Kurtz—it was ordered I should never betray him—it was written I should be loyal to the nightmare of my choice" (p. 141). Similarly for Razumov, haunted by his guilt for informing on Haldin, fidelity comes down to choosing among nightmares.

In *Under Western Eyes*, although the dilemmas over fidelity and betrayal are just as strong as in the adventure tales, the options for even an imitation of heroic conduct are entirely absent. Conrad's entire heroic vocabulary reoccurs here to remind us that heroism is impossible. Echoing the ethics of the adventure tales, General T_____, who is seen as a stupid, repulsive boor, claims, "My existence has been built on fidelity" (p. 51), while the scheming, manipulative Peter Ivanovitch gloats over Razumov, "But you, at any rate, are one of *us*" (p. 208). Even Conrad's "secret sharer," Leggatt, finds a monstrous counterpart in Haldin, the similarly spectral criminal who invades Razumov's room appealing, like Leggatt, for a silent trust. Humanity has by its very nature so perverted the heroic aspirations of the earlier novels that the heroic world, always a tentative invocation of an unrealized ideal, has finally become quite meaningless. "What does fraternity mean?" Conrad asked in a letter to Cunninghame

Graham, "Fraternity means nothing unless the Cain-Abel business. That's your true fraternity."⁹ Once again, the human community is a perversion of the ideal in "Eden." In the end, the values of Razumov's social world are only the dark shadows of those presupposed in *The Nigger of the "Narcissus"* and *Lord Jim*; but if Conrad is benignly ironical, often sentimental, about Jim, he seems less caring and more bitter in his treatment of Razumov. How deeply Conrad hated his images of the modern world and how relentlessly he was committed to portraying them seems finally expressed in the way he turns his hatred inward, as it were, and destroys the last image of his naive, idyllic hero. Self-destruction seems the only way to escape the dilemmas of betrayal.

The final novel of interest to me is *Victory*, published in 1915, which stands as Conrad's last major work in the fiction of heroic adventure and the farthest logical extension of the social vision in *Nostromo, The Secret Agent,* and *Under Western Eyes.* As if answering Mikulin's icy challenge, "Where to?" after Razumov declares he will "retire," Conrad takes his hero in *Victory* away from Western Europe and back once again to the Malayan Archipelago, into the darkening twilight of his romanticism, to the island of Samburan. *Victory* is not, to be sure, a novel the caliber of *Nostromo* or even *Lord Jim*: it is the product of an advanced state of pessimism, resignation, and perhaps even apathy, and expresses only a simplified, though still ironical celebration of heroic fidelity and self-sacrifice. But unlike Conrad's later novels (*The Arrow of Gold, The Rescue, The Rover,* etc.), its literary value is enhanced by reading it next to the earlier adventure tales, as it reviews the heroic motifs and moral struggles of those stories in the atmosphere of imaginative impotence and despair. The hero of the novel, Axel Heyst, seems at times an enervated and defeated version of Kurtz the heroic exile, while Davidson, the occasional narrator and witness to Heyst's story, is like a Marlow diminished in stature and depleted of the resources of that inquiring mind. The hopelessness of the love affair between Heyst and Lena takes on an added dimension if it is read next to that of Jim and Jewel. And it is easier to appreciate Heyst's seemingly irrational guilt over Morrison's death if we consider the consequences of social commitments in *Lord Jim* and *Under Western Eyes.* The island itself, finally, with its deserted buildings and eerie silence, is the ruin of both a pastoral and a commercial dream, and we can't help thinking of Jim's search for a new life on Patusan when, in the middle of the story as Heyst and Lena withdraw from the outside world, Heyst ironically believes that "Nothing can break in on us here" (XV, p. 223).

Victory has been intriguingly psychoanalyzed by Bernard Meyer in *Joseph Conrad: A Psychoanalytic Biography* and by Frederick Crews in a review of Meyer's book.[10] And indeed, the novel sometimes reads like a Freudian case study, especially in the celebrated scene where Lena surreptitiously disarms Ricardo of his knife, hides it in her skirts, and watches the criminal grovel at her feet ignominiously making love. But I don't think it is taking the starch out of *Victory* (any more than it ought to be) to argue that impotence, in reference to Heyst, should apply to his fear of social relationships in general, and that his frustration as Man and Protector is to be seen as part of a larger, metaphorical pattern of failure to sustain the dark paradise that the novel briefly and tenuously regains. It is useful to remark that Morrison, in a way parallel to that of Lena, poses a similar threat to Heyst's emotional insularity, and that Heyst's willful seclusion from "the world" suggests a larger denial of social commitment than the incontestably abundant sexual metaphors alone may account for. Why this sexual language is particularly striking here is, I think, because romantic love becomes the last diminished arena in which Conrad explores the possibilities for regaining a heroic world.

In *Victory* we may witness one more time the conflict in Conrad's imagination between romantic aspirations and a moral despair. But now, both alternatives are sapped of their power. For Heyst, the spiritual and moral paucity inherited from the earlier novels finds expression not in a language of intense, tormented, and barely intelligible introspection, as in parts of "Heart of Darkness," but in the arid, academic records of Heyst's father and in his own less virulent and less scornful skepticism. The elder Heyst is described as the "silenced destroyer of systems, of hopes, of beliefs" (p. 175), "who had spent his life in blowing blasts upon a terrible trumpet which had filled heaven and earth with ruins, while mankind went on its way unheeding" (p. 175). Heyst knows "that something of his father dwelt yet on earth—a ghostly voice, audible to the ear of his own flesh and blood" (p. 219), a voice which he himself speaks in when he says, "Truth, work, ambition, love itself, may be only counters in the lamentable or despicable game of life" (p. 203). For Heyst, all Conrad's ethical cornerstones—work, fidelity, love—are part of a "truth" which, as in *The Nigger of the "Narcissus,"* is a game, a myth, an illusion. At the same time, however, the characterization of Heyst's father as a misanthropic Gabriel and the written record of his prophetic despair perhaps speak for the man that Conrad feared he himself had become. Almost by way of protest, and perhaps in response to the dying embers of romance from the earlier tales, Conrad has Heyst reflect:

> There must be a lot of the original Adam in me, after all. . . . this primeval ancestor is not easily suppressed. The oldest voice in the world is just the one that never ceases to speak. If anybody could have silenced its imperative echoes, it should have been Heyst's father,

with his contemptuous, inflexible negation of all effort; but apparently he could not. There was in the son a lot of that first ancestor who, as soon as he could uplift his muddy frame from the celestial mould, started inspecting and naming the animals of that paradise which he was so soon to lose. (pp. 173–74)

The conflict in *Victory*, as it takes shape, is between the imperatives of Heyst's mythical and his biological fathers, between his spiritual and his intellectual legacies: between paradise and the fallen world.

I need not dwell for long on the development of Heyst's struggle, for the last clause of the previous passage tells the story in a nutshell. It is worthwhile to add, though, that against Heyst's precept that "he who forms a [human] tie is lost," that "the germ of corruption has entered his soul." (p. 200). Lena and Heyst seem to make a genuine attempt to understand each other, an attempt made all the more touching by their inability to do so. Lena cannot comprehend the nature of Heyst in his dark, mysterious silences, and Heyst approaches Lena as if she were "a script in an unknown language" (p. 222). The contrast between them resonates with echoes from the adventure tales: she is simple, trusting, heroic; while he, like Marlow, like the professor in *Under Western Eyes*, like Conrad himself, is a pur-veyor of words. Once again, human corruption displays itself in the lan-guage of social relationships, in language in general. As in *The Nigger of the "Narcissus"* all human ties are corrupt — even the most noble of them — because they are either perversions or unsuccessful imitations of the pre-social community in the myth of Eden. Heyst's "language," associated with the vocabulary he learns from his father's books, is insistently implicated as the institutional foundation of the fallen world; and closely associated with language, "Thinking," as Conrad says in his Author's Note to this novel, "is the great enemy of perfection." Although Heyst's love for Lena makes him suddenly care about life again, he is doomed from the start. The holocaust at the end of the novel is, with a subtle insistence, adumbrated in the apocalyptic imagery throughout the story. From the start we may be sure Heyst's love will fail.

Lena, however, emerges the victor of *Victory*, the hero that Heyst could not become, and in the process she joins Conrad's gallery of idealized women: Emily Gould with her schools and hospitals, Natalie Haldin with her naive and good-hearted optimism, Kurtz's Intended with her tragic devotion. Indeed, as Conrad's career progressed, the figures of the naive Singleton and the uncorrupted Jim give way to women who are highly romanticized and morally flawless. It is true that Conrad could not imagine "real women" in his fiction; but this was a limitation that in one sense he could turn to his advantage, for it is the unreality of these women, particularly Lena, that allows them to belong to at least a rhetorical and stylized version of Conrad's lost heroic world.[11]

In truth, however, Conrad's vision of the social ideal is never more than a blurred evocation and is never even imagined except vaguely as something lost. Perhaps the idea that this loss is permanent, that the loss itself is never more than a myth in the first place, accounts in large part for the differences between Conrad and the visionary tradition in English literature that I have represented by Milton and Wordsworth. Conrad's vision, finally, seems trapped within the temporal and finite constructs of the mortal world, trapped within his celebrated style, within a language beyond which he can only imagine the destruction of that language — and with it, culture, history, and the self. The only absolute in Conrad, according to the logic of the heroic journey, is the fate which Kurtz, Jim, Decoud, and Heyst all share: all destroy themselves and disappear, like the drowned seaman in Dana, beyond the comprehensible world.

When we assess Conrad's bearing upon English fiction, we may easily forget that Conrad preceded other novelists we call "modern" by an entire generation. When *Almayer's Folly* appeared in 1895, D. H. Lawrence was only ten years old, James Joyce only thirteen. Conrad was not personally acquainted with Lawrence or Joyce or Virginia Woolf. Seemingly he did not read them; to the best of my knowledge he left no direct evidence that he was even aware of them. True, his friendship with Edward Garnett supplied a thin link between Conrad and modern fiction, but whatever influence was exercised devolved only upon the younger writers. D. H. Lawrence in 1912 wrote Garnett in response to some Conrad stories Garnett had sent Lawrence:

> The Conrad, after months of Europe makes me furious — and the stories are *so good*. But why this giving in before you start, that pervades all Conrad and such folks — the Writers among the Ruins. I can't forgive Conrad for being so sad and for giving in.[12]

Virginia Woolf saw Conrad as an honorary patriarch of modern fiction, noting at the same time: "there is something exotic about the genius of Mr. Conrad which makes him not so much an influence as an idol, honoured and admired, but aloof and apart."[13] In more dramatic but otherwise similar terms, Ford Madox Ford recalled Conrad as "an amazing being . . . [who] could create a whole world and give to himself the aspect of a Sir Francis Drake emerging from the territory of the Anthropophagi and the darkness of the Land of Fire."[14] Lawrence, Woolf, and Ford in these remarks seem to share that broad sense of Conrad as a prophet and adventurer whose heroic ordeal took him to the brink of the modern world; and it is this kind of response that I have tried to account for more fully in this book. Now, after insisting upon the differences between Conrad and earlier novelists and distinguishing between the social and visionary imaginations, I would like to suggest a more problematical relationship between Conrad and two novelists, Lawrence and Joyce, considered indisputably modern: Lawrence, because among modern novelists he seems closest to Conrad's imagination; and Joyce, because he seems the most distant.

If Lawrence did not quite understand Conrad's "giving in," I think he did understand what it meant to be a "Writer among the Ruins." And reading a novel like *The Rainbow* next to Conrad's fiction, we are bound to notice a broad and pervasive similarity in images, metaphors, and characterizations. Marlow's contempt for our "sheltering conception of light and order which is our refuge" (*Lord Jim*, p. 313) is shared by Ursula Brangwen, who sees mankind as a camp within a universal darkness vainly and foolishly crying out, "Beyond our light and our order there is nothing" (p. 437 in the Viking edition). Later, reminiscent of Marlow in "Heart of Darkness" (and his implicit commentary upon the heroic self in adventure fiction), Ursula says of mankind, "They assume selves as they assume suits of clothing" (p. 448). Shortly thereafter, in a moment when Anton Skrebensky transcends his spiritual limitations, he sees society "performing tricks" (p. 449) in a way that recalls Marlow's circus metaphors in "Heart of Darkness." And when Skrebensky later turns back and professes his allegiance to this society, he sees Ursula, who wants to destroy her social bonds, as "the darkness, the challenge, the horror" (p. 482), which scans the complex of images associated with Kurtz, who also has godlike aspirations. Granting that the exact tone and character of Conrad and Lawrence mark these men as writers of two different temperaments, I would nonetheless insist that their resemblances in vocabulary are accompanied and accented by even further and more intimate parallels between them. Both presupposed in their fiction the myth of a paradise lost,[15] and both saw history as a degeneration of the social ideal. Both imagined the end of a cultural order, and both despised a modern world dominated by consciousness and mechanization. Both, finally, aspired to self-fulfillment in a visionary atmosphere characterized metaphorically by images of darkness and formless space; both sought to regain the perfect social community.

But where Lawrence most differs from Conrad is in his belief that the lost paradise may yet be rediscovered through a kind of cosmic love, through a unity between man and woman that does, finally, transcend the limitations of a fragmented, constricted, fallen world. Ironically, it is essentially in this way that the imagination of Lawrence, unlike Conrad's, may remain both visionary and social at once. Conrad's Razumov, in a moment of terrible understanding, realizes that in society "he no longer belonged to himself" (p. 301); and Heyst similarly fears that in his commitment to Lena "he no longer belonged to himself" (p. 244). But in almost the exact same terms, Lawrence's Tom Brangwen realizes with a fear that is preliminary to his triumph in love that "he did not belong to himself" (p. 35). Conrad, who, like Lawrence, hates the isolated ego, nonetheless clings to it as the last imaginable form of human existence, the only alternative to one's absorption into darkness. The triumph of Tom Brangwen is that he is able to overcome his fears and his limitations, to cast off both an individual and narrowly social identity, and achieve a transcendent union with his wife Lydia. For Conrad, on the other hand, the ideal community exists only as a paradise vaguely approximated within the imagination of isolated man; even its mythical and historical roots are undermined. In Conrad's historical vision, moral progress is impossible, and this is one way in which *Nostromo* differs from Lawrence's historical vision in the continuity between *The Rainbow* and *Women in Love*. Taken together, these may be seen as novels simultaneously about the liberation of the self and the progress toward an ideal love during the course of several generations of an English family—a liberation and progress counterpointed and complicated by the increasing threats to such aspirations in the development of a mechanized world. In contrast, *Nostromo* offers no possibility of such liberation, no vision of heroic community, no redemption through love. Conrad allows industrialism to stand for progress in *Nostromo*, but only by ignoring the most haunting implications of the novel could we say that the problems of Costaguana have been resolved, for human community remains a fiction subtly undermined by the anarchy of the social world. The one tale of Conrad's in which human community does seem to "work" is "The Secret Sharer." But significantly, this is the story in which human fellowship is identified complexly with fantasy, in which we suspect that the captain is "mad." The community in "The Secret Sharer" consists of one person really: Conrad and his spectral self. It is a wonderful and weird moment in fiction, but a fleeting one at that.

If Lawrence may be partly indebted to Conrad for his fictional ambience, the modern novel departs from Conrad (and Lawrence) with James Joyce. No less than Conrad, Joyce was aware of the breakdown of old forms of order, and like Conrad he sought to redefine the self in the modern world. But in *Ulysses*, Joyce sees the self created out of the accumulations of the past among which man must somehow give form to his innermost feelings. Although there is a persistent sense of cultural nostalgia in Joyce, and a staggering review of lost literary and historical forms, there is virtually no sense in *Ulysses* that there ever existed a precultural or a presocial self, or that the inner resources of man are not grounded in the institutions he has created to express them. For Conrad, of course, history is a wholesale falsification of the ideal self, a betrayal of the time of nonhistorical innocence; for Conrad history is a mythical extension of consciousness, the outward expression of a corrupted state of mind. Unlike Conrad, Joyce is not concerned with the imagination of a transcendent human community, but rather with locating and expressing the self and the human community among both the monuments and the debris of history. In at least one very important sense, therefore, Joyce and Conrad represent different strains in modern fiction. For while both are the champions of the personal and subjective in human experience, Joyce is the great classicist of modern fiction, while Conrad is the great romantic.[16]

Perhaps the best epitaph written for Conrad's heroic journeys was his own reaction to the outbreak of World War I, the event that left no doubt among his contemporaries that mankind had entered a new era. When the war began, Conrad was (almost symbolically) on a sentimental journey back to Poland and the places of his youth. Later he wrote of the evening that war was declared, saying: "All the past was gone, and there was no future, whatever happened; no road which did not seem to lead to moral annihilation."[17] That, too, was the legacy of his fictional journeys; it is obvious why no one could follow him. It is no wonder that even he, if he were to continue writing, had to find a different path from Marlow's in his last years.

It is true, as many critics point out, that Conrad frequently evokes the perfection of human society in the form of the seamen's community, that he celebrates the virtues of fidelity and service, that he identifies language with action—that, in short, he allows himself a coherent code of ethics for both his conduct and his artistic endeavors. But in all these instances, I would suggest, Conrad has tried to become the simple laborer of his Preface and has put his faith in an ideal that privately he distrusts. One of the ideas I have emphasized most is that Conrad usually rejects heroic formulas, that he undermines the language upon which his conception of heroism seems to rely. Fidelity, service, action, and work are all compromises in the effort to recover an unimaginable ideal. Understanding this, we will be better able to appreciate the status of art in the Preface and elsewhere. Art for Conrad is only a way of mediating between chaos and the ideal. Based as it is upon the principle of fidelity and the Pateresque absorption of consciousness into sense impressions, art recalls the principles of the seamen's world aboard the *Narcissus* in its tentative grasp upon order, in its dogged and futile resistance to the darkness that surrounds it and the anarchy implicit within. Hence, Conrad admires those writers like Flaubert who could fashion a literary world through a scrupulously engineered style; hence he pays tribute to Frederick Marryat, whose artistic fidelity is explicitly identified with his fidelity to the naval service.

It was not simply physical fatigue, then, and in one sense not even a depletion of his creative energies that accounts for Conrad's decline. This decline is implicit in his writing from the start; what he did was to realize it during the course of his career, the way Marlow finally discovers that all is lost in the heart of darkness. And during this journey that shapes his career, Conrad was in one crucial way unlike the novelists who are indisputably called modern. His imagination was controlled not by the classical nostalgia of Joyce, the delicate irony of Ford, or the vision of a transcendent love in Lawrence. These are writers who may delight in the exploration of human relationships and who try to redefine the relationships between individuals and their culture in the modern world. Conrad's imagination, rather, was controlled by a myth that he inherits from Wordsworth, and before him Milton: the myth that man lost his innocence once he became conscious of himself. In Conrad's world, social experience is a symptom of man's decadence. Hence, his spiritual journeys are carried out in painful isolation, while his political novels are panoramic canvasses for his sweeping visions of social chaos. In Conrad, man has stepped from a dream into a nightmare, and the shock is permanent. The end of self-discovery is not Beauty and Truth, but the inescapable consciousness of a paradise lost.

Notes

Notes to Introduction

1. H. G. Wells, from his *Experiment in Autobiography*, quoted in Jocelyn Baines, *Joseph Conrad, A Critical Biography* (New York: McGraw-Hill Book Company, 1967), p. 234.

2. All quotations from Leavis are taken from *The Great Tradition* (New York: New York University Press, 1967).

3. Ian Watt compares and contrasts Conrad with the French Symbolists in *Conrad in the Nineteenth Century* (Berkeley: University of California Press, 1979), pp. 180–87.

4. The specialness of Milton's and Wordsworth's poetic visions and voices has been commented upon in many places. On Milton, see especially Anne Davidson Ferry, *Milton's Epic Voice, The Narrator in Paradise Lost* (Cambridge: Harvard University Press, 1967). The following remarks are especially useful:

   > A heavenly vision (and it is useful to Milton that the word means at once what is seen and the act of seeing) is not like other sights or ways of seeing. It is an internal sight which penetrates to "invisible" truths not equatable with our superficial knowledge, and it has a completeness of form, a wholeness of shape and clarity of design different in kind from our fragmentary impressions. Uniqueness of form in song or vision expresses uniqueness of meaning. (p. 147)

   and:

   > . . . the relation of the speaker to his characters and his readers [in *Paradise Lost*] is not social, and therefore his language could not be either the language of private conversation or of public speech. (p. 180)

   With regard to Wordsworth, Harold Bloom's remark is helpful: "The Romantic movement is from nature to the imagination's freedom (sometimes a reluctant freedom), and the imagination's freedom is frequently purgatorial, redemptive in direction but destructive of the social self." See Bloom's "The Internalization of Quest Romance" in *The Ringers in the Tower, Studies in Romantic Tradition* (Chicago & London: The University of Chicago Press, 1971), p. 16. Conrad is generally not thought of in terms of Milton and Wordsworth as I have presented them here. However, Royal Roussel's argument in *The Metaphysics of Darkness* (Baltimore and London: The Johns Hopkins Press, 1971) bears upon mine in very suggestive ways. Consider, for example:

   > Conrad is concerned with man's need to find a social or intersubjective ground for his self. . . . But in Conrad's world this search never takes place entirely on the human level. It always occurs within the context of the fundamental alienation of conscious-

ness from its metaphysical source. Consequently, for most of his adventurers the voyage is not directed toward the discovery of a human parent but toward the ultimate origin of consciousness itself. (p. 12)

5. Roger Sale's term for what I am talking about is the "Myth of Lost Unity." See his *Modern Heroism, Essays on D. H. Lawrence, William Empson, & J. R. R. Tolkien* (Berkeley: University of California Press, 1973), p. 5 ff.

6. Two books have helped me collect these allusions to *Paradise Lost*: Hugh Kenner's *Dublin's Joyce* (Bloomington: Indiana University Press, 1956), p. 87, and Richard Poirier's *The Comic Sense of Henry James* (New York: Oxford University Press, 1967), p. 246.

7. The best known proponent of this theory is Zdzislaw Najder. See, for example, his paper, "Conrad and the Idea of Honor" in Zyla, Wolodymyr T. and Aycock, Wendell M., eds., *Joseph Conrad: Theory and World Fiction* (Lubbock: The Texas Tech Press, 1974), pp. 103–14.

8. See especially Ian Watt's "Conrad Criticism and *The Nigger of the 'Narcissus'*" in *Nineteenth-Century Fiction*, 12:4, pp. 257–83, which argues that Conrad asserts a sense of communal values that link him in his optimism to Wordsworth. Also relevant is Watt's article, "Joseph Conrad: Alienation and Commitment" in *The English Mind*, edited by Hugh Sykes Davies and George Watson (Cambridge: University Press, 1964), especially pp. 264–65 and 268–78.

9. Margery Sabin makes some very useful comparisons between English literature and French romanticism and antiromanticism in *English Romanticism and the French Tradition* (Cambridge: Harvard University Press, 1976).

Notes for Chapter 1

1. Richard Henry Dana, *Two Years Before the Mast* (New York: The Modern Library, 1936), p. 8. All subsequent references to *Two Years Before the Mast* will be to this edition.

2. D. H. Lawrence, *Studies in Classic American Literature* (New York: The Viking Press, 1964), p. 114.

3. Rudyard Kipling, *Captains Courageous* (New York: Doubleday, Page & Company, 1924), p. 286.

4. This term is used by Georg Lukács in *The Historical Novel* (London: Merlin Press, 1962) in discussing Scott, pp. 33–41.

5. See Lukács, pp. 33–41 for his description of Scott's hero.

6. Joseph Conrad, "Tales of the Sea" in *Notes on Life and Letters* (New York: Doubleday, Page & Company, 1925), Vol. III of the Kent edition, p. 56. Unless otherwise noted, all subsequent references to Conrad's works will be to this edition of the collected works.

7. James Fenimore Cooper, *The Sea Lions* (New York: G. P. Putnam's Sons, n.d), Mohawk edition, p. 169. All subsequent references to *The Sea Lions* will be to this edition.

8. Compare Dana's description of an iceberg, which is considerably more dramatic than Cooper's, but similar in its general tone and in its metaphors of sublimity:

And there lay, floating in the ocean, several miles off, an immense irregular mass, its top and points covered with snow, and its centre of a deep indigo colour. This was an iceberg, and of the largest size, as one of our men said who had been in the Northern Ocean. As far as the eye could reach, the sea in every direction was of a deep blue colour, the waves running high and fresh, and sparkling in the light, and in the midst lay this immense mountain island, its cavities and valleys thrown into deep shade, and its points and pinnacles glittering in the sun. All hands were soon on deck, looking at it, and admiring in various ways its beauty and grandeur. But no description can give any idea of the strangeness, splendour, and, really, the sublimity of the sight. Its great size, — for it must have been from two to three miles in circumference, and several hundred feet in height — its slow motion, as its base rose and sank in the water, and its high points nodded against the clouds; the dashing of the waves upon it, which, breaking high with foam, lined its base with a white crust; and the thundering sound of the cracking of the mass, and the breaking and tumbling down of huge pieces; together with its nearness and approach, which added a slight element of fear, — all combined to give it the character of true sublimity. (p. 320)

I do not know whether Cooper knew of this description when he wrote his own, but it is such a response to the vastness of nature that in part links these two writers.

9. This quotation appears in Thomas Philbrick, *James Fenimore Cooper and the Development of American Sea Fiction* (Cambridge: Harvard University Press, 1961), p. 239.

10. Ibid., p. 239.

11. Stephen Crane, *The Red Badge of Courage* in *The Works of Stephen Crane*, Wilson Pollett, ed. (New York: Alfred A. Knopf, Inc., 1925), vol. I, p. 24. All subsequent references to *The Red Badge of Courage* will be to this edition.

12. Compare Isaiah 1:3: "They shall beat their swords into plowshares, and their spears into pruninghooks: nations shall not lift up sword against nation, neither shall they learn war any more."

13. My sense of contemporary fiction has been greatly influenced by the essays and reviews of Richard Poirier, although the responsibility for the formulations here belongs to me.

14. See M. H. Abrams, *Natural Supernaturalism, Tradition and Revolution in Romantic Literature* (New York: W. W. Norton & Company, Inc., 1971) for a discussion of Wordsworth's debt to Milton. See especially pp. 21-32.

15. Compare in *Paradise Lost*:

    I sung of Chaos and *Eternal Night*
    Taught by the heav'nly Muse to venture down
    The dark descent and up to reascend,
    Though hard and rare . . . (III, 18-21)

16. See Anne Davidson Ferry's *Milton's Epic Voice* (Cambridge: Harvard University Press, 1967) for an extensive discussion of Milton's narrator.

17. David Ferry, *The Limits of Mortality* (Middletown, Conn.: Wesleyan University Press, 1959), p. 40. My thinking about Wordsworth has been greatly influenced by this book.

18. Geoffrey H. Hartman, *Wordsworth's Poetry, 1797-1814* (New Haven and London: Yale University Press, 1964), p. 250.

19. D. Ferry, op. cit., p. 29.

20. Ibid, p. 171.

21. Hartman, op. cit., p. 226.

22. For another opinion on the relationship between Conrad and Wordsworth, compare Ian Watt in "Conrad's Preface to *The Nigger of the 'Narcissus*,'" *Novel*, vii, 2, Winter 1974, 101–15, and Watt's more recent *Conrad in the Nineteenth Century*, pp. 76–85.

23. See also Watt, "Conrad's Preface to *The Nigger of the 'Narcissus*,'" pp. 104, 105, 112.

24. Letter to Sidney Colvin, March 18, 1917, in G. Jean-Aubry, *Joseph Conrad, Life and Letters* (New York: Doubleday, Page & Co., 1927), vol. II, p. 185.

25. For a good study of the relationship between Conrad's letters and his fiction, see Edward W. Said, *Joseph Conrad and the Fiction of Autobiography* (Cambridge: Harvard University Press, 1966), particularly in his discussions of the problematical relationships between Conrad's past and present.

26. Letter to R. B. Cunninghame Graham, Jan. 31, 1898, Jean-Aubry I, p. 186.

27. Letter to Edward Garnett, Sept. 16, 1899, in Edward Garnett, ed., *Letters from Joseph Conrad*, 1895–1924 (Indianapolis: Bobbs-Merrill Company, 1928), p. 155.

28. Letter to R. B. Cunninghame Graham, January 1898, Jean-Aubry I, p. 222.

29. Letter to Edward Garnett, March 23, 1895, in Jean-Aubry I, p. 186.

30. See J. Hillis Miller's chapter on Conrad in *Poets of Reality* (Cambridge: Harvard University Press, 1965), which presents Conrad's nihilism as the culmination of nineteenth-century pessimism. That Miller includes Conrad in a book about poets does not, of course, hurt my case.

31. Compare from *Paradise Lost*:

    So much the rather thou, Celestial Light,
    Shine inward, and the mind through all her powers
    Irradiate; there plant eyes; all mist from thence
    Purge and disperse, that I may see and tell
    Of things invisible to mortal sight. (III, 51–55)

32. This is a major difference between my thesis and that of David Thorburn in *Conrad's Romanticism* (New Haven and London: Yale University Press, 1974). Basically, Thorburn argues for an anti-apocalyptic strain in Conrad's fiction that allies him with Wordsworth in his celebration of simplicity and human solidarity. I am suggesting that such values are byproducts of Conrad's romanticism and are meant to salvage some measure of morality from the chaos of the heroic journey. I rely partly on the relative thinness and melancholy of Conrad's affirmations of brotherhood and the powers of art. What were compelling notions in Wordsworth degenerate into romantic rhetoric in Conrad, a phenomenon verifiable in the way that Conrad in his fiction consistently identifies human order with rhetorical order.

33. See especially Bernard Meyer, *Joseph Conrad: A Psychoanalytic Biography* (Princeton University Press, 1967) and most recently Peter J. Glassman, *Language and Being, Joseph Conrad and the Literature of Personality* (New York and London: Columbia University Press, 1976).

34. This preface appears in Walter F. Wright, ed., *Joseph Conrad on Fiction* (Lincoln, Nebraska: The University of Nebraska Press, 1964), and the quotation is taken from p. 235. This book is a very useful collection of Conrad's critical writing.

35. Zdzislaw Najder suggests that the virtues of fidelity and honor derive from an essentially Polish tradition of aristocratic chivalry. Such a view is not incompatible with mine, but I think the vocabulary of Conrad's code of ethics is more closely associated with his idea of the seamen's community. See Najder's article, "Conrad and Rousseau's Concepts of Man and Society" in *Joseph Conrad, A Commemoration*, ed. Norman Sherry (New York: Harper and Row Publishers, Inc., 1971), pp. 77–90.

36. Compare Thorburn's comments on this similarity, pp. 149–51.

37. See also Roussel's discussion of Conrad's "primal darkness," p. 3 ff.

38. M. H. Abrams describes this kind of journey in relation to German and English romanticism in *Natural Supernaturalism*, p. 235.

39. D. Ferry, op. cit., p. 43.

Notes for Chapter 2

1. Albert Guerard, *Conrad the Novelist* (Cambridge: Harvard University Press, 1958), p. 107.

2. Frederick Karl, *A Reader's Guide to Joseph Conrad*, rev. ed. (New York: Farrar, Strauss and Giroux, 1969), p. 109.

3. Joseph Conrad, *Tales of Hearsay and Last Essays* (London: J. M. Dent & Sons Ltd, 1963), p. 94.

4. Morton Dauwen Zabel, *Craft and Character* (New York: The Viking Press, 1957), p. 180.

5. Ibid., p. 181.

6. Guerard, op. cit., p. 124.

7. See Marvin Mudrick's spirited attack on the use of mythical categories in criticism of Conrad's novels, in "Conrad and the Terms of Modern Criticism," *Hudson Review*, 7(Autumn 1954):419–26.

8. Guerard, op. cit., p. 108.

9. See also Marvin Mudrick's complaint about Conrad's "persistent self-dramatizing and sentimentalizing impulse" in "Conrad and the Terms of Modern Criticism," p. 421. Mudrick's objections are elaborated in "The Artist's Conscience and *The Nigger of the 'Narcissus,'*" *Nineteenth-Century Fiction*, 11:288–97, March 1957. The criticisms of Conrad's stylistic ornamentation are long-standing, contemporaneous, in fact, with the first publications of his works. Many of his admirers take care to say that they like him *despite* his excesses. Consider, for example, Robert Adams's statement that "Critics disagree about him because there is so much puffy chatter to disregard even in the best Conrad. . . ," in *Partisan Review*, 28:1 (1961), p. 128.

10. This connection between Conrad and Dickens occurred to me after I read Robert Garis's *The Dickens Theatre* (Oxford: Clarendon Press, 1965), from which I borrowed some of my critical terminology in describing the Donkin passage. Other critics such as Paul Wiley, Marvin Mudrick, and Frederick Karl have noted other connections between Conrad and Dickens, and Conrad himself said that he read him. I am convinced that the relationship is worth pursuing even further than it has been in criticism.

11. Needless to argue in any detail, the significance here is metaphorical, although Conrad was probably subject to some of the same prejudices as the rest of his culture.

12. Guerard, op. cit. p. 107.

13. Ibid., p. 111.

14. Ibid., p. 109.

15. Robert S. Ryf, *Joseph Conrad*, Columbia Essays on Modern Writers (New York: Columbia University Press, 1970), p. 14.

16. For a discussion of "fallen language" and "Satanic rhetoric" in *Paradise Lost*, see Anne Davidson Ferry, *Milton and the Miltonic Dryden* (Cambridge: Harvard University Press, 1968), pp. 40-57 and 69-76. While I have no external evidence that Conrad read *Paradise Lost*, I am sure he absorbed the Miltonic imagination in ways that may elude critical formulation. Anne Ferry's remark that in *Paradise Lost*, "the drama of corruption is acted out in the progressive degeneration of human language" (p. 71) applies equally as well to *The Nigger of the "Narcissus"* and in much the same way.

17. See also Watt, *Conrad in the Nineteenth Century*, especially pp. 94-125 on "Solidarity." Much in this discussion is compatible with my views, but there is a difference in emphasis.

18. See Marvin Mudrick, "The Artist's Conscience and *The Nigger of the 'Narcissus*,'" p. 292 ff.

Notes for Chapter 3

1. Letter to R. B. Cunninghame Graham, Dec. 14, 1897, in Jean-Aubry I, p. 215.

2. Royal Roussel's characterization of Conrad's journey back into a primal darkness to the source of consciousness is generally compatible with mine, and Albert Guerard's commentary on the "journey within" is instructive, though I would take issue with some of his moral terminology. J. Hillis Miller's discussion of the "darkness" as a "metaphysical entity" (27 ff.) is also good. The best extended commentary on "Heart of Darkness" that I know of is contained in James Guetti's *The Limits of Metaphor* (Ithaca: Cornell University Press, 1967). Guetti suggests not only that the darkness is unimaginable, but also that the idea of the darkness itself is a contrivance of Marlow designed to maintain his sense of moral order:

   > I do not mean to imply, however, that the redefinition of "darkness" as nothingness is ever accomplished for Marlow; we must remember that, as he says, he drew back his "hesitating foot," and because he did he is able to take refuge in the idea of a "darkness," the idea of powers beyond the imagination responsible for the defeat of the imagination. To Marlow's moral sensibility such an idea is essential; he must have a meaning, even if he himself suspects its artificiality. (pp. 66-67)

   In my own discussion, I try to relate Marlow's journey and his subsequent retreat to the idea of heroism, and to compare Marlow's heroism with that of Kurtz. Also, I try to give this "darkness" that Roussel, Miller, Guerard, and Guetti talk about a genealogy in the literature of visionary romanticism. The volume of criticism on "Heart of Darkness" is, of course, considerable, but the story has not yet been discussed as a logical extension of visionary romanticism.

3. James Guetti, *The Limits of Metaphor, A Study of Melville, Conrad, and Faulkner*, (Ithaca: Cornell University Press, 1967), p. 57 ff.

4. Cf. Guetti, p. 50. Guetti's remarks on Kurtz's "vision," a vision that is self-negating, one that does not "see," provides a good way for understanding Kurtz as the Wordsworthian traveller who has journeyed too far. (See pp. 65–66 in *The Limits of Metaphor*.)

Notes for Chapter 4

1. See Conrad's correspondence with *Blackwood's Magazine* in *Joseph Conrad, Letters to William Blackwood and David S. Meldrum*, William Blackburn, ed. (Durham, North Carolina: Duke University Press, 1958), pp. 27 and 54 especially.

2. See *Letters to William Blackwood*, pp. 54–104. For another account and some different ideas on the writing of *Lord Jim*, see Eloise Knapp Hay, "*Lord Jim*: From Sketch to Novel" in *Twentieth Century Interpretations of Lord Jim*, ed. Robert E. Kuehn (Englewood Cliffs, New Jersey: Prentice-Hall, Inc., 1969), pp. 53–67. Originally this article appeared in *Comparative Literature*, 12(Fall 1960), 289–309.

3. Letter to David S. Meldrum, Nov. 25, 1899, in *Letters to William Blackwood*, p. 75.

4. Letter to David S. Meldrum, Jan. 9, 1900, in *Letters to William Blackwood*, pp. 82–83.

5. I think that the similarities between *Lord Jim* and *The Red Badge of Courage* are such that a good case could be made that Conrad was very much influenced by the Crane novel. This pairing, it seems to me, works a lot better than the one still more commonly made between *The Nigger of the "Narcissus"* and *The Red Badge of Courage*. In his combination of youthful naiveté and introspection, in his modesty and "commonness," in his literary fantasies of heroism, Jim is almost unique among Conrad's other heroes, while he is a lot like Fleming. But my purpose here is simply to suggest the comparison and to allow my discussion to develop still within the context of the adventure tales I discussed in chapter 1. I shall return to Crane, however, in my last chapter.

6. Sale, op. cit., p. 245.

Notes for Chapter 5

1. Guerard, op. cit., p. 121.

2. Meyer, op. cit., pp. 166–67.

3. Letter to J. B. Pinker, October 1909, in Jean-Aubry II, p. 103.

4. Letter to Pinker, Jean-Aubry II, p. 103.

5. The best first-hand information on Conrad's breakdown is contained in Jessie Conrad's two biographies of her husband: *Joseph Conrad: As I Knew Him* (Garden City: Doubleday, 1926), and *Joseph Conrad and His Circle* (New York: Dutton, 1935).

6. Letter to Hugh Clifford, May 10, 1910, in Jean-Aubry, II, p. 109.

7. Guerard, op. cit., p. 23.

8. "I can't tell you what pleasure you have given me by what you say of the "Secret Sharer," — and especially of the swimmer. I haven't seen many notices, — three or four in all: but in one of them he is called a murderous ruffian, — or something of the sort. Who are those fellows who write in the Press? Where do they come from? I was simply knocked over, — for indeed I meant him to be what you have seen at once he was. And as

you have seen, I feel altogether comforted and rewarded for the trouble he has given me in the doing of him, for it wasn't an easy task." Letter to John Galsworthy, 1913, in Jean-Aubry II, pp. 143–44.

Notes for Chapter 6

1. "I could not explain why he disappoints me—why my enthusiasm withers as soon as I close the book. While one reads, of course he is not to be questioned. He is the master of his reader to the very last line—then—apparently for no reason at all—he seems to let go his hold" (letter to Edward Garnett, Dec. 5, 1897, in Jean-Aubry I, p. 211).

2. See Robert Kiely, *Robert Louis Stevenson and the Fiction of Adventure* (Cambridge: Harvard University Press, 1965), p. 167.

3. Stanley E. Fish's section on Plato in *Self-Consuming Artifacts* (Berkeley: University of California Press, 1972), pp. 1–21, discusses the visionary imagination in terms compatible with my own, thereby suggesting to me ways in which Conrad's sensibility may be seen as part of an even larger literary tradition.

4. Irving Howe, *Politics and the Novel* (New York: Avon Books, 1970), p. 103.

5. F. R. Leavis, *The Great Tradition* (New York: New York University Press, 1967), pp. 200–201.

6. Hugh Kenner, *Gnomon* (New York: McDowell, Obolensky, Inc., 1956), p. 167.

7. See also Edward W. Said, *Beginnings, Intention and Method* (New York: Basic Books, Inc., 1975). Said's discussion of *Nostromo* (pp. 100–137) is for the most part compatible with mine.

8. See Irving Howe, p. 90, for a similar analysis of Razumov's public roles.

9. Letter to R. B. Cunninghame Graham, Feb. 8, 1899, Jean-Aubry I, p. 269. This letter contains much more that anticipates Conrad's vision of society in his political novels and his reaction to that society. For instance:

   L'homme est un animal méchant. Sa méchanceté doit être organisée. Le crime est un condition nécessaire de l'existence organisée. La société est essentiellement criminelle,—ou elle n'existerait pas. C'est l'égoïsme qui sauve tout,—absolument tout,—tout ce que nous abhorrons, tout ce que nous aimons. Et tout se tient. Voilà pourquoi je respecte les extrêmes anarchistes—"Je souhaite l'extermination générale."

10. See Frederick Crews, "The Power of Darkness," in *Partisan Review*, 34:4, pp. 515–17.

11. For different ideas on Conrad's political vision, see Avrom Fleishman's *Conrad's Politics, Community and Anarchy in the Fiction of Joseph Conrad* (Baltimore: The Johns Hopkins Press, 1968). Fleishman provides an excellent study of Conrad's intellectual backgrounds, although his reading of the political novels differs from mine. He places more weight, for example, upon Natalie Haldin's idealism than I do. I see primarily the corruptions of human community in the political novels and view Natalie's hope as Conrad's wistful concession to the last measure of human decency he sees in the world.

12. Letter to Edward Garnett, Oct. 30, 1912, in *The Letters of D. H. Lawrence*, ed. Aldous Huxley (New York: The Viking Press, 1932), p. 68.

13. Virginia Woolf, "How It Strikes a Contemporary," in *The Common Reader* (New York: Harcourt, Brace & World, Inc., 1953), p. 239.

14. Ford Madox Ford in a review quoted by Baines, op. cit., p. 443.

15. My comparison between Conrad and Lawrence is made possible partly by Roger Sale's brilliant chapter on Lawrence in *Modern Heroism*, which discusses Lawrence in the context of the "Myth of Lost Unity."

16. For more on Joyce's "classicism," see Hugh Kenner's exceptional study, *Dublin's Joyce* (Bloomington: Indiana University Press, 1956).

17. Joseph Conrad, "First News," in *Notes on Life and Letters*, p. 178.

Bibliography

Abrams, M. H. *Natural Supernaturalism, Tradition and Revolution in Romantic Literature.* New York: W. W. Norton & Company, Inc., 1971.

Adams, Robert M. "Views on Conrad." *Partisan Review*, 28, No. 1 (January-February 1961), 124-30.

Baines, Jocelyn. *Joseph Conrad, A Critical Biography.* New York: McGraw-Hill Book Company, 1967.

Blackburn, William, ed. *Joseph Conrad, Letters to William Blackwood and Davis S. Meldrum.* Durham: Duke University Press, 1958.

Bloom, Harold. "The Internalization of Quest Romance." In *The Ringers in the Tower, Studies in Romantic Tradition.* Chicago: The University of Chicago Press, 1971.

Conrad, Jessie. *Joseph Conrad and His Circle.* New York: Dutton, 1935.

_____. *Joseph Conrad: As I Knew Him.* Garden City: Doubleday, 1926.

Conrad, Joseph. *Complete Works.* Kent edition, 26 volumes. Garden City: Doubleday, Page & Company, 1925.

Cooper, James Fenimore. *The Sea Lions.* Mohawk edition. New York: G. P. Putnam's Sons, n.d.

Crane, Stephen. *The Red Badge of Courage.* In *The Works of Stephen Crane*, vol. I, edited by Wilson Pollett. New York: Alfred A. Knopf, Inc., 1925.

Crews, Frederick. "The Power of Darkness." *Partisan Review*, 34, No. 4 (Fall 1967), 507-25.

Dana, Richard Henry. *Two Years Before the Mast.* New York: The Modern Library, 1936.

Ferry, Anne Davidson. *Milton's Epic Voice, The Narrator in Paradise Lost.* Cambridge: Harvard University Press, 1967.

_____. *Milton and the Miltonic Dryden.* Cambridge: Harvard University Press, 1968.

Ferry, David. *The Limits of Mortality.* Middletown, Conn.: Wesleyan University Press, 1959.

Fish, Stanley E. *Self-Consuming Artifacts.* Berkeley: University of California Press, 1972.

Fleishman, Avrom. *Conrad's Politics, Community and Anarchy in the Fiction of Joseph Conrad.* Baltimore: The Johns Hopkins Press, 1968.

Garis, Robert. *The Dickens Theatre.* Oxford: Clarendon Press, 1965.

Glassman, Peter J. *Language and Being, Joseph Conrad and the Literature of Personality.* New York: Columbia University Press, 1976.

Guerard, Albert. *Conrad the Novelist.* Cambridge: Harvard University Press, 1958.

Guetti, James. *The Limits of Metaphor, A Study of Melville, Conrad, and Faulkner.* Ithaca: Cornell University Press, 1967.

Hartman, Geoffrey H. *Wordsworth's Poetry, 1797-1814.* New Haven: Yale University Press, 1964.

Hay, Eloise Knapp. "*Lord Jim*: From Sketch to Novel." In *Twentieth Century Interpretations of Lord Jim*, edited by Robert E. Kuehn. Englewood Cliffs, New Jersey: Prentice-Hall, Inc., 1969. Orig. in *Comparative Literature*, 12 (Fall 1960), 289-309.

Howe, Irving. *Politics and the Novel*. New York: Avon Books, 1970.

Huxley, Aldous, ed. *The Letters of D. H. Lawrence*. New York: The Viking Press, 1932.

Jean-Aubry, G., ed. *Joseph Conrad, Life and Letters*. 2 vols. Garden City, New York: Doubleday, Page & Co., 1927.

Karl, Frederick. *A Reader's Guide to Joseph Conrad*, rev. ed. New York: Farrar, Strauss and Giroux, 1969.

Kenner, Hugh. *Dublin's Joyce*. Bloomington: Indiana University Press, 1956.

_____. *Gnomon*. New York: McDowell, Obolensky, Inc., 1956.

Kiely, Robert. *Robert Louis Stevenson and the Fiction of Adventure*. Cambridge: Harvard University Press, 1965.

Kipling, Rudyard. *Captains Courageous*. New York: Doubleday, Page & Company, 1924.

Lawrence, D. H. *Studies in Classic American Literature*. New York: The Viking Press, 1964.

Leavis, F. R. *The Great Tradition*. New York: New York University Press, 1967.

Lukács, Georg. *The Historical Novel*. London: Merlin Press, 1962.

Meyer, Bernard. *Joseph Conrad, A Psychoanalytic Biography*. Princeton: Princeton University Press, 1967.

Miller, J. Hillis. *Poets of Reality*. Cambridge: Harvard University Press, 1965.

Mudrick, Marvin. "The Artist's Conscience and *The Nigger of the 'Narcissus.'*" *Nineteenth-Century Fiction*, 11, no. 4 (March 1957), 288-97.

_____. "Conrad and the Terms of Modern Criticism." *Hudson Review*, 7, no. 3 (Autumn 1959), 419-26.

Najder, Zdzislaw. "Conrad and the Idea of Honor." In *Joseph Conrad: Theory and World Fiction*. Edited by Wolodymyr T. Zyla and Wendell M. Aycock. Lubbock, Texas: The Texas Tech Press, 1974, pp. 103-14.

_____. "Conrad and Rousseau's Concepts of Man and Society." In *Joseph Conrad, A Commemoration*. Edited by Norman Sherry. New York: Harper and Row Publishers, Inc., 1971, pp. 77-90.

Philbrick, Thomas. *James Fenimore Cooper and the Development of American Sea Fiction*. Cambridge: Harvard University Press, 1961.

Poirier, Richard. *The Comic Sense of Henry James*. New York: Oxford University Press, 1967.

Roussel, Royal. *The Metaphysics of Darkness*. Baltimore: The Johns Hopkins Press, 1971.

Ryf, Robert S. *Joseph Conrad*. Columbia Essays on Modern Writers. New York: Columbia University Press, 1970.

Sabin, Margery. *English Romanticism and the French Tradition*. Cambridge: Harvard University Press, 1976.

Said, Edward W. *Beginnings, Intention and Method*. New York: Basic Books, Inc., 1975.

_____. *Joseph Conrad and the Fiction of Autobiography*. Cambridge: Harvard University Press, 1966.

Sale, Roger. *Modern Heroism, Essays on D. H. Lawrence, William Empson, & J.R.R. Tolkien*. Berkeley: University of California Press, 1973.

Thorburn, David. *Conrad's Romanticism*. New Haven: Yale University Press, 1974.

Watt, Ian. "Conrad Criticism and *The Nigger of the 'Narcissus.'*" In *Nineteenth-Century Fiction*, 12, no. 4 (March 1958), 257-83.

_____. *Conrad in the Nineteenth Century*. Berkeley: University of California Press, 1979.

_____. "Conrad's Preface to *The Nigger of the 'Narcissus.'*" In *Novel*, 7, no. 2 (Winter 1974), 101-15.

_____. "Joseph Conrad: Alienation and Commitment." In *The English Mind*. Edited by Hugh Sykes Davies and George Watson. Cambridge: University Press, 1964, pp. 257–78.

Woolf, Virginia. "How It Strikes a Contemporary. In *The Common Reader*. New York: Harcourt, Brace & World, Inc., 1953, pp. 236–46.

Wright, Walter F., ed. *Joseph Conrad on Fiction*. Lincoln, Nebraska: The University of Nebraska Press, 1964.

Zabel, Morton Dauwen. *Craft and Character*. New York: The Viking Press, 1957.

Index